Pursuing Perfection

Content note: please note that this book contains descriptions of and reflections on eating disorders, disordered eating, sexual abuse, domestic violence, body-image problems, fatphobia and disability, and their intersections with racism, misogyny and ableism. This may be triggering for some readers.

Pursuing Perfection

Faith and the Female Body

Edited by Maja Whitaker

scm press

© Maja Whitaker 2025

Published in 2025 by SCM Press
Editorial office
3rd Floor, Invicta House,
110 Golden Lane
London EC1Y 0TG, UK

www.scmpress.co.uk

SCM Press is an imprint of Hymns Ancient & Modern Ltd
(a registered charity)

HYMNS Ancient
&Modern

Hymns Ancient & Modern® is a registered trademark of
Hymns Ancient & Modern Ltd
13A Hellesdon Park Road, Norwich,
Norfolk NR6 5DR, UK

British Library Cataloguing in Publication data
A catalogue record for this book is available
from the British Library

ISBN: 978-0-334-06558-6

EU GPSR Authorised Representative
LOGOS EUROPE, 9 rue Nicolas Poussin, 17000, LA ROCHELLE, France
E-mail: Contact@logoseurope.eu

Typeset by Regent Typesetting
Printed and bound in Great Britain by
CPI Group (UK) Ltd

Contents

List of Contributors		vii
Acknowledgements		xi

1 Introduction
  Maja Whitaker — 1

2 Christian Hope through an Embodied *Telos*
  Amanda Martinez Beck — 7

3 Mirrors, Pedestals and a Cross: The Cult of Perfection
  and the Beauty of Self-sacrifice
  Jessica J. Schroeder — 24

4 Idolizing Thinness: Critiquing the False Claims of
  Diet Culture
  Jennifer Bowden — 43

5 Desire and Discipleship: Towards Body Acceptance
  Kristy Botha — 60

6 Unspeakable Fat, Unspeakable Beauty: Fatness,
  Apophasis and the Overflowing of Excess
  Hannah Bacon — 77

7 Perfectly Able, Beautiful and Slim: Desired Bodies in the
  New Creation, Shamed Bodies in the Old
  Maja Whitaker — 99

8 Are We Having Great Sex Yet? Women, Their Bodies
  and Their Pleasure
  Lisa Isherwood — 115

9 'How Is Your Beloved Better Than Others, Most Beautiful
   of Women?': Song of Songs 5.9–16 and the Primary
   Prevention of Domestic Abuse   133
   Erin Martine Hutton

10 A Shameful Perfection: Racism and the Religion
   of Thinness   153
   Michelle Mary Lelwica

11 Conclusion   173
   Maja Whitaker

A Liturgy and Benediction   179
Index of Bible References   181
Index of Names and Subjects   185

List of Contributors

Professor Hannah Bacon is Professor of Feminist Theology at the University of Chester, with a special interest in the relationship between gender, theology and the body. Her research looks at how Christian theology might inform and transform contemporary social discourses to do with fat and weight loss. She is the author of *Feminist Theology and Contemporary Dieting Culture: Sin, Salvation and Women's Weight Loss Narratives* (T&T Clark, 2019).

Amanda Martinez Beck is a fat activist and body peace coach specializing in the intersection of human dignity, body liberation and religion. She is the author of *Lovely: How I Learned to Embrace the Body God Gave Me* (Our Sunday Visitor, 2018) and *More of You: The Fat Girl's Field Guide to the Modern World* (Broadleaf Books, 2022), and the co-creator and co-host of the *Fat & Faithful* podcast. She began the @your_body_is_good Instagram account to teach herself and others that the purpose of the human body is connection, not perfection. Her writing has been featured in various outlets, including *Christianity Today* and *America Magazine*. She lives in Texas with her family.

Kristy Botha is currently studying for her PhD in Practical Theology at Palm Beach Atlantic University, Florida. Her research interests are related to women, body image and Christian discipleship. She was born in New Zealand but is currently living in Florida with her husband and four boys. Kristy has been involved in church ministry in Sydney, London and South Africa. Currently, she and her husband are campus pastors for Journey Church, Boynton Beach.

Jennifer Bowden is a registered nutritionist (MSc Dist) with a Graduate Diploma in Theology. She is currently completing a PhD, critically examining how religious and cultural narratives shape women's perceptions of their bodies and their dietary practices, and offering an alternative, theologically faithful response to diet culture that encompasses a more holistic understanding of health and well-being. Jennifer is married with two sons and has written a weekly nutrition column and major feature stories for current affairs magazines and national newspapers in New Zealand for over 17 years.

Erin Martine Hutton is an Australian poet and academic, and Moderation and Inclusion Manager at the Australian College of Theology. Her research interests are interdisciplinary, often at the intersections of history, literature and theology. She is just shy of completing her PhD, which explores how Song of Songs might help us to prevent domestic abuse.

Professor Lisa Isherwood is Professor of Feminist Liberation Theologies at the University of Wales, and believes theology to be a communal project spurred on by notions of radical equality and empowered by divine companionship. Her work explores the nature of incarnation within a contemporary context and includes such areas as the body, gender, sexuality and eco-theology. She is the author, editor or co-editor of 28 books, including *The Fat Jesus: Feminist Explorations in Boundaries and Transgressions* (Darton, Longman & Todd, 2007), and the executive editor of the *International Journal of Feminist Theology*.

Dr Michelle Lelwica is a professor of religion at Concordia College in Moorhead, Minnesota, where she teaches courses on the intersection of religion, gender, race, culture and the body. Dr Lelwica has done groundbreaking research and writing about the religious dimensions of eating and body image problems. She is the author of *Shameful Bodies: Religion and the Culture of Physical Improvement* (Bloomsbury Publishing, 2017), *The Religion of Thinness: Satisfying the Spiritual Hungers behind Women's Obsession with Food and Weight* (Gürze Books, 2010) and *Starving for Salvation: The Spiritual Dimensions of Eating Problems among American Girls and Women* (Oxford University Press, 1999), as well as scholarly articles and popular blogs that explore women's conflicted relationships with their bodies. Her latest book is *Hurting Kids: What Incarcerated Youth Are Teaching Me about Whiteness, Compassion, Accountability, and Healing* (Cascade Books, 2024). Dr Lelwica is also the mother of two young men.

Dr Jessica J. Schroeder is a writer, editor and entrepreneur. A self-described 'practical theologian', she earned her PhD in Systematic Theology at Wheaton College, where she wrote about the role beauty plays in human knowledge of God. She is also a graduate of Denver Seminary and Colorado Christian University, holding an MA in Theology and BA in Theology with a concentration in Biblical Studies and a minor in Worship Arts. Topics that most interest her include theology's intersection with beauty, delight, food, nutrition, stewardship, climate and ecology. Brought up in the sturdy Midwest, she resides near the foothills of the Colorado Rocky Mountains with her (Colorado native) husband, where they regularly enjoy tea, wine, homemade sourdough bread and mountain hikes.

Revd Dr Maja Whitaker is Academic Dean and lecturer in Practical Theology at Laidlaw College in New Zealand. Her interest in body theology in particular is shaped by her background in anatomical science and her experience as a mother to four daughters. She is the author of *Perfect in Weakness: Disability and Human Flourishing in the New Creation* (Baylor University Press, 2023). She is committed to spiritual formation and helping others understand how to follow the way of Jesus in contemporary cultural contexts. This includes reflecting on Christian thought and practice in relation to modern cultural ideologies about human flourishing in general and the diversity of bodies in particular.

Acknowledgements

Scripture quotations marked (ESV) are from The ESV® Bible (The Holy Bible, English Standard Version®), copyright © 2001 by Crossway, a publishing ministry of Good News Publishers. Used by permission. All rights reserved.

Scripture quotations marked (NIV) are taken from The Holy Bible, New International Version (Anglicised edition) copyright © 1979, 1984, 2011 by Biblica (formerly International Bible Society). Used by permission of Hodder & Stoughton Publishers, an Hachette UK company. All rights reserved.

Scripture quotations marked (NKJV) are taken from the New King James Version®. Copyright © 1982 by Thomas Nelson. Used by permission. All rights reserved.

Scripture quotations marked (NLT) are taken from the New Living Translation, copyright © 1996, 2004, 2015 by Tyndale House Foundation. Used by permission of Tyndale House Publishers, Inc., Carol Stream, Illinois 60188. All rights reserved.

Scripture quotations marked (NRSVA) are taken from the New Revised Standard Version Bible: Anglicized Edition, copyright © 1989, 1995 National Council of the Churches of Christ in the United States of America. Used by permission. All rights reserved worldwide.

Scripture quotations marked (NRSVUE) are taken from the New Revised Standard Version Updated Edition. Copyright © 2021 National Council of Churches of Christ in the United States of America. Used by permission. All rights reserved worldwide.

I

Introduction

MAJA WHITAKER

A semester of research leave had offered me a schedule that was more spacious than usual, so amid the academic work I decided to try my hand at pottery by enrolling in a local community education course. I knew that I was coming to this as a raw novice, but I had not realized the scope of what I would learn alongside the physical skills. In class we reassured ourselves that if we wanted perfectly symmetrical and smooth pots we would go out and buy something cheap and mass-produced. Our teacher reminded us that it is the hand-crafted pieces, with organic forms and fingerprints even, that are most highly prized as pieces of art. This was, I like to think, more than mere comfort for egos bruised by the slow pace of the learning process, as yet another pot collapsed on the wheel or swung wildly out of true. It was almost meditative, the process of sitting at the wheel, learning how to draw out what might be with a balanced and gentle touch, when the temptation to force and assert my vision for the piece forever crouched at my elbow. It offered a new way for me to learn the limits of my control: whatever vision I might have in my mind, my hands cannot necessarily create it. While one's skills increase over time (hopefully), even the experienced potters who taught us spoke about their ongoing experience of needing to sur-render to the process and accept what is given. The inevitable fragility continues through the processes of firing and glazing, given the vagaries of how clay and glaze interact with heat and air, and even the chance dropping on the floor.

As an ever-recovering perfectionist, I found this learning space to be a needed ego-corrective as it re-anchored me to my learnings about the limits of my power in the world and the necessity of submission to mystery in every area of my life. Alongside this I felt an invitation to creativity and fluidity, to dial down my constant attention to managing myself so tightly to ensure that I was showing up just right – not too little and not too much. While my experience is of course my own, this tension is characteristic of how many women describe their being in the world in general, and their being in their bodies in particular.

In 2023, the film *Barbie* struck a chord with viewers worldwide. The speech delivered by Gloria, played by America Ferrera, moved many women as she named so many of the ways in which women are expected to pursue perfection while navigating a multitude of tensions along the way. In reference to body size, she said, 'You have to be thin, but not too thin. And you can never say you want to be thin. You have to say you want to be healthy, but also you have to be thin.'[1] The pressure on women to conform to an 'ideal' body weight, regardless of the particularity of their body, is paired with a persistent denial of the force of that pressure, the reasoning behind it, and the payoffs of success. Similar dynamics are at play when it comes to beauty more broadly. Our bodies are conceived of as raw material to be shaped to fit an increasingly narrow vision of ideal aesthetic standards. As Heather Widdows (2018) has amply explored, the beauty ideal of 'thinness, firmness, smoothness, and youth' has become a global ideal and has taken on an ethical weight that often subsumes other goods. That is, we all feel that we must shape our bodies to meet this standard, regardless of the limits of our power to do so, the costs of this pursuit, and other conflicting values that we might hold. We have become the creator-artists of our body-projects. However, bodies are simply not that malleable. Even if they were unformed clay, which they are not, turning unformed clay into the piece that you envision is no easy task, however deep your desire may be.

These issues are not superficial or peripheral, though they have been treated as such in many male-dominated disciplines. They preoccupy, constrain and oppress many people, but women in particular. The appearance of our bodies, particularly of women's bodies, affects a range of tangible outcomes: social, vocational and economic. In work contexts, women deemed attractive are more likely to be given interviews when applying for a job (a call-back rate of 54 per cent versus 7 per cent; Busetta, Fiorillo and Visalli, 2013), and blonde women get paid more (Johnston, 2010). Men experience similar vocational outcomes in relation to height (Judge and Cable, 2004), and this is no less unfair, yet it is not followed by an expectation that a man would therefore engage in costly or harmful interventions to increase his height. Yet women consistently engage in practices that are costly and harmful to them, that endanger their well-being and limit their flourishing. It is because of this disproportionate burden that women carry that the voices and experiences of women are prioritized in this volume.

In response to all this, the Church and the Christian tradition should be offering an avenue to freedom and flourishing, and a generous invitation for all to belong. The first words spoken over the human person are the declaration that we, in our embodiment, are 'very good' (Gen. 1.31). From this start through to the promised consummation of resurrection, the grand narrative of Scripture affirms embodiment. All things being equal, the longer that we follow Jesus and immerse ourselves in Christian community, the better our body image should be. Yet research shows that while increased church attendance is causatively associated with an increase in general self-esteem and a positive attitude towards oneself, it does not positively affect body image (Bulbulia, 2022). Historically, the Christian tradition has struggled with the nature of people as embodied beings, often dismissing the body or viewing it as primarily something to be disciplined. These issues continue in contemporary Christian communities, which have too often uncritically promoted body-projects shaped by the aesthetic ideals of Western culture. These issues are starkly exposed in the hidden toxicity of diet culture and its questionable claims to produce health and well-being, which have been uncritically absorbed, Christianized and marketed from Christian celebrity platforms and the common pulpit.

In this volume, a rich assembly of established and emerging scholars offer perspectives from a range of disciplines on the female body and the pursuit of perfection within a broad Christian context. Issues around diet culture and body size predominate, in recognition of the persistence of fatphobia as a systemic bias, but the net is cast far wider than this. The various contributions move from foundational concepts, through diet culture in particular, to exploring implications in broader social contexts.

In the opening chapter (Chapter 2), 'Christian Hope through an Embodied *Telos*', Amanda Martinez Beck frames up the lure and deceit of both ableism and asceticism, pointing us towards the pursuit of hope rather than the perfection of our bodies. Her explanation of the *telos* of the body as loving God and loving neighbour provides a firm ground for our approach to a range of issues.

Jessica Schroeder (Chapter 3) uses the metaphors of mirrors and pedestals in contrast to the cross to critique and refine our understanding of the nature of beauty. Beauty is that which 'rightly pleases or ought to please with respect to what it is', rather than objective aesthetic standards that appeal to us either intuitively or by accident of our cultural location. This conceptual clarification offers us a way to critique cultural beauty standards while still pursuing true beauty, theologically defined.

Jennifer Bowden (Chapter 4) draws on her professional expertise as a nutritionist to offer a robust critique of diet culture. She exposes the falsity of its key claims on the grounds of nutritional science and a biblical anthropology that both honours and celebrates the reality of our embodiment.

Kristy Botha (Chapter 5) explores the lived experience of disordered eating and conformity to diet culture through the lens of desire and discipleship. She exposes the painful reality of shame and body hatred as the normal experience of many women which, in addition to the inherent damage these do, distracts and distorts our pursuit of more important values. She points us towards an integrated vision of beauty and offers much to reflect on as we consider our spiritual formation as individuals and communities.

Hannah Bacon (Chapter 6) exposes our prejudicial assumption of knowingness towards fat people and our tendency to view fat women in particular as 'objects that are talked about rather than as subjects with a voice'. She explores the eschatological expectations of Augustine and the elements of apophasis, indeterminacy and excess within this, leading us towards an open posture that 'hear[s] to speech the embodied sayings of fat women'.

Maja Whitaker (Chapter 7) critiques assumptions around the nature of perfected embodiment by exploring the common expectations of the nature of our future resurrected bodies in relation to disability, beauty and body size. The simmering discontentment with the body that characterizes modern Western culture leads us to shape those bodies as reflexive projects of the self, at the same time as deferring our hoped-for bodies to eschatological fulfilment. She offers a vision of diverse bodies flourishing in the new creation as a corrective to the body shaming that persistently pervades culture both inside and outside the Church.

Lisa Isherwood's chapter (Chapter 8), 'Are We Having Great Sex Yet? Women, Their Bodies and Their Pleasure', does not make easy reading, particularly as the issues of harm and global injustice cannot merely be considered at arm's length. She names the paradox whereby 'Women are encouraged to gain control over the surfaces of their bodies but to give away all control in social relations, intercourse and pleasure', and offers an alternative vision for both sex education and liturgy.

Erin Martine Hutton's contribution (Chapter 9) exemplifies how this work has significant outcomes in ways that are perhaps unexpected, moving as she does from biblical scholarship to the primary prevention of domestic abuse. Her interdisciplinary and gender-transformative approach troubles the interpretation of concepts associated with 'femi-

4

ninity' and 'masculinity' in a way that plays out in real-world contexts of deep harm.

The book draws to a close with Michelle Lelwica's confronting exposure of the racist roots of what she has termed the 'Religion of Thinness' (Chapter 10). Her vulnerable narration of her own experience of an eating disorder and her exploration of the complicity of the pursuit of thinness with systemic racism invites the reader to correspondingly courageous reflection.

At the end of each chapter we offer questions for personal reflection and/or group discussion. The intention here is to support you, the readers, in the work of contextualization and application, both personal and communal. In that work, I encourage you to attend to those things that the Spirit is drawing your attention to. You may wish to take some of these chapters into discussion in a small-group setting, in which case the questions are offered as entry-points to the loving and life-giving wrestling that we can do together. Some of these questions will land for you, others will seem less relevant. Some may be triggering and best avoided, or engaged in carefully with whatever support you know that you need. If you are discussing these in a group, hold space for others' stories and others' silence. Disclosure may be discomforting for both the one sharing and those listening – take the time to love one another carefully.

As an editor I am immensely grateful for what each author has offered of themselves and of their scholarship in these chapters. Many of these authors have shared their personal stories. I encourage you to hold these thoughtfully and, perhaps also in doing so, to sense a spacious invitation to consider your own. May the contributions of these authors give you the confidence to reflect on your own stories and on those of your community. May you do so with boldness – critically examining the root causes, the harmful implications and our complicity in these – but also with compassion: taking aim at social dynamics and biases rather than at individuals and bodies. Let us not merely shift the blame around. In all this, practise kindness, to yourself and to others, as these chapters deal with difficult issues, some relating to harm and trauma. But let kindness not lead to passive insincerity. The counter-cultural invitation here is to what Lisa Isherwood describes as 'radical incarnation', which calls us to 'shout out how beautifully and awesomely we are made in the body we have'.

Note

1 *Barbie*, 2023. Directed by Greta Gerwig, Warner Bros Pictures.

Bibliography

Bulbulia, J., 2022, 'Religions in New Zealand Since 2009', *Flourish: The Good News of Science-Engaged Theology*, Carey Baptist College, 18–19 July, Auckland, New Zealand.

Busetta, G., Fiorillo, F. and Visalli, E., 2013, 'Searching for a Job is a Beauty Contest', *Munich Personal RePEc Archive*, no. 49825.

Johnston, D. W., 2010, 'Physical Appearance and Wages: Do Blondes Have More Fun?', *Economics Letters*, vol. 108, no. 1, pp. 10–12.

Judge, T. A. and Cable, D. M., 2004, 'The Effect of Physical Height on Workplace Success and Income: Preliminary Test of a Theoretical Model', *Journal of Applied Psychology*, vol. 89, no. 3, pp. 428–41.

Widdows, H., 2018, *Perfect Me: Beauty as an Ethical Ideal*, Princeton, NJ: Princeton University Press.

2

Christian Hope through an Embodied *Telos*

AMANDA MARTINEZ BECK

'All bodies are good bodies' is a phrase I learned years ago as a hashtag on social media in my early days in the fat-acceptance movement. At that time, I couldn't even bring myself to say the word 'fat' because it had been weaponized against my body from my earliest memory. Nowadays, the word 'fat' is a mere descriptor of this body, much like 'short' or 'brunette' or any other term I use to describe the flesh I inhabit. Now, I am a fat activist, working to bring justice to all people no matter their body size. This is quite a task, especially in a culture that tells us that perfection – aka thinness – is the goal for our bodies. For those of us in less than perfect bodies (which is actually *all* of us), these cultural demands can leave us feeling hopeless. We are left asking, 'Is there any hope for *my* body?'

The answer for the Christian is 'Yes' – there is hope for our bodies! This hope is rooted in what I call the embodied *telos* of the human body. This embodied *telos*, along with a fundamental belief in the goodness of the human body, a theology of hope, and the narrative value of our bodies, will redefine the Christian approach to inhabiting our bodies from one of hopelessness to one filled with the hope, joy and love of the resurrection of Jesus.

The goodness of the body

In *Nicomachean Ethics*, Aristotle says something quite radical in our understanding of the nature of things: that all things are directed towards their *telos* – their purpose or end. For Aristotle, when something fulfils its purpose, it is good. When we are presented with a statement such as 'All bodies are good bodies', we are forced to ask, 'What makes a body *good*?' To put it in Aristotelian terms, a body is good when it fulfils its purpose. That begs the question: 'What is the purpose of the human body?' For that, I turn to Jesus' call to us as his followers – to love God and to love our neighbour as ourselves. I posit that the purpose of the human body is to have a relationship with God, with others and with oneself. Because anyone – no matter their size, strength or ability – can have a relationship with God, others and themselves, every *body* is a good body because it fulfils its purpose.

If the appeal to ancient philosophy does not convince you of the goodness of the human body no matter what, the Scriptures and church history can speak to that. If we start at the beginning, we hear God affirming that the creation of humans in bodies is 'very good' (Gen. 1.31, ESV). Our physical bodies are a significant part of God's very good creation, so much so that we would be nothing but disembodied spirits without them. By default, we have to see our bodies as part of that very good creation. The *Catechism of the Catholic Church* puts this idea plainly, quoting the Vatican II document *Gaudium et spes*:

> Man, though made of body and soul, is a unity. Through his very bodily condition, he sums up in himself the elements of the material world. Through him they are thus brought to their highest perfection and can raise their voice in praise freely given to the Creator. For this reason man may not despise his bodily life. Rather he is obliged to regard his body as good and to hold it in honor since God created it and will raise it up on the last day. (Quoted in *Catechism of the Catholic Church*, 2000, para. 364)

Through our human bodies, we relate and are connected with all of creation. Relationship with God, others and oneself is the beating heart of the human condition.

On the goodness of the human body, church history gives us substantial guidance, particularly on the flesh-and-blood humanity of Jesus. The Athanasian creed, formulated sometime in the first five centuries of Christianity, stated that Jesus is 'completely God, completely human, with a rational soul and human flesh'. The councils of Ephesus (AD 431) and Chalcedon (AD 451) affirmed the hypostatic union of Jesus, that in Christ there are two natures – human and divine – and that Jesus is fully human (body included!) while being fully God. In other words, the goodness of God in Jesus dwells in a fully human body. It is often preached that Jesus' presence at the wedding of Cana implies the goodness of marriage – how much more does that incarnation of Jesus imply the goodness of the human body?

The purpose of the body

Now that we have established the goodness of the body, whether we look at Scripture, church history or an Aristotelian perspective, we move towards why the purpose of our body matters. There is a frequent disconnect between what the Christian faith teaches about the human body and how Christians feel about their own bodies. This disconnect makes it nearly impossible for the Christian to live in the hope of the resurrection. Instead of pursuing hope, Christians have pursued perfection of their bodies. However, if we look at our experiences, this pursuit of perfection has not satisfied us but rather left us hopeless and on the edge of despair for our bodies. Before we address the pursuit of hope, let's look at how we have been pursuing perfection. It happens in one of two ways when it comes to our bodies – ableism or asceticism.

Ableism and asceticism

In a Christian understanding of a person, each human being lives an incarnational reality, an indivisible fusion of body and soul. All too often, however, Christian calls to consider our *telos* appeal only to our souls, leaving our bodies to fend for themselves. Left behind, our bodies are either pulled towards the culturally sanctioned *telos* of bodies – physical perfection, which I call ableism – or the other extreme – neglect, which I refer to as asceticism. The tension between these twin extremes of bodily perfection and bodily neglect leaves many Christians wondering what their bodily aim should be. Some Christians adopt ableism as a faith-driven goal for their body, focusing on things like strength, thinness and ability in order to perfect their physical form. Alternatively, some Christians adopt asceticism as a faith-driven goal for their body, focusing on things like fasting and the rejection of desire in order to fulfil their purpose. One only has to look at the Christian self-help shelf in a bookshop to see what the fat activist J. Nicole Morgan calls 'diet devotionals', books intended to help the faithful Christian lose weight, through ableism and asceticism. These diet devotionals serve up Scripture alongside popular dieting tactics. They encourage prayer to request the spiritual strength to stay with the diet. And they give adherents hope that *this* time they will lose weight 'God's way' and keep it off.

I have experience with both approaches. I've begged God in prayer to make me thin and able so I could do great things for the kingdom. I have studied and memorized verses like Philippians 4.13 and Romans

12.1–2 to help me focus on eating less and exercising more. I have fasted and prayed, rejecting my physical desires for more 'godly' spiritual ones. But none of these tactics remotely helped me become smaller. In fact, I have only got fatter as time has gone on. And I am far from the only one with an experience like this. From a young age, with all the messaging from television, magazines, school and even church, I have understood that to be successful I need a certain type of body. Along with these messages, I also heard in church that my body needed to be disciplined into submission through asceticism. And, most often, a sign of this faithful asceticism was thinness. Like many Christians, I believed that the purpose of my body was to be of use to God, and to be used by God meant being thinner, stronger, abler. For years I assumed a place as a second-class Christian because I thought that my body disqualified me from full and authentic Christian living. However, the more I read the Scriptures and the teachings of the Church throughout its 2,000-year history, the clearer it became to me: God's economy is an upside-down kingdom. When the world champions the rich, the powerful and the strong, God champions the weak, the broken and the dispossessed. Further than that, it became evident that the Western Church must make a fundamental break with our culture's perceptions and preconceived notions about bodies: which ones are to be elevated or denigrated. And it's all based on the incarnation of Jesus. All too often we in the Western Church think of bodies as a necessary evil, something we must feed, clothe and care for in order to get on with the actual valuable work of the kingdom. We can tend to take a dualistic view of ourselves in which we divide our soul from our body and say to ourselves, 'Soul good, body bad'.

Do our bodies matter to God? The answer is a resounding 'Yes', but some Christians live as if there are two distinct realities – the spirit, which is concerned with the things of God, and the flesh, which is concerned with the things of this world. In this asceticism mindset, the body is looked down on and treated with disdain. Asceticism is an extreme way to think about the body, and it has its roots in dualism: the kind of thinking in which the spirit is good and worthy of time and care while the body is bad and not worthy of time and care. Jesus' hypostatic union – fully God while at the same time fully human – contradicts this dualism in a powerful way. The incarnation of God in Jesus says that bodies are as valuable as spirits. We have a saviour who is both God and human, not one or the other, and that is a resounding affirmation of the goodness of the human body! Neglect of the body has no place in a robust Christian theology.

On the other hand, some Christians live as if the body is the outward physical sign of inward spiritual health. In this ableist mindset, the body is held to nearly impossible standards of health and ability. With roots in the prosperity gospel, this way of thinking about the body prioritizes health and wellness as signs of a disciplined spirit. This is a very common view of the body in twenty-first-century Christian circles. People who fall outside of the standards of bodily perfection are seen as lacking or, even more strikingly, as failures.

The problem with asceticism is that the incarnation indicates that our bodies are good and worthy of care. The problem with ableism is that Christian teaching values the least of these, including the infirm and the disabled. The reality of our bodies in God's kingdom is far from these mindsets, and we must start by investigating what the purpose, or *telos*, of a body is. The purpose of the body for the ascetic is for it to be overcome. The purpose of the body for the ableist is for it to be without flaw. Both of these purposes are deficient. Jesus did not become incarnate so that he could overcome his body. Jesus did not exist in a perfect body, nor did he ask his followers to seek bodily perfection. What Jesus *did* ask his followers to do was to love God with all that they are and to love their neighbour as themselves. The purpose of the human body can be found within this framework for living; the purpose of the body is relationship with God, with our neighbours and with ourselves.

A new framework: neighbour-care

Can X (formerly Twitter) change the course of a life? I know it did for me – or, rather, encountering the words of another human, in the person of J. Nicole Morgan, author of *Fat and Faithful: Learning to Love Our Bodies, Our Neighbors, and Ourselves* (2018). I had been reading Paul's letter to the Colossians 2, where he wrote:

> Therefore, if you died with Christ from the basic principles of the world, why, as though living in the world, do you subject yourselves to regulations – 'Do not touch, do not taste, do not handle,' which all concern things which perish with the using – according to the commandments and doctrines of men? These things indeed have an appearance of wisdom in self-imposed religion, false humility, and neglect of the body, but are of no value against the indulgence of the flesh. (Col. 2.20–23, NKJV)

When read in the light of dietary restrictions and food practices, it was clear to me that Paul urged freedom and not dietary regulation. Our culture emphatically tells us that food issues are the locus of self-control and bodily autonomy. A person with a well-regulated diet and a fit body should be the best of us, by our culture's logic. But Scripture disagrees – these food rules have no value against the indulgence of the flesh. It begs the question: 'What does have value against the indulgence of our flesh?'

Like a good millennial, I took my question to X and Morgan's response changed my life. She said, 'Loving our neighbour as ourselves.' Loving our neighbours as ourselves – this is of value against the indulgence of the flesh. All of a sudden, it made perfect sense. The gospel was not just good news for my soul – it was good news for my body as well. I didn't have to follow a set of rules to achieve heaven or the perfect body. All God was asking of me was to love God and to love my neighbour as myself. That was, and continues to be, revolutionary. It has drastically changed the way I see my body and the way I pattern my life in this body. The greatest and second commandments – love God and love your neighbour as yourself – continue to turn the world upside down. And that is precisely where I locate the purpose of the human body: relationship with God, with others and with myself.

Morgan's view of God and bodies would change me even more, par-ticularly when I encountered her definition of one of the seven deadly sins in historic Christianity: gluttony. With her neighbour-care frame-work, Morgan (2018) said that gluttony isn't about overeating or having one too many cupcakes. Rather, it is about loving our neigh-bour as ourselves. Her definition of gluttony is consumption that harms our neighbour. The traditional concept of gluttony – overindulgence in food or drink – places the blame at the individual level alone. Morgan's definition shifts our priorities from making sure we are not eating 'too much' in a given setting to looking at the ways our choices harm or help the people around us. It changes the calculus from merely an individual one to a systemic one, a calculus that requires the transformation of society. It is one that requires what we pray every week in the Lord's prayer: that God's kingdom would come and God's will would be done on earth as it is in heaven. Through the words and friendship of J. Nicole Morgan, I have reshaped my life to a neighbour-care framework, which fits perfectly with the purpose of my body: relationship with God, with others and with myself. From this framework and with this purpose, we can start to reclaim hope for our bodies.

Hope and the Christian

As Emily Dickinson so eloquently stated, 'Hope is the thing with feathers.' Hope is what allows us to take flight amid turmoil and despair. The positivity researcher Barbara L. Fredrickson spoke of the benefits of hope:

> Hope literally opens us up. It removes the blinders of fear and despair and allows us to see the big picture. We become creative, unleashing our dreams for the future. This is because deep within the core of hope is the belief that things can change. No matter how awful or uncertain they are at the moment, things can turn out for the better. Possibilities exist. Belief in this better future sustains us. It keeps us from collapsing in despair. It infuses our bodies with the healing rhythms of positivity. It motivates us to tap into our signature capabilities and inventiveness to turn things around. It inspires us to build a better future. (Fredrickson, 2009)

As Fredrickson emphasized, hope is undeniably a powerful emotion to have at one's disposal. But in my work as a fat activist, I talk with a lot of people about losing hope for their bodies. After a dieting failure (or repeated dieting failures), it's easy to believe that hope is lost, that we will never attain the goal of perfection or thinness or strength or ascetic closeness to God. That feeling of hopelessness is very real and has a notable impact on the daily life of a person who finds themselves without hope – a body without hope cannot see the bigger picture. Dreams for the future are shackled, even to the point of dying. I believe that so many of us have lost hope for our bodies, however, because our hopes are focused on the wrong goal. If perfection is impossible, it is inevitable that we are going to feel like failures. Resetting our goals is necessary.

Hope theory

A secular definition of hope might be helpful. According to hope theory, pioneered by C. R. Snyder in the 1990s, hope is a positive psychological state that has three components: goals, pathway and agency. Goals are natural in the human condition; we set forth with things we want to accomplish on a daily basis. Goals can be long term or short term, but the point is that we set them and expect ourselves to fulfil them. In order to achieve our goals, we need agency (the belief that we can fulfil a goal) and a pathway (the plan to get to the goal). According to Snyder's hope theory, hope is found where our agency and our pathways intersect. We have hope when we have goals that we believe we can accomplish because we have a plan. Weight loss is a very common goal, so much so that Snyder even uses it as an example of a long-term goal in his seminal 2002 article 'Hope Theory: Rainbows in the Mind'. To have a weight-loss goal is ubiquitous; it seems that no matter one's size, one can always be thinner. Snyder posits that there are two types of goals: approach goals and avoidance goals. In an approach goal, someone is attempting to come closer to a target; for example, an approach goal would be to have a thinner body. An avoidance goal is something that a person is trying to avoid; for example, an avoidance goal would be not to get fat.

As stated before, according to Snyder, the two components of hope that get us towards our goal are agency thinking and pathways thinking. Agency thinking has to do with belief and motivation that we can accomplish a goal. Pathways thinking has to do with our plan to accomplish the goal. When those two come together successfully, we have hope that we will accomplish the goal. When we are lacking in either agency or pathways thinking, we do not have hope. Consider the woman who has a goal to lose 30 pounds. Her agency thinking is boosted by all the weight-loss ads that claim such a loss is a matter of willpower; she certainly wants to lose weight and is motivated by the way our society praises thinness and denigrates fatness. Her pathways thinking is encouraged by the weight-loss ads she has seen; they imply that by exercise and eating 'right', anyone can lose any amount of weight. Therefore, she has hope that she can accomplish her goal of losing 30 pounds. What happens when her planned pathways to lose weight do not work? She loses hope. Repeated struggles to lose weight fail her, and her shame increases. Eventually, she is at the bottom, having no hope that her body will ever be thinner. It's easy for her to equate her lack of success with a lack of personal worthiness.

When our hope is placed in an approach goal like thinness or perfection or an avoidance goal like not getting fat, the odds are that we will ultimately lose hope. This loss of hope happens because we have unconsciously formatted our body goals to the pattern of our culture, where bodily perfection reigns supreme. Using what we now know is the purpose of the human body – relationship – we can reformulate our goals and align with Christian hope, one that will not disappoint us or our bodies. This, however, requires a robust theology of hope.

A theology of hope

Hope is a hard thing to pin down. It's commonly defined as a feeling or desire for something in the future. The Bible speaks of hope as something promised to the people of God. Jeremiah 29.11 is one of the most famous verses dealing with such a promise – 'For I know the plans I have for you,' declares the LORD, 'plans to prosper you and not to harm you, plans to give you hope and a future' (NIV). The apostle Paul speaks of God as the God of hope in Romans 15.13 – 'May the God of hope fill you with all joy and peace as you trust in him, so that you may overflow with hope by the power of the Holy Spirit' (NIV). *The Catechism of the Catholic Church* says that 'Hope is the theological virtue by which we desire the kingdom of heaven and eternal life as our happiness, placing our trust in Christ's promises and relying not on our own strength, but on the help of the grace of the Holy Spirit' (*The Catechism of the Catholic Church*, 2000, para. 1817). According to these religious definitions, hope is something we can possess in an anticipatory manner, rooted in our belief and expectation.

For many believers, their Christian hope is founded on a theology that points to eternity in heaven, which many imagine as the strumming of harps on a cloud for ever. Such pie-in-the-sky thinking has left many people of faith in the precarious tension of loving Jesus but not wanting to leave earth to join the (boring) heavenly choir. There is good news for these believers, however, according to the New Testament theologian N. T. Wright. In his 2008 book *Surprised by Hope*, Wright argued that our far-and-away ideas of heaven and the afterlife are not as close to early Christian belief as we think them to be.

Our hope for the future, according to Wright, is contained within the resurrection of Jesus of Nazareth. The resurrection of Jesus does not mean that we 'go to heaven' when we die; rather, it is the first fruits of the life to come, a foretaste of our destiny. Undoubtedly, the earliest Christians believed that Jesus Christ was physically raised from the dead, but according to Wright there is more to the resurrection than that. The resurrection means a new transformed and incorruptible body – and not just for Jesus, but for his followers too. Life after death is not a disembodied heavenly chorus; it's a flesh-and-blood reality in the new heavens and new earth! This has radical implications for our physical bodies. Just like the body of Jesus is renewed and transformed after the resurrection, so ours will be too. That is the hope for the human body – to be renewed and transformed into a new creation alongside Jesus Christ, in relationship with God, others and oneself. The hope for our bodies is the resurrection of Jesus Christ, a hope that we will share at his second coming when we are raised again physically to walk in the newness of life. This hope in the resurrection is transformational for our bodies, especially when all hope seems lost.

One cannot talk about a Christian theology of hope without mentioning the German theologian Jürgen Moltmann, whose book *Theology of Hope* has influenced an entire generation to see hope as fundamentally rooted in the resurrection of Jesus Christ. Not only does Moltmann see hope as fundamental to the Christian faith, he sees within it the path to the end of the age. For Moltmann, eschatology is not merely a study of the end times; eschatology is hope:

> Eschatology means the doctrine of Christian hope, which embraces both the object hoped for and also the hope inspired by it. From first to last, and not merely in the epilogue. Christianity is eschatology, is hope, forward looking and forward moving, and therefore also revolutionizing and transforming the present. (Moltmann, 1993, p. 16)

That is to say, we have hope for what is to come, but that hope does not only allay the fears of the future – it energizes and encourages us to live our faith now. In this way, hope is an indispensable mechanism for living a fruitful life of faith. And how do bodies play into this eschatological hope? As Wright (2008) told us, and as Christianity has preached for thousands of years, our resurrection into a physical body awaits us. By Moltmann's reasoning, the hope of these resurrected bodies energizes and encourages us to live fully into our present bodies, spurred on to faith and joy even while we wait for Jesus to make all things new.

Moltmann also saw hope and *telos* intertwined: 'The Christian hope is directed towards a *novum ultimum*, towards a new creation of all things by the God of the resurrecting of Jesus Christ' (Moltmann, 1993, p. 33). We pursue hope through our embodied *telos* – relationship with God, with others and with ourselves – now and in our resurrected bodies. This hope tells a new story, one that 'opens a future outlook that embraces all things, including also death' (p. 34). Where we place our hope determines how we live right now, and as the goal to be thinner or perfect fades, the goal of living an incarnated reality with the resurrected Jesus blossoms. Such a way of living will produce a new frame of mind, spurring new stories for our present bodies and replacing the negative stories we currently hold.

The narrative of new bodies

One of the most striking stories in the Scriptures is the tale of Jacob wrestling with the Angel of the Lord. In Genesis 32, we are told that, 'Jacob was left alone; and a Man wrestled with him until the breaking of day' (Gen. 32.24, NKJV). When daylight approaches, the Man demands for Jacob to release him, but instead of obeying, Jacob demands a blessing. The Man indeed blesses Jacob, but he also does two other things: the Man gives Jacob a new name, and he injures his hip so that he must now walk with a limp. The new name, Israel, is ambiguous, but some scholars think it means 'He who wrestles with God'. This story is so significant because not only does this new name come to represent the whole people of God, but God gives Jacob – now Israel – a wound he will carry with him for the rest of his life. This could just be a story of encounter with God, ignoring the physical manifestation of being touched in the hip socket. However, the Hebrew tradition holds this wound as precious and transformative, even to the point that the Israelites changed their dietary rules to accommodate it (see Gen. 32.31–32).

Following in the footsteps of the Hebrew tradition to make meaning out of physical suffering, the early Christians do the same. We see that in the story of the cross. Shane Clifton said that even 'the disciples – and the risen Jesus – experienced this meaningfulness retrospectively. In the midst of suffering there is no meaning to be had – no adequate explanation. Only on looking back does it become apparent that God, in his providential grace, has imbued the cross with meaning' (Clifton, 2018, p. 42). Much like the storied significance of the cross, our bodies take on narrative meaning when we look back at what we have experienced and attempt to make meaning from our suffering and experiences. This is what I call 'prophetic memory', the meaning-making of past events for the sake of our faith. The Scriptures are filled with such prophetic memory, from the creation of the world to the exodus from Egypt to the cross and the resurrection. In fact, making meaning out of stories and directing them towards a specific *telos* is a hallmark of Judeo-Christian theologies. According to Stanley Grenz, 'the development of a *telos*-directed narrative is among the most significant theological contributions of the biblical communities (Grenz, 2000, p. 343). As we study the Scriptures, we tease out stories along a redemptive arc to speak to our current situation. What we do with the bodies in Scripture is no less a story-making endeavour, one that brings us into encounter with weakness and brokenness. And we must make stories out of that reality.

The story of a disabled God

One day, as I was praying in front of a large crucifix, these words pressed themselves into my heart: 'My body tells my story.' I looked up at Jesus depicted on the cross and considered what this could mean, that Jesus' body told his story. It was, is, a wounded and broken body – did that mean only a wounded and broken story? No, it is not just pain and suffering; there is great love, joy and hope. I remember asking myself, 'So what story is my body telling?'

Shortly after the resurrection, when Mary Magdalene goes to the tomb to tend to Jesus' body, she runs into Jesus but does not recognize him, thinking he is a gardener (John 20.11–18). In fact, not recognizing Jesus in his resurrected body seems to be a theme – neither on the road to Emmaus nor at the miraculous catch of fish do Jesus' disciples recognize him at first. When Jesus appears to them through locked doors in Jerusalem, they actually know it's him, but they think he is a ghost. Jesus stands before them in his resurrected body and proves his flesh-and-blood humanity with undeniable proof: his wounds from the crucifixion. He stands before them in a resurrected – but still broken – body.

Maja Whitaker has argued that these marks on Jesus' body are not scarred over; they are wounds somehow still open, changed but recognizable as tender marks of his suffering: 'Christ's wounds, still persisting, have been transfigured somehow' (Whitaker, 2022, p. 285). Indeed, Jesus' wounds are not something that will disappear from his resurrected body. When the disciples watch Jesus ascend into heaven in Acts 1, the angels tell them, 'Men of Galilee, why do you stand gazing up into heaven? This same Jesus, who was taken up from you into heaven, will so come in like manner as you saw Him go into heaven' (Acts 1.11, NKJV). 'This same Jesus' – the one with open wounds in his hands, side and feet – will return in the clouds. It can be inferred that the wounds of Jesus are here to stay.

Two inferences we can make about resurrected bodies from these stories are 1) such a body may look drastically different from what we would expect, and 2) the resurrected body has wounds. The narrative value of this wounded and unfamiliar body is important. While it is tempting to assume that our resurrected bodies will be perfect in form and function when we are raised again, the body of Jesus challenges such assumptions. With regard to form, Jesus still bears the wounds of the cross. When Thomas doubts, Jesus says, 'Put your finger here; see my hands. Reach out your hand and put it into my side' (John 20.27, NIV).

With regard to function, consider the image of Jesus that John gives us in Revelation: 'Then I saw between the throne and the four living creatures and among the elders a Lamb standing as if it had been slaughtered' (Rev. 5.6, NRSVA). Disability theologians like Whitaker (2022) and Tabita Christiani (2017) interpret this passage to mean that even in his resurrected body, presiding as king in the throne room of heaven, Jesus stands like a disabled person stands. Like Jacob his ancestor before him, Jesus is disabled. Christiani stated it succinctly and powerfully: 'Jesus the disabled God in his resurrection with pierced hands, feet, and side, is still disabled in front of the throne and empire of God' (Christiani, 2017, p. 36). In spite of his weakness – and perhaps *because* of it – Jesus reigns over all.

The storytelling symbol of a disabled God is transformative. Whitaker wrote:

> Christ's persisting wounds have symbolic power to subvert the pattern of the world which equates power, beauty and hyper-agency with glory, value and freedom. It suggests that the Christian hope does not lie in the 'perfect' unimpaired human bodies and minds achieving ultimate self-realization in the new creation, but in the gathering up of human persons and all creation into the presence of a loving God. (Whitaker, 2022, p. 291)

The perfection that our culture tells us to strive for cannot stand as the purpose for our bodies when encountering the weak and wounded resurrected Jesus.

What does this mean for our hope in the bodily resurrection of Jesus and his followers? It means that even in the resurrection, bodily weakness will not disappear. The story of a disabled God is a transformative paradigm for our thinking, especially about bodies. It means that our wounds, imperfections, weaknesses and disabilities can be a part of the story of redemption. And not only part of the story, but central to our identification and role in it. It means that God's goal for our bodies was never 'perfection' in the way our culture perceives it. (It means that in the resurrection we might even be fat!)

Rewriting our body stories

With narrative examples like the stories of Jacob's hip and Jesus' wounds, we have the opportunity to rewrite the story we are telling ourselves about our bodies. The stories we too often tell about our bodies focus on failure and insufficiency. These are stories of hopelessness and losing sight of the promises of God in Jesus. What we need is a *telos*-directed story about our bodies, one that has the resilience and narrative depth to handle our bodily trials, weaknesses and even failings. Thus it becomes vital that we have our body's correct purpose in mind: relationship, not perfection. When relationship with God, others and ourselves is seen as our body's *telos*, problems with our body become something to work through but not necessarily overcome. There is no perfect body waiting for us at the end of the story, so we do not have to strive to make such an end happen in our present reality. The hope of the resurrection can spur us on to joy and care for our present bodies, knowing that the new creation that awaits us is open to weakness and brokenness. This may seem like a letdown – are we not waiting for something better for our bodies? But at the end of our story, we have weakness without pain or tears (Rev. 21.4). We have to rewrite the stories of our bodies to align with our purpose. We can learn to lean into our weakness here and now because it is a part of who God has made us to be. There is meaning in our suffering, not because God wills it or wants to teach us something, but because we are sharing in the life of the wounded and risen Jesus. In this previous glorious fellowship, in the story of wounds and weakness, we have hope because our body's purpose is relationship, not perfection.

Practices of hope

These stories of weakness and brokenness leave room for hope – the hope of the resurrection, in which we will walk with a disabled saviour. Right now, though, we live in an in-between space, one where the resurrection of Jesus happened two millennia ago and one where we eagerly await his second coming and our receipt of our resurrected bodies in the new heavens and new earth. In this in-between, there are practices of hope – physical manifestations of hope, tangible reminders of our embodied *telos* and the stories our bodies are telling. There are many practices of hope, some with deep roots in Christian history like the laying on of hands, some with Jewish roots like observing the Sabbath, and others from Eastern spirituality like speaking mantras to centre oneself. However, there are two on which I want to focus: baptism and the Eucharist.

The first practice of hope is baptism, the Christian rite of initiation. The apostle Paul described baptism in Romans 6.4–5, saying, 'Therefore we were buried with him by baptism into death, so that, just as Christ was raised from the dead by the glory of the Father, so we might also walk in newness of life. For if we have been united with him in a death like his, we will certainly be united with him in a resurrection like his' (NRSVUE). As we journey through the world in this baptismal newness of life, we carry the symbol of baptism in our hearts and in our stories. Liturgical Christians do more than a one-and-done approach at baptism. It is true that the rite of baptism is a one-time act, but every time these liturgical Christians dip their fingers in holy water and mark themselves with the sign of the cross, they remember and renew their baptismal covenant. The practice of baptism and subsequent remembrances of the baptismal covenant bring hope of the future into our present reality. They spur us on to a deeper, more embodied faith in relationship with God, others and ourselves. Baptism roots our vision of hope in sharing in the resurrected body of Jesus Christ.

The Eucharist grounds us in fellowship with the disabled God. The disability theologian Nancy Eiesland spoke of the Eucharist 'incarnating the disabled God' in bread (Jesus' body, broken for us) and wine (Jesus' blood, poured out for us) (Eiesland, 1994, p. 129). When we participate in the Eucharist, we eat God, we drink God in, we become one with Jesus in his death and in his weak and wounded resurrection. Eiesland called the Eucharist 'a bodily practice of justice', saying that, 'hope and the possibility of liberation welling up from a broken body is the miracle of the Eucharist' (p. 128). For Eiesland, the Eucharist is an act of solidarity:

> The Eucharist as body practice signifies solidarity and reconciliation: God among humankind, the temporarily able-bodied with people with disabilities, and we ourselves with our own bodies. In the Eucharist, we encounter the disabled God, who displayed the signs of disability, not as a demonstration of failure and defect, but in affirmation of connection and strength. (Eiesland, 1994, p. 130)

Notice how this practice, from Eisland's perspective, leans into an embodied *telos* – relationship with God, others and ourselves. In these two practices of baptism and the Eucharist, we ground ourselves in the hope of the resurrection while opening ourselves up to the narrative power of the disabled God. We are rooted in an embodied *telos* and can therefore live with real hope.

Conclusion

As we embrace our embodied *telos* – relationship with God, others and ourselves – we find the hope that eludes us when our purpose is pursuing perfection, whether through ableism or asceticism. With an embodied *telos* directing us, we can set new goals based on relationship and tell new stories about our bodies along the way, as we are changed by our encounter with the disabled God. We employ our agency by enacting practices of hope like baptism and the Eucharist to re-energize ourselves on the journey.

Bibliography

Catechism of the Catholic Church, Catholic Church, 2000, 2nd edn, Huntington, IN: Our Sunday Visitor.

Christiani, T. K., 2017, 'Jesus the Slaughtered Lamb: A Disability Hermeneutics of Revelation 5', *In God's Image*, vol. 36, no. 1, pp. 31–6.

Clifton, S., 2018, *Crippled Grace: Disability, Virtue Ethics, and the Good Life*, Waco, TX: Baylor University Press.

Eiesland, N., 1994, *The Disabled God: Toward a Liberatory Theology of Disability*, Nashville, TN: Abingdon Press.

Fredrickson, B. L., 2009, 'Why Choose Hope?', *Psychology Today*, 23 March, https://www.psychologytoday.com/nz/blog/positivity/200903/why-choose-hope, accessed 21.08.2024.

Grenz, S. J., 2000, 'Eschatological Theology: Contours of a Postmodern Theology of Hope', *Review and Expositor*, vol. 97, no. 3, pp. 339–54.

Moltmann, J., 1993, *Theology of Hope*, Minneapolis, MN: Fortress Press.

Morgan, J. N., 2018, *Fat and Faithful: Learning to Love Our Bodies, Our Neighbors, and Ourselves*, Minneapolis, MN: Fortress Press.

Snyder, C. R., 2002, 'Hope Theory: Rainbows in the Mind', *Psychological Inquiry*, vol. 13, no. 4, pp. 249–75.

Whitaker, M. I., 2022, 'The Wounds of the Risen Christ: Evidence for the Retention of Disabling Conditions in the Resurrection Body', *Journal of Disability & Religion*, vol. 26, no. 3, pp. 280–93.

Wright, N. T., 2008, *Surprised by Hope: Rethinking Heaven, the Resurrection, and the Mission of the Church*, New York: HarperOne.

Questions for reflection and discussion

1   You might not have given it much thought, but take some time to prayerfully imagine your resurrection body: How does it feel? What is it doing? What does it look like? Then consider the risen Christ whose resurrection body is perfected but still wounded: How does this influence your imagining of your own resurrection body to come?

2   The author writes, 'The stories we too often tell about our bodies focus on failure and insufficiency.' What stories have you told about your body along these lines?

3   What new story for your body could you write in light of your reflection on the *telos* (purpose) of your body?

4   The author discussed baptism and Eucharist as practices of hope. How do you connect with these practices, and how might you experience them as more hope-centred? What other practices could you name that help you to lean into your embodied *telos*?

3

Mirrors, Pedestals and a Cross: The Cult of Perfection and the Beauty of Self-sacrifice

JESSICA J. SCHROEDER

A young girl looks in the bathroom mirror, squeezing at little spots on her face, wishing she could rid herself of the adolescent acne plaguing her skin. Her older sister seems to have perfect skin – well, perfect everything – turning heads wherever she goes. A teenager turns her backside to her full-length mirror, having barely squeezed into the pair of skinny jeans she bought last season. They just fit – or so she tells herself. Glancing down at a few magazines strewn across the floor, a sultry model brazenly scrutinizes her from the cover of one. Her countenance falls. She just wants to be good enough. A middle-aged mother sighs as she tugs disapprovingly at the wrinkles spreading across her face. She smiles a lot. Perhaps too much – the crow's feet just won't let up. Turning away from the mirror she sighs again as she steps on to the bathroom scales. The number glares back at her with a shaming taunt.

Such accounts are 'just another day in the life' of women across the globe. Too many women have been steeped in what I call 'appearance culture'. Admittedly, 'appearance culture' doesn't roll off the tongue, but I wish to avoid the term 'beauty culture', as 'beauty' is a term I wish to clarify, redeem and protect. We are plagued by images and messages declaring we must be thinner, prettier, sexier. Airbrushed models and computer-edited – not to mention computer-generated – images set the standard and are placed on pedestals. More extreme examples aside, these rather anaemic examples of the problem are nonetheless illustrative: women feel their bodies must be perfect. In order to feel good enough, to feel worthy, to feel beautiful, we feel we must achieve a certain (though arbitrary) standard of outward appearance. We strive, all too often in vain, to reach such heights. Even for those of us who do reach them – or who simply won the genetic lottery to make it more or less a given – life fails to attain greater meaning or satisfaction as a result. We feel just as empty, just as lacking, just as imperfect.

What if there were another narrative? What if we could redefine perfection; what if beauty had another set of criteria? Thanks be to God, we can and it does. In the face of appearance culture's ideal of 'bodily perfection', the Christian faith speaks a different word.

In this chapter, I will address the primary problem with appearance culture's ideal of bodily perfection, offer a solution to that problem, and finish with practical application. In short, the problem is that the cult of bodily perfection misunderstands beauty and thus leads us astray in our pursuit of perfection. As we shall see shortly, perfection is indeed an appropriate goal to pursue. However, both perfection and beauty – not to mention the way of reaching these – have been grossly ill-defined. The solution I will propose includes redefining perfection and our path to pursuing it as well as rediscovering true beauty, of which Jesus Christ is the prime example. Finally, application will focus on imitating Christ through contemplative prayer as a way of living out the proposed solution.

The problem: a misguided view of perfection

Having introduced the context in which women find ourselves today, we can now turn our attention to the problem inherent therein: the cult of bodily perfection misunderstands perfection and thus leads us astray. While the goal may be a good one in a general sense – that is, aiming for 'perfection' – it is a misguided one. Not only is the understanding of perfection incorrect (bodily 'perfection'), its way of achieving such a goal is also amiss (e.g. seeking some more or less arbitrary standard). Once we gain an understanding of what has gone amiss, we can then look more closely at how perfection ought to be understood.

The goal of bodily perfection is misguided namely because it misunderstands humanity's *telos*. We were made with the intent of moving towards perfection, yes, but appearance culture understands perfection as merely outward. Yet not only this, its 'vision' of outward perfection is largely arbitrary. It prizes thinness and a certain 'flavour' of 'beauty' (or, more accurately, attractiveness) over others.

As already noted, perfection is an appropriate goal. In Matthew 5.48 (ESV), Jesus declares to his disciples in his Sermon on the Mount, 'You therefore must be perfect, as your heavenly Father is perfect.' The pursuit of perfection is clearly appropriate. What remains to be clarified, however, is what exactly perfection is and, similarly, how we go about seeking it. While it will be the goal of the next two sections to treat these, here we shall continue to unravel the problem of society's pursuit of bodily perfection.

At the heart of appearance culture's misstep is a notion of perfection based on subjective perception and standards or, in other words, a notion of perfection based on human ideas rather than God's. Additionally, while it may seem unnecessary to address the misguided means of achieving an already incorrect goal, I believe there is also value in attending to these. One may still cling to faulty means, patterns or habits even if a goal has been redefined. Living steeped in a culture in which certain actions have become entrenched, we may be required to imagine a new way of being. What is amiss about the goal of bodily perfection is the fact that it is the seeking of human-set standards. 'Human-set' standards, as the words imply, are set by people and are thus more or less arbitrary standards rather than those grounded in the divine will. What is amiss about the means is that the seeking places a dual emphasis on appearance and self. I will start by addressing the second (the dual emphasis on appearance and self), which maps out the path for the pursuit of perfection. After this, I will treat the first – the goal based on human-set standards and thus arbitrary ones.

An initial examination of 1 Samuel 16.7 (ESV) illuminates the error of emphasizing outward appearance. In response to Samuel's assumption that Jesse's oldest son must be the Lord's anointed, 'The LORD said to Samuel, "Do not look on his appearance or on the height of his stature, because I have rejected him. For the LORD sees not as man sees: man looks on the outward appearance, but the LORD looks on the heart."' At risk of oversimplifying, this passage shows God's care for the inner person – the heart, one's character – over and above mere outward appearance. Other passages displaying a similar theme include Matthew 23, Romans 2 (especially vv. 25–29), John 7.24 and 2 Corinthians 5.12. If it is inappropriate to place undue emphasis on outward appearance for discerning the rightful heir to the throne, one's inward motives, the justness of an act, and more, then certainly it is inappropriate for outward appearance to be of primary importance in either assessing or pursuing perfection. In other words, to overemphasize mere outward appearance in pursuit of perfection is to be misguided. Moreover, it is to ignore what Scripture declares about God's priorities – what he values most highly. It is crucial to note, however, that shifting the emphasis away from outward appearance does not mean that beauty is unimportant for or unrelated to perfection. On the contrary, and as will become evident below, beauty is intimately tied to perfection. Key to this relationship is how we understand beauty – how it is defined. The point here is that outward appearance simply ought not to be our first and only measure for assessing beauty. Attractive outward appearance is frequently associated with inward or intrinsic goodness and beauty, but not always. It can be misleading.

Having addressed appearance, I will now turn briefly to the inappropriateness of emphasizing the self in seeking perfection. Surely one must focus on oneself to some extent in order to move towards the goal of perfection. At least, so it would seem. Growing towards perfection, however, occurs not when we focus on so-called 'self-improvement'. Rather, as we shall see in greater detail below, it is in self-giving, in opening ourselves up to the other – particularly to God – that we both exhibit true beauty and move towards perfection.

Now, concerning the arbitrariness of human-set standards, while not all human-set standards are necessarily arbitrary, when removed from God's word and his ways – as is typically the case in broader society today – they tend to stray into arbitrariness. Here I am using the word 'arbitrary' to refer to that which is established subjectively rather than grounded upon any necessary, external, objective foundation(s). The human-set standards of bodily perfection this book critiques have been determined by individuals' (and collectives of individuals') preferences rather than the intrinsic nature of things. Passages such as Romans 1.18–32, 8.5–8 and 1 Corinthians 2.6–16 reveal the stark contrast between the worldly, 'natural' person or approach and the ways of God, particularly those led and informed by the Holy Spirit. Our judgements ought to be based on what is, not merely on what we perceive or desire to be. The human heart is deceitful and the mind is liable to error.

Instead of basing our goal of perfection on human-set standards, the appropriate goal of perfection must be redefined with respect to perfection according to the Creator, the one who is perfect and desires his creation to reach perfection. From the very beginning, perfection has always been the goal. A robust theology of creation affirms that God created all that is not God, and that he declared it 'good'. Taking a cue from Irenaeus, we may also affirm that while we were indeed created good, we were on a trajectory towards perfection; we were not yet perfect (*Against Heresies*, 4.38). Moreover, God always had perfection in mind for us, but sin took us off that trajectory. Only through the death and resurrection of Jesus may we be set back on that trajectory aright (Farrow, 1995; cf. Brown, 1975). Indeed, perfection is not merely an appropriate goal. It has always been the goal. Trouble comes when we take God's view of perfection and twist it into our own image.

In summary, if the problem begins inside us – with our own subjective standards and thus definitions and means of pursuing perfection – then the solution is going to need to come from that which is external to us. We need objective standards from an objective reality to guide us.

The solution: redefining perfection, rediscovering true beauty

The solution to the problem of a misunderstood notion of perfection and an unfruitful means towards that goal is to redefine perfection and reset our course towards that goal on a promising trajectory. What is perfection, really? And how do we determine the correct path to reach this goal once it is defined?

Scripture sheds light on what true perfection is. First, we see that God the Father is perfect. As already mentioned, Jesus commands his disciples, 'You therefore must be perfect, as your heavenly Father is perfect' (Matt. 5.48, ESV). Second, we see that God's will is perfect. In his letter to the Romans, Paul sharply contrasts the ways of the world with the will of God, which he describes as 'good and acceptable and perfect' (Rom. 12.2, ESV). Third, we see that perfection has to do with lacking no good thing. For example, in Matthew 19, Jesus interacts with a rich young man seeking eternal life. Jesus tells him to keep the commandments, to which the young man responds, '"All these I have kept. What do I still lack?" Jesus said to him, "If you would be perfect, go, sell what you possess and give to the poor, and you will have treasure in heaven; and come, follow me"' (Matt. 19.20–21, ESV; cf. James 1.4). On the flip side, we might add that to be perfect is to be complete or full in goodness, truth and beauty. In light of these three affirmations, we can summarize: to be perfect is to be like God.

To better understand Jesus' command to 'be perfect, as your heavenly Father is perfect', we need to examine its broader context. In Matthew 5, Jesus says:

> You have heard that it was said, 'You shall love your neighbour and hate your enemy.' But I say to you, Love your enemies and pray for those who persecute you, so that you may be sons of your Father who is in heaven. For he makes his sun rise on the evil and on the good, and sends rain on the just and on the unjust. For if you love those who love you, what reward do you have? Do not even the tax collectors do the

same? And if you greet only your brothers, what more are you doing than others? Do not even the Gentiles do the same? You therefore must be perfect, as your heavenly Father is perfect. (Matt. 5.43–48, ESV)

The context leading up to this command is revealing. A key takeaway from this passage is that, while we are certainly called to love our neighbours, loving those who love us is easy ('Do not even the tax collectors do the same?'). The unique mark of perfection highlighted here is the ability to love extravagantly, which includes loving even one's enemies. Jesus charges the disciples to be perfect as their heavenly Father is. We see clearly in all four Gospel accounts that Jesus practises what he preaches. He loves his enemies in many ways, but most particularly in his obedience in going to the cross. Romans 5 depicts this extravagant love in self-sacrifice, painting the picture rather starkly:

For while we were still weak, at the right time Christ died for the ungodly. For one will scarcely die for a righteous person – though perhaps for a good person one would dare even to die – but God shows his love for us in that while we were still sinners, Christ died for us. Since, therefore, we have now been justified by his blood, much more shall we be saved by him from the wrath of God. For if while we were enemies we were reconciled to God by the death of his Son, much more, now that we are reconciled, shall we be saved by his life. More than that, we also rejoice in God through our Lord Jesus Christ, through whom we have now received reconciliation. (Rom. 5.6–11, ESV)

Not only does Paul sum up the glorious reconciliation we receive through the death and resurrection of Jesus Christ, he highlights our position as 'sinners', 'the ungodly', even God's 'enemies' at the very time of Jesus' obedience to go to the cross. This reconciliation made possible by the death and life of Jesus Christ sets us back on the trajectory to perfection. Moreover, in Jesus we have someone to imitate. Indeed, we are commanded to be perfect as our heavenly Father is perfect; we may also look to Jesus as the perfect example – the very image – of the Father's perfection.

In drawing an understanding of perfection from Scripture, what we do *not* see is an emphasis on outward appearance. But what about beauty? Beauty is intimately tied to perfection. It is crucial to address beauty while redefining perfection, in part because appearance culture poorly defines beauty just as it poorly defines perfection. Appearance culture's standards of beauty, on which it establishes its misguided goal of 'bodily perfection', are both predominantly external and largely arbitrary. Being 'beautiful' is based on the size of clothing one can squeeze into, the shape of one's silhouette and the number on the bathroom scales. At least for women, Western values have recently praised thinness as the ideal. In order to recognize the arbitrariness of such standards – even in the twenty-first century – one need only step into a 'non-Western' country. For example, a study comparing British and Ugandan undergraduates' ratings of the attractiveness of body types ranging from extremely thin to extremely obese found that Ugandans found the obese body types more attractive than did their British counterparts. Interestingly, this was even more so the case with female bodies than male (Furnham and Baguma, 1994). Admittedly, this study is rather dated. A more recent study done in Fiji shows that as 'non-Western' cultures are more and more affected by media produced in Western countries, Western ideals are becoming more common. In other words, women who otherwise may have previously valued their own bodies in a 'fuller' state are now more likely to seek the West's ideal of thinness, in part a result of what is associated with thinness: 'love, wealth, attention, and success' (Kong, 2007, pp. 29–30). As my husband recounted his own travels to Fiji, he noted that plump women tended to be prized and sought after as marriage partners. (Ironically, even a quick synonym search of 'plump' reveals the inclusion of words such as 'desirable', 'enviable', 'sought-after', 'prize' and 'advantageous'.) This at least may have been the case once. It appears that the more 'Western' a country becomes, the more appearance culture's values take root. In addition to the need to redefine beauty – to rescue it from arbitrariness and mere externality – it is important to address beauty because it is a mark of successful movement towards the appropriate goal of perfection.

Before providing a definition of beauty, I want briefly to address the faulty nature of basing beauty on external measures. In short, appearances can deceive. Outward appearance does not always match a thing's 'true substance'. For example, something may be outwardly attractive, yet ugly. Likewise, something may be 'unattractive', and yet beautiful. Examples on either side include, on the one hand, a musically attractive song whose lyrics, upon closer listening, are 'ugly' because of their content and meaning. On the other hand, consider an initially 'unattractive' lentil soup, whose true beauty is revealed upon tasting it. Mere outward appearance is insufficient to determine a thing's status as beautiful. We can turn to Scripture for support here as well. In addition to occasions like Jesus' indictment of the Pharisees' hypocrisy in Matthew 23.27,

Scripture contains several encouragements (even some commands) for women in particular not to place undue emphasis on the crafting of their external appearance; 1 Peter 3.3–4, Proverbs 31.30 and 1 Timothy 2.9 are notable. While these passages have unjustly been used against women to disparage personal grooming, they ought to be heeded for their wisdom: external beauty is fleeting and is not the substance that determines a person. Caring for one's body is an act of appropriate stewardship. At the same time, it can be taken to unhealthy – even ungodly – extremes. As such passages teach, it is the person's heart or spirit that truly determines beauty. These concepts will make better sense once we define beauty.

Beauty, in the most basic sense, is that which, being perceived, rightly pleases or ought to please with respect to what it is. Beauty's distinction from attractive outward appearance comes down to whether it 'rightly pleases or ought to please'. An attractive outward appearance may please on first glance, but a deeper assessment is required to assess an object's true status with regard to beauty. Admittedly, as far as the definition is concerned, 'pleases' is a tame word. Yet while there certainly is beauty that takes our breath away, there is also a beauty that delights in a minimal way – it *pleases*. Roger Scruton describes 'minimal beauty' as beauty 'in the lowest degree'. It still qualifies as beauty but, in his words, it 'might be a long way from the "sacred" beauties of art and nature which are discussed by the philosophers' (Scruton, 2011, pp. 7–8). Unfortunately, examples of minimal beauty tend to be ignored. Rather than denying maximal experiences of delight in beauty, this definition advocates a capacious notion of beauty, making room for the inclusion of all manner of what counts as beautiful. In other words, instead of considering only the Grand Canyon, Beethoven's 'Moonlight Sonata' and Bernini's sculptures 'beautiful', a capacious notion of beauty allows for beauty to encompass everyday wonders such as a cleverly chosen cardigan, the delicate uncoiling of a fern frond, and a well-set table.

Considering the phrase 'with respect to what it is', what would we say of a properly functioning plumbing system? Is it beautiful? At first blush, many would likely argue 'No', but such claims tend to rest on particular notions of what beauty is (e.g. especially overly 'maximal' definitions of beauty). When we affirm minimal beauty, however, we are capable of seeing a well-ordered and well-functioning system as beautiful. The way scientists often speak about the natural world is evidence of this. While it admittedly may be easier to speak of the human nervous system as 'beautiful' than a home plumbing system, these two have more in common than we might initially think. If we call one beautiful, why not the other? The opinions we readily express with regard to beauty may be more rooted in sheer habit than we realize. Returning to the phrase in question, beauty entails a sense of 'oughtness'. That which pleases with respect to what it is takes into account the unique reality of the given thing. A thing's beauty is to be judged according to objective, not subjective, standards. The occasion of 'fittingness', 'rightness' or 'ought-ness' being displayed strikes us with a sense of beauty. This can range from baseline minimality all the way up to the most extreme maximal level.

It also merits noting that beauty is not merely visual. The concept of perception in this definition includes all sensory intake. While we may not be used to referring to gastronomic delights or velvety tactile experi-ences as beautiful, I think this has more to do with our relative emphasis on visual metaphors and language habits than on whether the term ought to be applied in such cases. Again, this comes down to familiarity and habit. Initial awkwardness due to unfamiliarity with a concept does not make it inappropriate or wrong.

Another question may arise at this point – namely, whether beauty may encompass abstract realities such as love, justice, goodness, kind-ness and the like. Initially, these seem to be 'non-perceivable', at least in their 'essence'. These 'universals', however, are only known through particular instantiations, which are perceivable. How else do we know love than through relationship with others or observing interactions between others, whether in real time or through story? How else do we know justice than by particular examples we can perceive in some way? In this sense, then, we can affirm that beauty encompasses abstract uni-versals, in part because they are only known in and through perceivable particulars. But what about abstract particulars, such as an idea in one's mind? Arguably, these things are beautiful as well. They rightly please or ought to please, and perhaps we may consider a person's imagining as a sort of 'seeing' – seeing with the mind's eye.

As a final note on definition, in light of this chapter's consideration of perfection, we might add the nuance of beauty being that which pleases God. As Creator, God is Source of all goodness, truth and beauty. He himself *is* Goodness, Truth and Beauty. Moreover, since God is perfect, his judgement is perfect. If something is truly beautiful, it will please him.

Beginning to apply this definition, how do we gain a firmer under-standing of what is truly beautiful? How do we know what rightly pleases, what *ought* to please, what pleases God? Returning to 1 Samuel 16, this passage demonstrates what is beautiful in God's sight. Moreover, it is an indictment against the world's faulty notion of beauty, which is founded on mere appearance:

> When they came, he looked on Eliab and thought, 'Surely the LORD's anointed is before him.' But the LORD said to Samuel, 'Do not look on his appearance or on the height of his stature, because I have rejected him. For the LORD sees not as man sees: man looks on the outward appearance, but the LORD looks on the heart.' Then Jesse called Abinadab and made him pass before Samuel. And he said, 'Neither has the LORD chosen this one.' Then Jesse made Shammah pass by. And he said, 'Neither has the LORD chosen this one.' And Jesse made seven of his sons pass before Samuel. And Samuel said to Jesse, 'The LORD has not chosen these.' Then Samuel said to Jesse, 'Are all your sons here?' And he said, 'There remains yet the youngest, but behold, he is keeping the sheep.' And Samuel said to Jesse, 'Send and get him, for we will not sit down till he comes here.' And he sent and brought him in. Now he was ruddy and had beautiful eyes and was handsome. And the LORD said, 'Arise, anoint him, for this is he.' Then Samuel took the horn of oil and anointed him in the midst of his brothers. And the Spirit of the LORD rushed upon David from that day forward. (1 Sam. 16.6–13, ESV)

Interestingly, this passage does not comment on David's character directly. Contextually, it is both evident and assumed that the Lord looks on David with favour for reasons other than external appearance, not to mention birth order, life circumstance or line of work. Verse 7 declares God's priorities, clearly describing what pleases him: 'Do not look on his appearance or on the height of his stature ... For the LORD sees not as man sees: man looks on the outward appearance, but the LORD looks on the heart.' The fact that David is chosen, especially as the youngest (or 'smallest') – and as a shepherd, which would have been unheard of – reveals the application of verse 7 to the anointing of David over against any of his brothers. It was David's heart – his character, the 'inner man' – that pleased God. And yet this passage does not teach that external appearance is of no value. Curiously, David is described as attractive (he was 'ruddy', 'had beautiful eyes' and 'was handsome' (v. 12)). However, these qualities were not what caused God to look on him with favour; again, 'man looks on the outward appearance, but the LORD looks on the heart' (v. 7). The theme we can draw from this passage both to understand true beauty and to counter appearance culture's notion of bodily perfection is this: pleasing character is of more value to God than pleasing appearance. While 1 Samuel 16 is admittedly only one example, Scripture carries this theme throughout; 1 Peter 3.3–4, already mentioned above, is one such example. While there are certainly other matters at play in the broader context, at minimum it showcases the worth of the inner person over appearance, particularly in God's sight (compare this with Matthew 23 and Proverbs 31 as well as others cited above concerning outward appearance).

Now, turning to address how beauty is intimately tied to perfection, we can affirm that something cannot be perfect without being beautiful. Beauty is one of three transcendental properties of being, typically referred to as 'the transcendentals'. Her sisters are truth and goodness. All three are properties of being and are described as 'convertible' or 'co-extensive', both with being and with one another (Schindler, 2013, p. 64; McInroy, 2014, p. 138). This 'convertibility' means they necessarily coexist and that one may, in a sense, be exchanged for another. On the most basic level, what is the case for one is necessarily so for the others as well. Being is most essential; truth, goodness and beauty are each ways to describe being, non-redundantly describing different aspects (McInroy, 2014). This non-redundance rests on being's all-inclusive nature; although beauty may describe being differently from truth or goodness, none of these three sisters can add anything to beauty (McInroy, 2014). The transcendentals coexist – are convertible – such that, as von Balthasar says, 'That which is truly true is also truly good, and beautiful, and one' (von Balthasar, 1993, p. 116). Considering the 'convertible' nature of the transcendentals, the relationship between beauty and perfection extends to the other transcendentals: something must be good and true to be perfect. This is evident both in God's own nature and in creation as he spoke it into existence. First, as to God's nature, he is perfect. He is also good, true and beautiful – not to mention being the Source of these things. Moreover, because he is perfect, he is *perfectly* good, true and beautiful. Second, turning to creation, God created all things good. Yet they were imperfect. They were indeed good, and on a trajectory towards perfection, but not yet perfect. While something can be good without being perfectly good, so it can be beautiful without being perfectly beautiful. Once something reaches perfection, it attains perfection of those qualities. Good becomes perfectly good; beautiful becomes perfectly beautiful. Thus, we can assert that if something is not beautiful – if it is *ugly* – then it is arguably 'not on its way' to perfection. A thing's status with regard to beauty based on 'stasis' alone can be misleading – that is, if viewed as merely sitting along a static spectrum. While some things are static, one must also consider whether that thing is 'in motion', moving either towards or away from beauty (and perfection). Based on the definition of beauty as that which pleases or ought to please, if something is on its way to perfection, it necessarily is beautiful. When something that was ugly 'in stasis' begins to move towards beauty, it becomes beautiful by virtue of its movement in that good direction: it is pleasing and ought to please. Thus, a central way of understanding beauty in light of perfection is as a mark of moving towards perfection.

It is worth taking a moment, for the sake of clarity, to define ugliness. If beauty is that which, upon perceiving, rightly pleases or ought to please, then ugliness can be described as that which renders what was beautiful no longer pleasing, or to the point where it is not right that it would please. Ugliness is that which, if it pleases, it pleases wrongly and ought not to do so. Ugliness is not a 'thing' in itself but, like evil, ought to be understood in terms of privation. Ugliness is privation of beauty. Upholding the concept of minimal beauty, it is vital to clarify that ugliness is not a result of 'lesser degrees' of beauty. Something may not be as beautiful as it could be and may not yet be ugly (Johnson, 2020, pp. 33–4). This makes room for both that whose beauty has faded (e.g. a vase of wilting flowers) and that which is minimally pleasing (e.g. a simple piece of pottery, especially one already well formed and fired, yet still to be glazed). Ugliness is not an inevitable consequence of minimal beauty, faded beauty or, necessarily, of beauty muted by some external force (e.g. a tree burned by fire). Rather, ugliness is a desecration of beauty that then stands contrary to beauty. Ugliness is against. '[I]t becomes a challenge to God, a counter-argument in creation to the divine goodness and sovereignty' (Johnson, 2020, p. 34). Examples in Western culture commonly described as 'beautiful' that are not truly beautiful – do not rightly please – include attractive bodies dressed in such ways that objectify the person or encourage lust in onlookers, sexual intimacy outside of the bonds of the marriage covenant, and use of natural resources to produce seemingly good things in an exploitative manner. A common theme among these examples, in broad terms, is the pursuit of indulgence at the expense of goodness or truth. They may please some of those involved, but not rightly. Returning to the transcendentals' convertibility, when one is desecrated the others lose their integrity as well.

Before moving on, it is worth addressing something that has so far remained implicit: beauty is objective and is thus determined by objective standards, rather than subjective ones. While something may be more or less attractive to a given individual – for example, I may enjoy jazz music more than the reader – it has an objective reality with respect to beauty or ugliness regardless of one's subjective experience of it. To use the example of jazz, there is an objective reality to the beauty of good jazz music, whether a particular person 'likes' or 'prefers' it (or not). It is not our perception of something and subsequent judgement of it that grants it status as beautiful; rather, it is beautiful or not based on its reality before God. In fact, we may be in error about our judgements (see Scarry, 1999). To have 'good taste' or 'judgement', then, with respect to aesthetics is the ability subjectively to judge something in line with its objective reality. It is proper to call something 'beautiful' (subjectively – i.e. from one's own 'subjective' standpoint) when it is in fact beautiful ('objectively'). Yet a question remains: how can we know, truly, what is beautiful and what is not? If we are knowing subjects who only perceive in our own unique, embodied contexts, how do we attain such objective standards external to us? In a word, we cannot. Like 'truth' and 'person', as finite human beings, we may affirm that such things exist objectively even though they are beyond our ability sufficiently to define. Yet we have both God's word and his indwelling Holy Spirit to help guide us into all truth, which includes the right discernment of beauty. While we may err, we are ever learning and have the capacity to improve our 'taste'.

Having redefined perfection – in summary, to be like God – and rescued beauty from the clutches of subjectivism, how do we go about moving towards perfection? Now that we have a redefined goal, what means ought we to take to pave an appropriate path towards that goal? As hinted at in the passages of Scripture treated above, to be perfect like our heavenly Father, we must imitate Christ. Romans 5 brought fuller explanation to Jesus' command in Matthew 5, showing that perfection – namely, perfect love – looks like self-sacrificial giving, even (perhaps especially) on behalf of one's enemies. At risk of the claim to imitate Christ sounding like an implicit suggestion, we can turn elsewhere in Scripture to find commands along such lines. In several places, for example, Paul instructs his readers to 'imitate' or 'be imitators', either of God or of him as he imitates Christ. Thus, even when Paul sets himself as an example, Christ is his example (see e.g. 1 Cor. 11.1 and Eph. 5.1).

Before we can consider imitating Christ, however, we must recognize that it is impossible to move towards perfection without first being reconciled to God. Returning to Irenaeus, we may affirm that we were created good, on a trajectory towards perfection, but because of the Fall we fell from that 'path'. Our redemption through the death and resurrection of Jesus Christ – and our response of faith in him – puts us back on that trajectory towards perfection (see e.g. Rom. 8.1–11 and 2 Cor. 5.11–21).

Moving on to consider pursuing perfection by imitating Christ, we can begin by recognizing that the quintessential example of this self-sacrificial love is Jesus' death on the cross. With this paragon of self-sacrificial love in mind, what does it look like to imitate Christ in light of such an example? As we consider this, a crucial question stares us in the face: is the cross beautiful? If judging by mere appearances, one could easily make the claim that the cross is not beautiful. But we have already established that appearance alone does not determine a thing's beauty or ugliness. There is more to it. What about the act itself – that is, its intent? From one side, it could arguably be considered ugly; the cross is a method of gruesome, torturous execution. Yet from another vantage point – that is, from God's vantage point – the cross is an act of exquisite, self-sacrificial, divine love. From this point of view, how could the cross not be beautiful?

To explore this further, let us consider Aslan's death on the stone table in C. S. Lewis's *The Lion, the Witch and the Wardrobe*. The act of killing was carried out by the White Witch, but Aslan willingly accepted this death on Edmund's behalf. He chose it. What the White Witch and her cronies did to him was ugly, indeed. But Aslan's action? I think we could argue that it was beautiful – self-sacrifice of one strong and innocent on behalf of the guilty, especially the rather helpless and undeserving guilty. Moreover, Edmund was dubbed a traitor; that was why he was sentenced to death. Edmund had become Aslan's enemy. Translating consideration of Aslan's self-sacrifice to the cross of Christ, what the Romans and Jews did in killing the Son of God was ugly. It does not, and ought not to, please; this action brutally defiles the good, true and beautiful. In fact, it is an act of putting to death He Who Is Goodness, Truth and Beauty. And yet, when we consider the Son's act of obedience to the Father, his willingness to die, his loving self-sacrifice in taking on the sin of the world and being put to death for the salvation of his undeserving people, this act is stunningly beautiful.

What we see in the beauty of the cross is the beauty of self-sacrificial, self-giving love. But not all would agree that this is beautiful. Indeed, the notion of imitating Christ with regard to self-sacrifice certainly has its critics. Notable are various feminist critiques. For example, citing the feminist theologians Judith Plaskow, Susan Dunfee and Daphne Hampson, Frederick V. Simmons summarizes their concern with Reinhold Niebuhr's identification of love with self-sacrifice as not only ignoring women's experience, but having the potential to 'aggravate their sin by promoting undue self-abnegation'. Such an understanding of love is accused as proving 'pernicious to women and others struggling to cultivate a self of their own' (Simmons, 2021, p. 271; cf. Papanikolaou, 2003). Unfortunately, many feminist critiques tend to conflate self-sacrifice with oppression and abuse, viewing self-sacrifice as necessitating that the historically oppressed contribute to their own oppression. Self-sacrificial giving need not lead to such ends.

Rather than agree with the broader feminist perspective, we have an alternative in the likes of Sarah Coakley. While Coakley recognizes what she calls 'the (wholly understandable) emphasis on "vulnerability" as an opportunity for masculinist abuse', she challenges the feminist critique that has no patience for holding a positive notion of vulnerability, submission, or self-giving and self-sacrifice (Coakley, 2002, p. 33, n. 65). She paints a different picture of self-sacrificial giving by affirming the possibility of opening oneself up to divine power in vulnerability and submission without fear of being 'battered' (pp. 34–5). Using contemplative prayer as her framework, Coakley argues that 'the apparently forced choice between dependent "vulnerability" and liberative "power" is a false one' (p. xv). In fact, she claims it is only in opening ourselves up and 'making space' for God to be God that we can be 'properly "empowered"' (p. 34).

Stepping beyond the notion of power to consider perfection, Coakley's work is instructive in her positing of Christ's example of vulnerable self-giving as core to his perfection. Speaking of Christ in circumstances and places such as Gethsemane and Golgotha, she asks, '[W]hat … if the frailty, vulnerability and "self-effacement" of these narratives is what shows us "perfect humanity"?' (Coakley, 2002, p. 30). Moreover, what about the 'possibility of a "strength made perfect in (human) weakness" (2 Corinthians 12.9), of the normative concurrence in Christ of non-bullying divine "power" with "self-effaced" humanity' (p. 31)? Going beyond helping us to retain safely the notion of self-sacrifice as imitable – and not only capable of being imitated, but also desirable of doing so – she provides a framework for understanding Christ's acts of self-giving love and vulnerable openness to the Father as part of, perhaps even central to, his perfection. Coakley's alternative to the feminist critique of self-sacrifice enables us to look to Christ – especially in his cross – as the epitome, the perfect example, of self-giving love. In him we find not only the solution to the problem of ill-defined notions of perfection and beauty, but also an example to follow in pursuing both true beauty and perfection.

Application: imitating Christ through contemplative prayer

Above, I presented the solution to the problem of a misunderstood notion of bodily perfection as redefining perfection and beauty, and resetting our course towards the appropriate goal of perfection, particularly through imitation of Christ. What does this look like practically? While the world pursues the 'latest and greatest' ways to adapt one's outward appearance, what is the faithful follower of Jesus to do? What actions ought we to take to pursue perfection and foster true beauty towards that end? While there is much that could be said here, I will focus on one primary practice: contemplative prayer.

Drawing further on the work of Sarah Coakley, we can tangibly imitate Christ through the practice she suggests in her response to feminist critiques. For Coakley, the human is both vulnerable and empowered in the practice of contemplative prayer. She claims:

> What I have elsewhere called the 'paradox of power and vulnerability' is I believe uniquely focused in this act of silent waiting on the divine in prayer. This is because we can only be properly 'empowered' here if we cease to set the agenda, if we 'make space' for God to be God. (Coakley, 2002, p. 34)

Ironically, while we probably tend to think of pursuing perfection as an active striving, the posture of contemplative prayer cuts against such grains. It is in this stillness, openness, receptivity and willingness to be met and filled that we may begin our pursuit. As Coakley further explains this practice, we can see how it is linked to imitating Christ:

> [T]his practice is profoundly transformative, 'empowering' in a mysterious 'Christic' sense; for it is a feature of the *special* 'self-effacement' of this gentle space-making – this yielding to the divine power which is no worldly power – that it marks one's willed engagement in the pattern of the cross and resurrection, one's deeper rooting and grafting into the 'body of Christ'. 'Have *this* mind in you', wrote Paul, 'which was also in Christ Jesus'. (Coakley, 2002, p. 35; her italics)

At risk of losing the thread of perfection to a focus on empowerment, let us recognize that Coakley considers engagement in this practice 'one's willed engagement in the pattern of the cross and resurrection'. Recall how Romans 5 informs Jesus' words in Matthew 5. Jesus himself became the prime example of perfect love through self-giving, showing uniquely in these acts of sacrificial love that he is perfect as his heavenly Father is. Contemplative prayer provides us with a practical pattern to engage, which enables us to imitate Christ's openness to the Father's will and his subsequent obedience to the path set before him through such connection to the Father.

For any who may still be concerned about this path of imitating Christ as openness to abuse, Coakley assures us:

> [T]his rather special form of 'vulnerability' is not an invitation to be battered; nor is its silence a silenc*ing*. (If anything, it builds one in the courage to give prophetic voice.) By choosing to 'make space' in this way, one 'practises' the 'presence of God' – the subtle but enabling presence of a God who neither shouts nor forces, let alone 'obliterates'. No one can *make* one 'contemplate' (though the grace of God invites it); but it is the simplest thing in the world *not* to 'contemplate', to turn away from that grace. Thus, the 'vulnerability' that is its human condition is not about asking for unnecessary and unjust suffering (though increased self-knowledge can indeed be painful); nor is it (in Hampson's words) a 'self-abnegation'. On the contrary, this special 'self-emptying' is not a negation of self, but the place of the self's trans-formation and expansion into God. (Coakley, 2002, pp. 35–6; her italics)

Here in this passage we come to a theme central to Coakley's work but not yet addressed here: kenosis. For Coakley, a particular version of kenosis is 'not only compatible with feminism, but vital to a distinctly Christian manifestation of it' – namely, one that embraces certain spiritual paradoxes (e.g. 'losing one's life in order to save it'; certainly, self-sacrificial love would fall into this camp as well) (Coakley, 2002, p. 4). For Coakley, kenosis – while commonly assumed to mean an emptying or 'relinquishing' of some variety or measure of divine power – is the refusal to grasp particular forms of ('false and worldly') power in the first place. Also worth considering is another alternative she offers, which is kenosis as a way of revealing divine power in ('intrinsic') humil-ity rather than in grasping (pp. 7–8, 11). Additionally, Coakley suggests a 'spiritual extension' of 'Christic' kenosis, which she says 'involves … a regular and willed *practice* of ceding and responding to the divine' (p. 34; her italics). The self-emptying, self-giving of kenosis need not reawaken fears of powerlessness. Rather, the passage giving us the very word 'kenosis' is yet one more charge calling us to imitate Christ:

Have this mind among yourselves, which is yours in Christ Jesus, who, though he was in the form of God, did not count equality with God a thing to be grasped, but emptied himself, by taking the form of a servant, being born in the likeness of men. And being found in human form, he humbled himself by becoming obedient to the point of death, even death on a cross. (Phil. 2.5–8, ESV)

Once again, Jesus is our example. Following his lead, in contemplative prayer and thus through humble openness to the will of the Father we may become what he desires us to be. To re-emphasize what Coakley stated, 'this special "self-emptying" is not a negation of self, but the place of the self's transformation and expansion into God' (Coakley, 2002, p. 36).

Finally, revisiting the notion of true beauty, Paul's words in 2 Corinthians 4 may be a comfort to us as we press on faithfully, pursuing perfection and true beauty in the midst of a misguided culture. As time goes on and our outward beauties begin to fade, while our society advocates supplements, creams and treatments of various kinds, we can stand firm on the truth that we both possess in ourselves, and carry, a beauty that far outshines anything the world can offer. We need not – and *ought* not to – lose heart. 'Though our outer self is wasting away, our inner self is being renewed day by day.' We can call to mind that, whatever circumstances we may be facing, 'this light momentary affliction is preparing for us an eternal weight of glory beyond all comparison, as we look not to the things that are seen but to the things that are unseen. For the things that are seen are transient, but the things that are unseen are eternal' (2 Cor. 4.16–18; cf. vv. 6–11, ESV).

Bibliography

Brown, Robert F., 1975, 'On the Necessary Imperfection of Creation: Irenaeus' *Adversus Haereses* IV, 38', *Scottish Journal of Theology*, vol. 28, no. 1, pp. 17–25.

Coakley, Sarah, 2002, *Powers and Submissions: Spirituality, Philosophy and Gender*, Oxford: Blackwell.

Farrow, Douglas, 1995, 'St. Irenaeus of Lyons: The Church and the World', *Pro Ecclesia*, vol. 4, no. 3, pp. 333–55.

Furnham, Adrian and Baguma, Peter, 1994, 'Cross-Cultural Differences in the Evaluation of Male and Female Body Shapes', *International Journal of Eating Disorders*, vol. 15, no. 1, pp. 81–9.

Johnson, Junius, 2020, *The Father of Lights: A Theology of Beauty*, Grand Rapids, MI: Baker Academic.

Kong, Melissa, 2007, 'Beauty Ideals & Body Image: Suva, Fiji', *Independent Study Project (ISP) Collection*, 217, https://digitalcollections.sit.edu/isp_collection/217, accessed 21.08.2024.

McInroy, Mark, 2014, *Balthasar on the Spiritual Senses: Perceiving Splendour*, Oxford: Oxford University Press.

Papanikolaou, Aristotle, 2003, 'Person, Kenosis, and Abuse: Hans Urs von Balthasar and Feminist Theologies in Conversation', *Modern Theology*, vol. 19, no. 1, pp. 41–65.

Scarry, Elaine, 1999, *On Beauty and Being Just*, Princeton, NJ: Princeton University Press.

Schindler, D. C., 2013, *The Catholicity of Reason*, Grand Rapids, MI: William B. Eerdmans.

Scruton, Roger, 2011, *Beauty: A Very Short Introduction*, Oxford: Oxford University Press.

Simmons, Frederick V., 2021, 'Love', in Robin Lovin and Joshua Mauldin (eds), *The Oxford Handbook of Reinhold Niebuhr*, Oxford: Oxford University Press, pp. 263–80.

von Balthasar, Hans Urs, 1993, *My Work: In Retrospect*, San Francisco, CA: Ignatius Press.

Questions for reflection and discussion

1 What is something you have considered beautiful that, on reflection, may in fact be ugly? Or, on the other side of this, what is something you have considered ugly that may in fact be beautiful, even if only 'minimally'?

2 After reading this chapter, how would you reckon with the words of Isaiah 53.2, taking them to be speaking about Jesus?

3 How might the reflections in this chapter equip you to face appearance culture's faulty ideals in your everyday life?

4 How does Coakley's practice of contemplative prayer strike you? How might you begin integrating this practice into your life? What do you hope to see as real-life benefits of this practice?

4

Idolizing Thinness: Critiquing the False Claims of Diet Culture

JENNIFER BOWDEN

Bulimia nervosa was largely unheard of in Fiji until the 1990s, when Western television shows were introduced to the small Pacific Island nation. The impact on Fijian teenage girls of a Western diet of glamorous soap operas and ads portraying White Western women became rapidly apparent. 'I want their body', explained one Fijian teenager (Becker, 2004, p. 546). After three years of exposure to Western television, critical indicators of disordered eating appeared among the Fijian teenage girls, with some 11 per cent inducing vomiting to control their body weight. While 74 per cent reported feeling 'too big or fat' sometimes, 83 per cent stated that television had influenced their feelings or their friend's feelings about their body shape or weight (Becker et al., 2002, pp. 510–11).

The profound influence of Western television on Fijian teenage girls is one mechanistic example of diet culture in action. Primarily a Western phenomenon, diet culture is a belief system that equates thinness with health, gives social status to weight loss, prioritizes control and restriction of foods and exercise behaviours, moralizes food choices and contributes significantly to body dissatisfaction (Faw et al., 2021). Diet culture's messaging provides a largely unseen guide for how to think, behave and what to value in Western culture. These messages are communicated through television and other media, such as magazine ads for women's shapewear, derogatory jokes about fat bodies and overt statements in diet books, including faith-based diet books such as Lysa TerKeurst's book *I'll Start Again Monday* (2022), in which she reveals her long-held desire for a thinner body (p. 15).

Culture also communicates through covert, subliminal messages and metaphors. The most effective metaphors become models that create world views. Diet culture's well-known metaphors include: 'You are what you eat' and 'calories in versus calories out' (Rubino et al., 2020,

p. 489). These perpetuate the belief that health outcomes depend solely on individual efforts and that sufficient willpower will produce weight loss. These claims are false. Body weight is not a proxy for health and weight-loss diets do not work in the long term. Instead, diet culture and the multi-billion-dollar diet industry cause irreparable physical and emotional harm to millions of women. Yet broader culture and the Church still promote diets as a path to a healthier and happier life for women.

In this chapter, I will outline the harms caused by diet culture before exploring through the lens of biblical anthropology, nutrition research and sociological research how this false belief system ignores current science and does not align with Scripture. I will show that women's well-being is better served by holistic health solutions that honour their embodied unitary state as human beings made in the image of God, rather than diets that cause physical and emotional harm, all while discriminating against these women, who are held personally responsible for not digesting their bodies down to the glorified thin body ideal.

The pervasive harm of diet culture: healthism, weight stigma and the oppression of women

Diet culture's ethos of individual responsibility for fatness emerges from the Western ideology of 'healthism', which promotes health as a super-value, not merely a means to a good life but the ultimate definition of it (Crawford, 1980). Healthism positions responsibility for health problems at the individual level, even when social or political factors outside the individual's control (such as a Westernized processed food supply) contribute to poor health. Because weight is equated with health, fatness is thus perceived as an individual irresponsibility. People with fat bodies are viewed as unwilling to control their lifestyle with diet and exercise, and stereotyped as lazy, greedy, unintelligent, unsuccessful, lacking self-discipline and willpower, and thus morally reprehensible.

This framework materializes in pervasive weight stigmatization that causes emotional and physical damage on a global scale, and yet it is a widely acceptable bias in Western cultures. These negative stereotypes routinely result in discriminatory behaviour towards overweight individuals in the workplace, healthcare, public health policies, education, the media and personal relationships (Rubino et al., 2020). Women are disproportionately impacted by weight stigma and discrimination, which leads to gender inequalities in employment and education.

Women are disproportionately impacted in part because women are consigned to the role of a body in Western cultures, where physical beauty is typically their primary source of social capital. Women in neoliberal economies are expected to self-regulate their body weight to enhance their social capital rather than blame systemic issues. Compliance is enforced powerfully through disgust, with disgust probably the dominant mechanism that links obesity to weight stigma and discrimination. For example, the word 'fat' is often used as a personal insult to discredit women in particular, this specifically gendered criticism being founded on the understanding that women's social capital largely depends on their attractiveness (Hamera, 2019). While viewing women purely as bodies was a notable aspect of New Testament culture (Nelson, 1979), it is unbiblical and Jesus did not adhere to this world view; instead, he honoured and encouraged women to be his disciples (e.g. Luke 10.38–42; 11.28; John 4.4–30). Moreover, discrimination of any kind, including weight discrimination, is counter to Scripture's command to love our neighbours as ourselves (Gal. 5.14).

Women internalize the pervasive messages of diet culture. So much so that 84 per cent of American women are dissatisfied with their bodies (Runfola et al., 2013), and 93 per cent of young Spanish women want to change at least three areas of their body (Aparicio-Martinez et al., 2019). Age provides no relief, with over 60 per cent of Austrian women aged 60–70 years dissatisfied with their body (Mangweth-Matzek et al., 2006). Body dissatisfaction is both more common and more severe among women than in men, and it is more closely associated with a woman's feelings of self-worth. This body dissatisfaction increases the risk of anxiety, depression, low self-esteem and eating disorders (Faw et al., 2021). Furthermore, as I will explain in more detail later, almost all weight-loss diets inevitably fail (Ge and Hitchcock, 2020), which compels women to adopt increasingly more extreme diet behaviours in pursuit of the ideal of the thin body (Aparicio-Martinez et al., 2019).

Sadly, rather than critiquing diet culture and defending its victims, the Christian Church has adopted the diet-culture paradigm and reproduced its harmful messages (Parasecoli, 2015). Subtle and overt messages about body weight are routinely dispensed from the pulpit. This includes contributing to the vilification of fat bodies by linking fatness to sinfulness (Gerber, 2012). Many are the ways that Western churches fat-shame their congregation while proof-texting the apostle Paul's message that your body is a temple (1 Cor. 6.19–20; Kidd, 2023). A plethora of faith-based diet books and programmes have emerged in the last century, many endorsed or written by influential male evangelical leaders like

Charles Stanley, T. D. Jakes and Pat Robertson. Indeed, many popular Christian authors and pastors have adopted the diet-culture paradigm and encouraged their followers to do likewise. Gwen Shamblin's book *The Weigh Down Diet* (1997) and her Weigh Down Ministries became a multi-million-dollar global diet empire. Other examples include *The Hallelujah Diet* (Malkmus, Shockey and Shockey, 2006), *The Maker's Diet* (Rubin, 2020), *The Daniel Plan* (Warren, Amen and Hyman, 2013) and Lysa TerKeurst's book *I'll Start Again Monday* (2022).

While faith-based diet books ostensibly focus on health, they share the same preoccupation with body image as secular weight-loss books (Parasecoli, 2015). Moreover, they are based on questionable theology and trivialize the gospel. For example, foods are categorized as good or evil (Warren, Amen and Hyman, 2013, pp. 80–2, 107–14), with claims that 'unhealthy' foods defile the body (Griffith, 2004, pp. 208–13), directly contradicting Scripture (e.g. Matt. 15.10–11; Luke 10.7–8). Others incorrectly frame the prophet Daniel's decision not to consume royal food and wine in Nebuchadnezzar's household as a nutrition decision (Griffith, 2004, p. 208). These faith-based diet books woefully neglect the responsibility of teachers to handle Scripture rightly (2 Tim. 2.15).

Faith-based diet books and programmes also adhere to inaccurate diet-culture beliefs, such as: 1) fat bodies are unhealthy and therefore weight loss will improve health; 2) constantly modifying and monitoring one's body is normal; 3) weight loss leads to happiness; 4) overeating and inactivity result in someone becoming overweight, so eating less and exercising more will produce weight loss. However, these beliefs do not reflect current science, and in this chapter I will critique each in turn.

In addition, the constant modification and monitoring of one's body promoted by diet culture is anything but natural. Instead, it reflects a futile commitment to a secular rather than Christian world view. God calls Christians to *not conform* to the patterns of this world but to discern his will (Rom. 12.2). Yet fat activists have singled out the Christian Church as a 'happy bedfellow with diet culture' (Kidd, 2023, p. 166). Ill-informed beliefs about diet culture are even promoted in theology texts (John, 2022; Koenig, VanderWeele and Peteet, 2024). The Church has neglected to examine whether diet culture's beliefs actually promote health or align with orthodox Christian doctrine, particularly biblical anthropology (Gerber, Hill and Manigualt-Bryant, 2015, p. 83). In the following sections, I will critique diet culture's claims through the lens of biblical anthropology, sociology, weight and health science before presenting an alternative view of health and well-being that better aligns with Scripture.

Diet culture claims that fat bodies are unhealthy

Lysa TerKeurst writes that her body's 'weight is a direct reflection of my choices and the state of my health' (2022, p. xv). However, body weight is not a proxy for health status, and weight loss does not automatically confer health benefits. Obesity does correlate with several chronic health conditions, but correlation does not imply causation: doctors do not advise men to grow their hair for improved cardiac health, even though male pattern baldness correlates with an increased risk of cardiac incidents (Chastain, 2022). Moreover, weight loss does not inevitably correlate with health improvements such as reduced blood pressure, cholesterol and glucose levels (Tomiyama, Ahlstrom and Mann, 2013). Instead, increases in physical activity and cardio-respiratory fitness are linked to more significant reductions in mortality risk than weight loss (Gaesser and Angadi, 2021). Furthermore, overweight people typically live longer than normal-weight people (Flegal et al., 2013), in part because overweight adults have better survival rates from chronic diseases than normal-weight adults. In short, body weight is not an accurate measure of health and losing weight does not make you healthier (Faw et al., 2021). In fact, 'there is considerable evidence that the focus on weight and weight loss is linked to diminished health' (Tylka et al., 2014, p. 3).

Despite this, health policies worldwide enact these diet-culture beliefs. Take the case of a Māori woman in New Zealand seeking fertility treatment. The patient had to drastically reduce her food intake and stop exercising to achieve the lower BMI criteria for publicly funded fertility treatment. Those changes reduced her weight to the required level but ironically resulted in her menstrual cycle ceasing. She explained, 'Just getting to the point where they were like, "you're healthy enough for us to see you" gave us more problems … it wasn't healthy at all' (Williams, 2020). BMI is a highly problematic measure that does not accurately predict health in the general population, especially for non-Europeans, yet it continues to guide public health policy (Rahman and Berenson, 2010; University of Otago, 2020).

Western healthcare models tend to focus solely on the physical dimension of health, revealing the ongoing influence of Cartesian dualism. However, a one-dimensional approach to health will fail to produce holistic well-being.

Both Scripture and science point us towards an understanding of a person as an embodied unitary being; the physical body is an essential part of God's good design. Yet dualist (or even trichotomist) accounts of a human being, influenced by Greek philosophy, persist widely within the Church, and the soul is exalted as the essence of the 'real' self while the body is diminished and humiliated. Within this framework, commands to control and subjugate one's physical body into a thinner form through semi-starvation can appear reasonable, given the soul's superiority over the body. Diet culture treats the body as a disposable set of external machinery that is diminished and humiliated until it is fortuitously shed at death.

Given the holistic nature of the embodied human being, efforts to promote health and well-being must consider more than physical aspects such as body weight, which Western healthcare models are notorious for focusing on (Hunger, Smith and Tomiyama, 2020). In contrast, consider *Te Whare Tapa Whā*, an indigenous model of health developed as an expression of Māori concepts of well-being (Rochford, 2004). There are four aspects of well-being: *taha tinana* (physical), *taha hinengaro* (emotion), *taha whānau* (social) and *taha wairua* (spiritual), all of which must be attended to for the person to flourish. This multi-faceted framework explains a holistic understanding of health that aligns with a biblical perspective of a person as an embodied unitary being who thrives only in relationship with God, other and creation.

Non-diet approaches to health and well-being, such as the Health At Every Size (HAES) framework, also honour the multi-faceted account of health and well-being. The HAES approach encourages body size acceptance; recognizes that health and well-being are multidimensional and interconnected with physical, social, spiritual, occupational, emotional and intellectual aspects; honours hunger and fullness cues, along with food enjoyment; and promotes enjoyable movement rather than exercising for weight loss. This improves long-term health and well-being through improved metabolic fitness, lower blood pressure and lipids, improved energy expenditure, eating habits and psychological benefits. In contrast, diets produce short-term weight loss before weight regain occurs and few long-term health improvements (Bacon et al., 2005). Thus, the HAES approach has a more positive impact on long-term well-being than a weight-loss diet. Despite this, many remain invested in body weight as a proxy for health and dieting to improve overall health, even when evidence to support these beliefs is shaky at best, and those without 'good' thin bodies face ongoing discrimination both within and outside the Church.

Diet culture claims ceaseless bodily improvement is normal

In Western cultures, the body is seen as a project that forms one's self-identity, which should be worked on throughout one's life. While these body-projects vary based on gender and other social factors, they are all concerned with managing one's bodily appearance, given an awareness that the body is a billboard for one's personal brand. Thus, the body is valued as a project because it is a form of physical capital that influences one's social location (Shilling, 2012). The construction of a healthy body is one of the most common body-projects, but it is increasingly linked to physical appearance: a body that *looks* healthy and young, irrespective of whether it *is* healthy (Shilling, 2012).

For Western females, the idealized woman is thin, or at least without visible body fat (Aparicio-Martinez et al., 2019). While plus-size models are gaining popularity on social media as a result of more body-inclusive modelling, thinner models are still the online powerhouses (Anderson et al., 2022). However, not all women's bodies will digest themselves down to acceptable thinness. Our bodies are not all that malleable and cannot contort into any shape at the whim of Western culture's latest body fashions (Memon et al., 2020), as I will explain in more detail later. Thus, many women experience their bodies as being beyond their control while living in a culture that prizes bodily control. Moreover, less affluent women, who do not have the time and resources to spend on this body-project, are alienated. They are marked out through larger body sizes, resulting from eating cheaper foods that are fattier and more processed. In contrast, higher social classes are more able to select foods and activities that produce the thin-body ideal (Shilling, 2012). When the Church perpetuates diet culture it aligns itself with a social hierarchy that benefits dominant groups and harms those in lower socioeconomic groups.

This focus on the continual remodelling of the physical body is at odds with the implicit value of the physical body in Christian theology. The Word came to dwell among us, not in some ethereal, spiritual form, but in human flesh (John 1.14), and it was through his flesh that Christ accomplished our salvation (Rom. 8.1–4). Jesus remained embodied after the resurrection and in the ascension (Luke 24.36–43, 50–51), and has invited his followers to remember him by partaking in bread and wine, representing his body and blood. Yet the body has been treated as suspect, second-rate and even disposable throughout the Christian tradition. The changeability of the human body has been viewed as problematic (Bynum, 2017), and women, with their unpredictable and leaky, menstruating, lactating bodies, have been deemed physiologically flawed (Mercer, 2018). However, Scripture affirms that bodies matter to God (Nelson, 1995, p. 59). We are to offer our bodies to God in worship (Rom. 12.1), rather than control and continually modify them in superficial ways.

Diet culture claims that weight loss leads to a happier life

'Nothing tastes as good as skinny feels' (as Kate Moss claimed in the early 2000s) could be the slogan for all that diet culture promises; the happiness and enjoyment derived from achieving the ideal thin body supposedly outweighs the pleasure of eating delicious food. This claim is extended through slogans, mantras and images (Lelwica, 2010): diet ads often claim that their products improve self-esteem and increase attractiveness; celebrities are used to endorse diets, implying that their enviable life and success are linked to their thin body; and diet trans-formation photos routinely show a glum 'before' body contrasted with a smiling 'after' one. These messages breed and perpetuate the belief that women should pursue happiness and self-worth through diets and weight loss. However, dieting and a thinner body do not automatic-ally produce a happier life; they more often cause psychosocial harm (Memon et al., 2020). While weight loss may reduce the weight discrim-ination that women experience, suggesting that women lose weight to avoid discrimination is unethical. It is discrimination, not fatness, that we must eradicate.

Weight bias aside, adults with a higher BMI typically have better psy-chological well-being than their peers with a lower BMI (Archangelidi and Mentzakis, 2018). Similarly, people who have lost weight are more likely to report feeling depressed than weight-maintainers (Jackson et al., 2014). Indeed, prolonged semi-starvation (as occurs during dieting) produces depression, emotional distress and irritability (Memon et al., 2020). Dieting also leads to a preoccupation with food, increased emo-tional responsiveness, dysphoria and distractibility, and binge-eating episodes once food is available (Polivy, 1996). Given most dieters must stay in an energy-restricted state long term, they also experience these adverse emotional sequelae long term. Christian ex-dieters explained to me how dieting created mood changes and an obsessive self-focus:[1]

Overall, dieting makes me extremely self-focused and takes away men-tal energy from what I should be doing. It zaps the joy out of daily life

... I'm a more relaxed, joyful, and productive wife and mom when dieting is off the table.

Mood changes as a result of dieting impacted relationships with families and communities, noted another woman: 'The scale – how many mornings did this put me in a bad mood around my family?!' When the diets inevitably failed, these women experienced tremendous guilt and poor self-worth:

> When I was dieting, the guilt I felt if I gained weight just pushed me further into disordered eating and disregulation. I felt so self-conscious of my body all the time, worried if I was being judged for my round tummy and thick lower half.

A worrying association exists between dieting and an escalation to eating disorders, which significantly impact quality of life and mortality risk (Memon et al., 2020). In contrast, intuitive eating is *inversely* associated with various eating pathologies, body image disturbances and psychopathology. Intuitive eating is an adaptive eating style that encourages tuning in to internal cues of hunger, fullness and satisfaction. It honours the embodied experience of the unitary nature of human beings and diametrically opposes weight-loss diets that treat the body as a kind of machinery that can be modified at will through semi-starvation. Notably, intuitive eaters have a more positive body image, self-esteem and well-being (Linardon, Tylka and Fuller-Tyszkiewicz, 2021). Combining a holistic approach to health and well-being, such as the HAES approach, with intuitive eating produces better overall well-being and happiness.

Despite this, the pursuit of a thin body is painted as the ultimate purpose for Western women (Lelwica, 2010), who are compelled to dedicate their time, energy and resources to this pursuit, which becomes a vocation for life, with the promise of happiness and fulfilment awaiting. In reality, diet culture fails to deliver the promised thin body and happiness while dangerously distracting these women from taking their place as equals in society (Isherwood, 2010) and engaging in community, vocation and mission. Diet-culture followers adopt a self-ward focus that seeks happiness by aligning to the secular ideal of a thin body rather than a God-ward focus. The process of discipleship involves shifting our attention away from self-interest and towards God and others. Transformation is to be towards Christlikeness not thinness, and it is those who live *this way* that Jesus describes as happy (Luke 6.20–26).

Diet culture claims that diets work if you have willpower

The body-project that diet culture promotes is underpinned by the assumption that a person can control body weight, and that weight loss is possible with sufficient willpower. In fact, diets have a high long-term failure rate, and evidence points instead to an unalterable weight set range for each person. In other words, dedicating one's life to the pursuit of thinness is a body-project doomed to fail.

Weight-loss diets are more likely to contribute to weight gain, independent of genetics, and may have actively worsened the 'obesity epidemic' (Memon et al., 2020). Notably, between one-third and two-thirds of dieters regain more weight post-diet than they lost on their diet (Mann et al., 2007). Yet the scientific community and corporate weight-loss companies continue to promote weight-loss diets and claim responsibility for short-term weight loss before hastily divesting responsibility for the subsequent inevitable weight regain. Such a blinkered view has led to scientific literature on weight management that does not meet evidence-based medicine standards (Aphramor, 2010).

While humans have free will to act of their own volition, the degree to which this extends remains a matter of debate. Many mental and physical processes are unconscious; these reflexive responses and involuntary actions cannot be considered an outworking of free will. For example, a leg jerking upwards after a tap on the knee. Similarly, the body has an automatic psychobiological response to sustained hunger that promotes eating and weight regain to sustain life, which occurs in dieters and famine victims.

The Minnesota Starvation Experiment conducted during the Second World War is a prime example of these automatic responses to an energy-restricted diet. The male participants had a limited daily intake of around 1,570 calories, slightly more than the 1,000–1,500 calories currently prescribed for women on low-calorie weight-loss diets. The men experienced significant hunger and an obsession with food, collected recipes and cookbooks, and dreamt about forbidden foods. They struggled with food restrictions, stole forbidden foods, ate food scraps from rubbish bins, and some experienced such significant psychological distress they were admitted to a psychiatric ward. When the men began a managed refeeding and then *ad libitum* phase to regain weight, several reported binge eating, and some overate to the point of vomiting or were hospitalized for gastric distension. Their drive to overeat remained for weeks after the food restriction phase ended, suggesting food restriction has a lasting effect on food-seeking behaviours (Eckert et al., 2018). The

Minnesota study and others affirm that psychobiological changes drive hunger and food-seeking behaviours in response to energy restriction, which explains in part why weight-loss diets are largely ineffective (Ge and Hitchcock, 2020). Yet, sadly, when these psychobiological changes drive similar food-seeking behaviours in dieting women, they are subjected to gaslighting and told to try harder.

Interestingly, the extent of the Minnesota men's overeating in the re-feeding phase correlated with the degree of prior food restriction and loss of body fat and fat-free body mass. This suggests feedback loops exist between body fat, fat-free body-mass levels and the body's hunger-appetite control centre, which controls food-seeking and eating behaviours (Dulloo, 2021). Psychobiological mechanisms also regulate energy expenditure when energy restriction occurs (Speakman et al., 2011). For example, the body can reduce its resting metabolic rate (RMR), which is the energy used at rest. After weight loss, a person's RMR declines significantly more than expected for the lower body weight, a phenomenon called metabolic adaptation, whereby the body's biology changes to counteract weight loss and encourage weight regain. The participants in the *Biggest Loser* television show experienced metabolic adaptation for six years after the show despite substantial weight regain. Some participants had an RMR 499 kcals per day less than expected even after regaining their lost weight, meaning they had to eat less and exercise more to maintain their higher pre-show weight (Fothergill et al., 2016). Researchers have proposed various theories to explain the altered food-seeking behaviours and down-regulated RMR in dieters, including the weight set point and settling point theories, which contend that each individual has a predetermined body weight point, or range, that their body actively seeks to maintain (Garvey, 2022). Undoubtedly, some form of active regulation drives psychobiological changes after energy restriction, triggering inevitable weight regain to sustain life, thus ensuring almost all diets fail in the medium to long term (Hunger, Smith and Tomiyama, 2020; Speakman et al., 2011).

While diet culture promotes the belief that with enough willpower everyone can control their body shape through dieting, this is untrue. People are complex, unitary, embodied beings designed to survive. When our food intake does not meet our energy needs, unconscious psychobiological changes occur that willpower cannot counteract. Our nature as unitary embodied beings means that we cannot manually adjust our body weight at will.

Honouring an embodied anthropology: a Christian perspective on diet culture

Scripture exhorts us to beware of false prophets who come in sheep's clothing but inwardly are ravenous wolves. Diet culture has cunningly seeped into the teaching and practices of the Christian Church, outwardly clothed in concerns about improving women's health. However, inwardly diet culture focuses on appearances, not true health; that is, on being *seen* to eat the right foods and being *seen* as having the right body size associated with good health, rather than on actual inward health. Thus, diet culture adds to the outward objectification and judgement of women's bodies and ultimately harms women's health.

The Church has unconsciously and uncritically absorbed diet-culture beliefs and widely reproduced and promoted them, as evidenced by the plethora of faith-based diet books, theological texts, and current evangelical leaders that express diet-culture beliefs. While the Church may be motivated by a desire to improve the health and well-being of women, it has instead contributed to their harm. Furthermore, while we could generously class this cultural blind spot of the Church as an unintentional oversight, Scripture calls the Church to examine critically the patterns of this world and not unthinkingly conform to them. In this regard, the Church has failed. Moreover, many churches actively avoid the topic of women's bodies, residing in what Nelson (1995) phrases as a Victorian-like era of not particularly liking human bodies or bodily related matters. However, if the Church does not teach women what their bodies are for and what health and well-being look like, then our culture will fill that void with its own beliefs. Diet culture has done appallingly well at this task, having taught Western women to hold their created bodies to an impossible standard, such that almost all Western women suffer from body dissatisfaction and desire a thinner body. Diet culture has created generations of women who are never satisfied with their embodiment and remain destined to birth further generations of clients for the multi-billion-dollar diet industry.

Diet culture creates a dysfunctional dynamic between women and their bodies and food by promoting false ideas, such as that only thin bodies are healthy, that thin bodies bring happiness and that it is normal and possible to continuously control and restrict foods and exercise behaviours throughout one's lifetime to produce the visual ideal of a thin body. However, the beliefs of diet culture contradict current science, theological anthropology and the truth of women's unitary embodied existence. There is resounding evidence that thin bodies are not automatically healthier than fat bodies, that thinness does not produce happiness (in fact, it often creates the opposite) and, finally, that the thin body ideal is not achievable for all because body weight is not amenable to alteration. Instead, body weight is unconsciously controlled at a set point or range, which no amount of willpower can overcome. Scripture and scientific evidence affirm that humans are embodied unitary beings, not a duality with a separate physical body. Thus, while diet culture falsely teaches women a disembodied anthropology that presumes they can control their body size by fighting their flesh, the truth is there is no separate soul that can control and downsize one's physical body at will.

Diet culture encourages the idea that failing to take action or achieve the thin body ideal is morally wrong, a view the Church has contributed to, thus endorsing the weight-based discrimination women face. However, discrimination against fellow humans based on their body size is biblically unacceptable, for all humans are made in the image of God (Gen. 1.26–27). While the definition of the *imago Dei* has long been debated, what is agreed is that to image God means to reflect God in creation. Thus, *all* humans somehow reflect or resemble God in creation – irrespective of their body size or shape – and therefore *all* human beings and their embodiment are good. Jesus outlined the moral implications of this when he commanded his followers to love God with their whole being, and to love their neighbour, who images God, as themselves (Matt. 22.37–40). We must honour the image of God by showing care, love and dignity to everyone (Cherry, 2017), irrespective of their body weight. A more holistic framework for health and well-being, such as the Māori model *Te Whare Tapa Whā* and the Health At Every Size paradigm (HAES), recognizes the unitary nature of human beings as reflected in Scripture.

The time is overdue for the Christian Church to cease its promotion of the disembodied diet-culture paradigm, which causes significant harm to women and is not consistent with either Scripture or current science. God calls the Church to love, serve and show compassion. Yet diet culture creates a toxic environment that encourages dissatisfaction, discrimination and disdain, resulting in the unethical treatment of many women based on their body weight. The Church must embrace a holistic approach to health and well-being that honours the embodied unitary nature of people rather than treating them as disembodied beings. In doing so, the Church will create a more caring and inclusive environment that honours all women as made in God's image and thus worthy of dignity, love and respect.

Note

1 The following quotes are taken from a Facebook support group 'Intuitive Eating for Christian Women', https://www.facebook.com/groups/intuitiveeating forchristianwomen, accessed 21.09.2023.

Bibliography

Anderson, J. B. et al., 2022, 'Shifting the Standard of Beauty: Beginning of the Body Inclusive Model', *Cureus*, vol. 14, no. 6, p. e25584.

Aparicio-Martinez, P. et al., 2019, 'Social Media, Thin-Ideal, Body Dissatisfaction and Disordered Eating Attitudes: An Exploratory Analysis', *International Journal of Environmental Research and Public Health*, vol. 16, no. 21, p. 4177.

Aphramor, L., 2010, 'Validity of Claims Made in Weight Management Research: A Narrative Review of Dietetic Articles', *Nutrition Journal*, vol. 9, no. 30, https://doi.org/10.1186/1475-2891-9-30.

Archangelidi, O. and Mentzakis, E., 2018, 'Body-Weight and Psychological Well-Being in the UK General Population', *Journal of Public Health*, vol. 40, no. 2, pp. 245–52.

Bacon, L. et al., 2005, 'Size Acceptance and Intuitive Eating Improve Health for Obese, Female Chronic Dieters', *Journal of the American Dietetic Association*, vol. 105, no. 6, pp. 929–36.

Becker, A. E., 2004, 'Television, Disordered Eating, and Young Women in Fiji: Negotiating Body Image and Identity During Rapid Social Change', *Culture, Medicine and Psychiatry*, vol. 28, pp. 533–59.

Becker, A. E. et al., 2002, 'Eating Behaviours and Attitudes Following Prolonged Exposure to Television among Ethnic Fijian Adolescent Girls', *British Journal of Psychiatry*, vol. 180, no. 6, pp. 509–14.

Bynum, C. W., 2017, *The Resurrection of the Body in Western Christianity, 200–1336*, expanded edn, New York: Columbia University Press.

Chastain, R., 2022, 'What Cis-Male Pattern Baldness Can Teach Us about Weight Science', *Weight and Healthcare*, 27 February, https://weightandhealthcare.sub stack.com/p/what-cis-male-pattern-baldness-can, accessed 21.08.2024.

Cherry, M. J., 2017, 'Created in the Image of God: Bioethical Implications of the Imago Dei', *Christian Bioethics: Non-Ecumenical Studies in Medical Morality*, vol. 23, no. 3, pp. 219–33.

Crawford, R., 1980, 'Healthism and the Medicalization of Everyday Life', *International Journal of Health Services*, vol. 10, no. 3, pp. 365–88.

Dulloo, A. G., 2021, 'Physiology of Weight Regain: Lessons from the Classic Minnesota Starvation Experiment on Human Body Composition Regulation', *Obesity Reviews*, vol. 22, p. e13189.

Eckert, E. D. et al., 2018, 'A 57-Year Follow-up Investigation and Review of the Minnesota Study on Human Starvation and its Relevance to Eating Disorders', *Archives of Psychology*, vol. 2, no. 3, pp. 1–19.

Faw, M. H. et al., 2021, 'Corumination, Diet Culture, Intuitive Eating, and Body Dissatisfaction Among Young Adult Women', *Personal Relationships*, vol. 28, no. 2, pp. 406–26.

Flegal, K. M. et al., 2013, 'Association of All-cause Mortality with Overweight and Obesity Using Standard Body Mass Index Categories: A Systematic Review and Meta-Analysis', *Journal of the American Medical Association*, vol. 309, no. 1, pp. 71–82.

Fothergill, E. et al., 2016, 'Persistent Metabolic Adaptation 6 Years After "The Biggest Loser" Competition: Persistent Metabolic Adaptation', *Obesity*, vol. 24, no. 8, pp. 1612–19.

Gaesser, G. A. and Angadi, S. S., 2021, 'Obesity Treatment: Weight Loss Versus Increasing Fitness and Physical Activity for Reducing Health Risks', *iScience*, vol. 24, no. 10, p. 102995.

Garvey, W. T., 2022, 'Is Obesity or Adiposity-based Chronic Disease Curable: The Set Point Theory, the Environment, and Second-generation Medications', *Endocrine Practice*, vol. 28, no. 2, pp. 214–22.

Ge, L. and Hitchcock, C. L., 2020, 'Comparison of Dietary Macronutrient Patterns of 14 Popular Named Dietary Programmes for Weight and Cardiovascular Risk Factor Reduction in Adults: Systematic Review and Network Meta-analysis of Randomised Trials', *British Medical Journal*, vol. 369, no. 8240, p. m696.

Gerber, L., 2012, 'Fat Christians and Fit Elites: Negotiating Class and Status in Evangelical Christian Weight-loss Culture', *American Quarterly*, vol. 64, no. 1, pp. 61–84.

Gerber, L., Hill, S. and Manigault-Bryant, L., 2015, 'Religion and Fat = Protestant Christianity and Weight Loss? On the Intersections of Fat Studies and Religious Studies', *Fat Studies*, vol. 4, no. 2, pp. 82–91.

Griffith, R. M., 2004, *Born Again Bodies: Flesh and Spirit in American Christianity*, Berkeley, CA: University of California Press.

Hamera, J., 2019, 'Weighty Anti-Feminism, Weighty Contradictions: Anti-fat Coverage and Invective in US Right-wing Populist Outlets', *Women's Studies*, vol. 48, no. 2, pp. 146–66.

Hunger, J. M., Smith, J. P. and Tomiyama, A. J., 2020, 'An Evidence-based Rationale for Adopting Weight-inclusive Health Policy', *Social Issues and Policy Review*, vol. 14, no. 1, pp. 73–107.

Isherwood, L., 2010, 'The Fat Jesus: Feminist Explorations in Fleshy Christologies', *Feminist Theology*, vol. 19, no. 1, pp. 20–35.

Jackson, S. E. et al., 2014, 'Psychological Changes Following Weight Loss in Overweight and Obese Adults: A Prospective Cohort Study', *PLOS ONE*, vol. 9, no. 8, p. e104552.

John, J., 2022, *Will I Be Fat in Heaven? & Other Curious Questions*, London: Philo Trust.

Kidd, A. E. B., 2023, *Fat Church: Claiming a Gospel of Fat Liberation*, Cleveland, OH: Pilgrim Press.

Koenig, H. G., VanderWeele, T. J. and Peteet, J. R., 2024, *Handbook of Religion and Health*, 3rd edn, New York: Oxford University Press.

Lelwica, M., 2010, *The Religion of Thinness: Satisfying the Spiritual Hungers Behind Women's Obsession with Food and Weight*, Carlsbad, CA: Gürze Books.

Linardon, J., Tylka, T. L. and Fuller-Tyszkiewicz, M., 2021, 'Intuitive Eating and its Psychological Correlates: A Meta-Analysis', *International Journal of Eating Disorders*, vol. 54, no. 7, pp. 1073–98.

Malkmus, G., Shockey, P. and Shockey, S., 2006, *The Hallelujah Diet: Experience the Optimal Health You Were Meant to Have*, Shippensburg, PA: Destiny Image.

Mangweth-Matzek, B. et al., 2006, 'Never Too Old for Eating Disorders or Body Dissatisfaction: A Community Study of Elderly Women', *International Journal of Eating Disorders*, vol. 39, no. 7, pp. 583–6.

Mann, T. et al., 2007, 'Medicare's Search for Effective Obesity Treatments: Diets are not the Answer', *American Psychologist*, vol. 62, no. 3, pp. 220–33.

Memon, A. N. et al., 2020, 'Have Our Attempts to Curb Obesity Done More Harm than Good?', *Cureus*, vol. 12, no. 9, p. e10275.

Mercer, C., 2018, 'The Philosophical Roots of Western Misogyny', *Philosophical Topics*, vol. 46, no. 2, pp. 183–208.

Nelson, J. B., 1979, *Embodiment: An Approach to Sexuality and Christian Theology*, London: SPCK.

Nelson, J. B., 1995, 'On Doing Body Theology', *Theology & Sexuality*, vol. 1, no. 2, pp. 38–60.

Parasecoli, F., 2015, 'God's Diets: The Fat Body and the Bible as an Eating Guide in Evangelical Christianity', *Fat Studies*, vol. 4, no. 2, pp. 141–58.

Polivy, J., 1996, 'Psychological Consequences of Food Restriction', *Journal of the American Dietetic Association*, vol. 96, no. 6, pp. 589–92.

Rahman, M. and Berenson, A. B., 2010, 'Accuracy of Current Body Mass Index Obesity Classification for White, Black, and Hispanic Reproductive-age Women', *Obstetrics & Gynecology*, vol. 115, no. 5, pp. 982–8.

Rochford, T., 2004, 'Whare Tapa Whā: A Māori Model of a Unified Theory of Health', *The Journal of Primary Prevention*, vol. 25, no. 1, pp. 41–57.

Rubin, J., 2020, *The Maker's Diet: Updated and Expanded: The 40-Day Health Experience that Will Change Your Life Forever*, Shippensburg, PA: Destiny Image.

Rubino, F. et al., 2020, 'Joint International Consensus Statement for Ending Stigma of Obesity', *Nature Medicine*, vol. 26, no. 4, pp. 485–97.

Runfola, C. D. et al., 2013, 'Body Dissatisfaction in Women across the Lifespan: Results of the UNC-SELF and Gender and Body Image (GABI) Studies', *European Eating Disorders Review*, vol. 21, no. 1, pp. 52–9.

Shamblin, G., 1997, *The Weigh Down Diet*, New York: Doubleday.

Shilling, C., 2012, *The Body and Social Theory*, 3rd edn, Thousand Oaks, CA: Sage Publications.

Speakman, J. R. et al., 2011, 'Set Points, Settling Points and Some Alternative Models: Theoretical Options to Understand How Genes and Environments Combine to Regulate Body Adiposity', *Disease Models & Mechanisms*, vol. 4, no. 6, pp. 733–45.

TerKeurst, L., 2022, *I'll Start Again Monday: Break the Cycle of Unhealthy Eating Habits with Lasting Spiritual Satisfaction*, Nashville, TN: Thomas Nelson.

Tomiyama, A. J., Ahlstrom, B. and Mann, T., 2013, 'Long-term Effects of Dieting: Is Weight Loss Related to Health? Weight-loss Diets and Health', *Social and Personality Psychology Compass*, vol. 7, no. 12, pp. 861–77.

Tylka, T. L. et al., 2014, 'The Weight-inclusive Versus Weight-normative Approach to Health: Evaluating the Evidence for Prioritizing Well-being over Weight Loss', *Journal of Obesity*, vol. 2014, http://dx.doi.org/10.1155/2014/983495.

University of Otago, 2020, 'BMI an Inconsistent Measure of Obesity for Māori and Pacific People', 12 June, https://www.otago.ac.nz/news/newsroom/bmi-an-incon sistent-measure-of-obesity-for-maori-and-pacific-people, accessed 21.08.2024.

Warren, R., Amen, D. and Hyman, M., 2013, *The Daniel Plan: 40 Days to a Healthier Life*, Grand Rapids, MI: Zondervan.

Williams, K., 2020, 'Māori and Pasifika "Definitely Disadvantaged" over BMI Fertility Treatment Requirement', *Stuff*, 3 December, https://www.stuff.co.nz/ national/health/123519860/mori-and-pasifika-definitely-disadvantaged-over- bmi-fertility-treatment-requirement, accessed 21.08.2024.

Questions for reflection and discussion

1 How does this chapter challenge or reinforce your beliefs or assumptions about being overweight?

2 Of the four key diet-culture claims highlighted by the author, which ones are you most aware of in your thinking and how?

3 What have been the key sources of these diet-culture claims in your life?

4 How might things change for you if you unravelled and rooted out these claims from your thinking? Would that change how you relate to yourself, God and others?

5

Desire and Discipleship:
Towards Body Acceptance

KRISTY BOTHA

In the opening pages of her book *Appetites*, Caroline Knapp describes her life as a 21-year-old woman struggling with anorexia, living on a strict diet, running miles a day, 'a stick-figure with a grimace' (Knapp, 2003, p. 1). She describes the diet she remained on for three years: 'One plain sesame bagel for breakfast, one container of Dannon coffee-flavoured yogurt for lunch, one apple and a one-inch cube of cheese for dinner.' She reflects on how she grew smaller and smaller, becoming a 'master' of her own appetite and body, yet confused by her inner life and longings. When I first started reading Knapp's memoir a couple of years ago, I was only two pages in, and I began to feel an ache in my heart. I saw the violence to self-understanding that comes with food and body problems. Knapp writes:

> I was cold all the time, even in summer, and I was desperately unhappy, and I had no idea what any of this meant, where the compulsion to starve came from, why it so drove me, what it said about me or about women in general or about the larger matter of human hungers. I just acted, reacted. (Knapp, 2003, pp. 1–2)

Knapp's struggle is not uncommon; in varying degrees many women (including myself) have experienced the reality of some kind of dis-ordered eating associated with a negative body image. We may or may not describe ourselves as having an eating disorder, but we might be preoccupied with the latest wellness trends, continually trying out new diets, new exercise routines or weight-loss medication. We may be familiar with that nagging voice reminding us of the 'imperfections' we need to work on. Sadly, many of us, like Knapp, are unaware of what drives our ambitions for self-improvement.

I was moved by Knapp's memoir because she was not only telling her own story, but she was also telling the story of many women around the world whose lives and potential are diminished because of a disconnected relationship with the body. Women live confined by feeling 'not good enough' – not thin enough, not pretty enough, not 'healthy' enough. The desire for thinness, health and wellness motivates women to continue the literal and metaphorical treadmill of self-improvement. Many women, and increasing numbers of men, live dissatisfied with their bodies. For some, it may just be a slight disappointment with one particular feature of their body or the wobbly bits here and there; for others, body dissatisfaction extends to a strong disgust at their body shape or size.

The issue of negative body image pervading contemporary Western culture is a deeply theological problem. Women are created to live fully alive, to flourish as integrated selves. When women's lives are diminished by negative body image and eating problems, it is not only individual women who suffer: the broader social body is depleted. In what follows, I will consider how Christian discipleship practices can become a 'body-turn' away from cultural obsessions of self-improvement towards desire for the kingdom of God. The human being is a 'loving thing' more than a 'thinking thing' or 'believing thing'; the desires that drive us impact our formation as human beings more than the way we think or even what we believe (Smith, 2009). A turn away from harmful body obsessions towards human flourishing requires awareness of how the deep historical roots of body hatred contribute to contemporary food and body problems; and an understanding of how embodied discipleship practices can turn our love towards the One who gives well-being in the most truthful sense of the word – well-being for one another and the whole of creation.

In the first part of this chapter, I will briefly reflect on how aspects within the historical Christian tradition have contributed to contemporary body and eating problems, and explore the role that body shame plays in the lives of contemporary women. The second part of the chapter will focus on how rituals and practices train our bodies towards a certain *telos*, and I will consider what it might mean for women to flourish in an integrated life – personally, holistically and communally as the body of Christ.

If human beings exist within 'webs of significance', as the anthropologist Clifford Geertz (1973, p. 5) suggests, then Christians exist within the 'webs' of culture and so are not immune to the pull of Western cultural body obsessions. The culture of self-improvement is not contained in the context of the 'secular' world; rather, dieting and weight loss are often praised in the context of Christian churches. The Church, however, has the potential to be the place where an integrated life can be practised, and embodied discipleship can turn us towards desire for the kingdom of God.

The build-up of body hatred

The Christian tradition carries a complex history in relation to attitudes towards the physical body. This chapter cannot give space to the depth of literature around Christian asceticism and fasting during the late antiquity and Medieval period. For the curious reader, I would recommend works such as Caroline Bynum's *Holy Feast and Holy Fast* (1987), Rudolph Bell's *Holy Anorexia* (1987), Veronika Grimm's *From Feasting to Fasting* (1996) and Joan Jacobs Brumberg's *Fasting Girls* (2000). These historical works clarify how social patterns of behaviour and ideas about women and food played into the lives of Christian women during this time. These studies are important for our journey towards body acceptance within contemporary culture. It is not the case that modern society has recently gone off track with our current attitudes towards the body and food. We need to recognize what Shelley Bovey describes as a tap-root of a 'two thousand year old hatred and fear of flesh' (1989, p. 27).

The prevailing narrative within historical Western theology and philosophy often describes the physical body as something to discipline and control for the sake of the 'spiritual' life. As Susan Bordo writes, 'that which is not-body is the highest, the best, the noblest, the closest to God; that which is body is the albatross, the heavy drag of self-realization' (2003, p. 5). In other words, the 'spiritual' is raised over and opposed to the 'physical'; the 'spiritual' is connected to the divine (the eternal things) and the 'physical' is connected to the earth (all that is coming to an end). This conception of a human being as a two-part physical and spiritual being (anthropological dualism) is rooted in the thought of Plato, who described the human being as an 'immortal soul imprisoned in a mortal body' (Murphy, 2006, p. 12). Here, the body is a mere shell for the soul until it returns to the spiritual realm. This dualistic thinking heavily influenced the early Church and still influences the Church today. To borrow Paula Gooder's phrase, most Western Christians today have an 'inner Plato' filtering the way we read Scripture and our bodies (2016, p. 18).

This influence continued into late antiquity and shaped the emerging Christian asceticism that celebrated the practice of fasting to the neglect of the practice of feasting (Grimm, 1996). Through the Medieval era, many Christian writers viewed self-denial as a symbol of holiness and virtue, and figures such as Eusebius, Athanasius, Jerome and Augustine of Hippo promoted health of the soul over health of the human body. Veronika Grimm identifies the reflexive relationship between the social body and the physical body: as early Christians perceived the world around them as a threat to the individual body and the body of the Church, practices such as fasting and chastity seemed to guard against the 'downright poisonous elements' of society (1996, p. 195). The ascetic practices were used as a pursuit of perfect imitation of Christ (*imitatio Christi*) in the submission to the will of the Father. For example, the pioneer of monasticism, St Anthony, after hearing the words of Jesus in Matthew 19.21, sold his possessions and fled to the desert for 40 days of self-denial in search of perfect communion with God. For St Anthony, a life of self-denial became a life of spiritual aliveness: 'The fibre of the soul is ... sound when the pleasures of the body are diminished' (Schaff and Wace, 1978, p. 7). Many monks and nuns followed Anthony's example, fleeing to the desert regions of Egypt and Palestine and, denying the self as they fasted, prayed and served in their pursuit of perfection in Christ. This monastic life was a lifetime of daily martyrdom: 'one "died" each day in countless attempts to "put on the mind of Christ" in humility, generous service, and a forgetfulness of self that would open the mind and heart to a new knowledge of God' (O'Donnell, 1990, p. 59).

This 'forgetfulness of self' is something women experience in dieting culture today. Lindsay Kite and Lexie Kite describe how the participants of their online body-image course reflect distance and detachment from their bodies, 'as if the women are outside observers of their own bodies', and the drive for a 'better' body comes from fearing what others see (Kite and Kite, 2021, p. 5). The difference is that the goal of self-denial for postmodern women is not perfect submission to Christ, as it was for the early monastic community, but rather a body that looks and feels 'perfect' according to cultural norms.

Self-starvation and self-denial through fasting reinforced the dualistic understanding of human beings: the body is abused so the soul can become holy. As one fourth-century Church Father affirmed: 'If the body is strong, the soul withers. If the body withers, the soul is strong' (Chadwick, 1958, p. 109). Caroline Walker Bynum (1987) tells the stories of religious Medieval women to explore how the symbolic meanings of food and bodies impacted their spirituality. She explains how self-starvation enabled women to gain religious and social power and a sense of control over their own lives. For Catherine of Siena (*d.* 1380), who died aged 33 from self-induced starvation, extreme fasting was connected to her ability to lead and influence in ways that would otherwise have been unattainable for her. There is a tension between self-harm and self-care here, as the pursuit of perfect control over the body provides a sense of identity despite the detrimental effect on the body. Similarly, for modern women, self-starvation remains a tool women use to gain autonomy, power and a place in society. Knapp, for example, in reflecting on her experience of anorexia writes: 'Starving, in its inimitably perverse way, gave me a way to address the anxiety I felt as a young, scared, ill-defined woman who was poised to enter the world and assume a new array of rights and privileges' (2003, p. 8).

The influence of anthropological dualism was reinforced by the European Enlightenment and the prevailing vision of rationalism, in which reason was supreme over body. Descartes (1596–1650) argued that a person is essentially 'a thinking thing', and the body a rejected superfluity. The influence of Cartesian dualism remained strong into the nineteenth century, influencing the advancement of a value system based on size and shape of the body.

Moral thinking about food and the body is evidenced in Christian diet devotionals that began to emerge in the United States and other parts of the Western world in the late 1900s. Lynne Gerber (2011) suggests that Protestant Christianity has played a significant role in establishing fat as a 'secular sin', adding moral and spiritual value to the secular weight-loss industry. Consider Presbyterian minister the Revd Charlie Shedd's *Pray Your Weight Away* (1957). Motivated by his personal weight loss of 100 pounds, Shedd's weight-loss advice stood on the belief that 'The fat you carry couldn't be within God's plan for you' (pp. 11–12). For Shedd, being fat represented spiritual weakness, and failure at weight loss represented a lack of faith in God. He writes: 'we fatties are the only people on earth who can weigh our sin' (pp. 11–12).

While Shedd explicitly asserts his claim that fat is a sin, I suspect that many of us implicitly view fat as a sin to be weighed in one way or another – whether that is in how we interpret the meaning of 'gluttony', which Scripture names as sinful, or in how we celebrate the person who has restraint with food as an 'inspiration'. However, fatness does not necessarily correlate with gluttony. Mary Louise Bringle considers the biblical texts that explicitly refer to gluttony and finds 'no condemnation of obesity' (1992, p. 56). Where Scripture mentions gluttony, it is a warning against patterns of consumption that might bring harm to others or to self; it is not describing the shape or size of the body. These passages are concerned with whether a person's life is aimed at the will of God or to self-will, not what the body looks like, and certainly not what it weighs. Bringle writes: 'Forbidden fruits are not forbidden in the Bible because they are fattening; fat-phobia, indeed, marks a fairly *anti*-biblical preoccupation' (1992, p. 56; her emphasis). Christian diet literature titles during the twentieth century are telling of the moral and spiritual link to weight loss: *Free to Be Thin* (Chapian and Coyle, 1979), *More of Jesus, Less of Me* (Cavanaugh and Forseth, 1976), *God's Answer to Fat – Loøse It!* (Hunter, 1975), *Help Lord – The Devil Wants Me Fat!* (Lovett, 1977), *Loving More, Eating Less* (McDaniels, 1988). Also, highly popular diet programmes such as Gwen Shamblin's 'Weigh Down Ministries' (1997) and the evangelical weight-loss programme 'First Place' (Lewis and Whalin, 2001) influenced millions of willing Christian dieters.

In addition to the false connections made between spiritual and moral life and slimming, the more concerning aspect of the diet and fitness movement within Protestant Christianity has been the racial undertones. The White-privileged market of the Christian dieting world points to what Sabrina Strings addresses in her book *Fearing the Black Body* (2019). The link of slimness to the violence of racial and class prejudice systems during and after the slave trade, as Strings points out, suggests a different kind of sin we should be worried about: the injustice done to other people. Does our concern for slimness perpetuate injustice towards those who are fat? Does fatphobic discourse within White evangelical churches continue to uphold racist attitudes? The biblical call to reconciliation, where 'There is neither Jew nor Gentile, neither slave nor free, nor is there male and female, for you are all one in Christ Jesus' (Gal. 3.28, NIV), challenges a hierarchy of bodies. God's plan for right relationships confronts ideologies within Western culture that would rank thin bodies as 'better' than fat bodies. When we start to see injustice playing a part in our self-improvement efforts, we can see the issue of body ideals is no trivial matter because it is not an individual concern only; rather, it is a serious issue with broad social implications.

Shame as a 'normal' way of life

The body-image researchers Kite and Kite (2021) report that 82.5 per cent of women participants in their online body-image course admit to appearance anxiety, causing them to stay away from events or turn down social invitations. When they asked the question: 'How do you feel about your body?' they received answers like: 'I feel like I'm too fat or not skinny enough for the world today'; 'It has never looked how I want it to. There is cellulite, scars, veins ... things I try hard to keep hidden.' Another respondent wrote: 'This is so weird for me to think about and even admit to anyone ... I certainly hide all of the time. I hide from old friends that I want to see so badly because I don't want them to see the "fat" me.' The concerns women express around the shame of body appearance could seem superficial or materialistic. However, rising numbers of women of all ages experience eating disorders and disordered eating: body shame poses a threat to human flourishing, with consequences for both the individual and the social body. Body shame can cause some women to withdraw or hide away, oppressed by the unattainable standards of Western culture. For other women, the shame of not measuring up to the 'thin ideal' can cause them to turn to disordered eating as an attempt to avoid or alleviate body shame.

I am particularly devastated by the way that the experience of shame has become the 'normal' emotion experienced in relation to one's body, so much so that for a woman not to be ashamed of her body may seem 'abnormal'. Courtney Martin describes this in the title of her book as *The Frightening New Normalcy of Hating Your Body* (2007). We tend to view our bodies as shameful because of our own 'failures' of self-control or discipline, rather than a result of the cultural 'web' in which we exist. Shame can become a deep habitual feeling that traps women in paralysing ways of being – passive, depressed and self-rejecting (Pattison, 2000, p. 7). For some women, body shame can be a discrete and tolerable feeling, whereas others experience shame as a constant state of everyday life in the body.

The diet industry uses shame tactics to build their market and to sustain their business as failed dieters return to the companies and become lifetime members. The former finance director of WeightWatchers, Richard Samber, told *The Guardian* in 2013 that their business comes from the 84 per cent who fail to keep off the weight (Peretti, 2013). Shaming before-and-after photos are typically used to send a message of the shameful self, transformed into a presentable body ready for the public eye. A testimonial on the Nutrisystem website reads: 'Before Nutrisystem, I was so ashamed of my weight that I would wear my baggy ER scrubs at home. That's not me anymore, and I'm a better nurse because of it.'[1] Testimonies of this kind are commonplace in advertising for weight-loss programmes. The message they relay is that the 'fat' self is to be feared and 'fixed' – the 'better' thinner self can hold her head high, proud of her slimming accomplishments.

The kind of shame driven by the Western weight-loss industry is either based around 'looking' out of shape (i.e. fat) or 'looking' like a health concern. The worrying thing is that weight and health are now commonly seen as one and the same, so that the pursuit of the 'thin ideal' and the pursuit of health are conflated. The invention of the 'obesity epidemic' has provided a way for proponents of diet culture to portray fat bodies as a risk to individuals, society and the economy. The fear of fat has become a health risk as well as an aesthetic concern, intensifying the supposed shamefulness of fat. The gloomy fact is that a high percentage of dieters are unable to maintain weight loss, continuing the cycle of shame and self-loathing.

The issue of body shame creates a tension when it comes to discussing a Christian response, because the Church, like any other social system, has often used shame to manipulate, order and control. The entrenched patriarchal Christian interpretation of the Genesis narrative that links women's bodies to sin and guilt enforces the inherent shame of the female body. Without questioning the patriarchal influence on theology, it can be easy to view shame as an appropriate state for Christian women – a way to keep us 'modest' and self-disciplined. However, we are called to human flourishing, to be people who reflect the image of God (Gen. 1.26–27), a 'new creation' in Christ (2 Cor. 5.17, NIV), living within the grace given to us through God's incarnation in Christ (John 1.14; Phil. 2.6–7). Thus we must face the way that body shame poses a threat to human flourishing and the call to live 'in Christ' (2 Cor. 5.17, NIV).

So far, this chapter has discussed the body as disciplined and controlled by early philosophers and mystics, the body that symbolizes morality and rejects diversity, and the body as shamed by Western culture. The journey towards body acceptance, at this stage, seems daunting. It is easy to see why diet companies make billions of dollars supporting the fight against the body! I will centre my response around three theological questions that will help move us towards a vision of body acceptance. First, how can Christian theology challenge anthropological dualism? Second, how can an understanding of true Christian character provide new ways of accepting body diversity? Third, how can embodied practices create a body-turn towards desire for the kingdom of God?

Towards body acceptance

Although the idea of human beings as a split body/soul is rooted in ancient Greek philosophy rather than biblical framings, anthropological dualism still persists in contemporary Christianity. In a recent Bible study group I attended, the teaching on the body read: 'the body acts as a temporary house or shell that contains our soul and spirit.' I could not help but hear echoes of Plato and his successors who downplayed the role of the body and elevated the soul as something separate and superior to the body. Gooder explains it well: 'In the minds of many, "spiritual" is the opposite of "physical"; the "spiritual" is associated with God and the "physical" with earth; the "spiritual" with all things good and the "physical" with all things bad' (2016, pp. 5–6). This distrust of the body is a far cry from the Hebrew roots of Christianity. As Gerhard von Rad explains, in Old Testament teaching, 'our bodies and passions and all creation blessings' are 'thoroughly worthy of trust' (1972, p. 203). Scripture affirms the human person as an embodied self – the whole person in constant relation with God and others.

Yet an unbiblical dualistic view of the human being persists, leaving many Christians ambivalent towards the body as the 'spiritual' life takes priority over the physical body. According to Elizabeth Kent:

> it matters a great deal whether when speaking of the body we are thinking of merely flesh and bones or a living, breathing canvas of meaning which encapsulates the very essence of a person. Whether we speak of *having* a body rather than *being* embodied reveals our relationship to the body. (Kent, 2013, p. 116; her emphasis)

If we believe that the body is not an essential part of a person but something we will leave behind when we die and go to heaven, why would our bodies be important for spiritual formation here on earth? Our anthropology shapes our practice, and the prevailing anthropological dualism has contributed to the Church's impotence in the face of the genuine body-needs of contemporary Christians.

Kent (2013) suggests that one of the reasons the Church has frequently failed to address disordered eating is her uncritical alignment with Western cultural attitudes that understand the body in individualistic terms and which prize autonomy. One consequence of this 'privatized belief' is our 'struggle to articulate a Christian response to the views of embodied identity and practices of the body with which we disagree because we are so firmly wed to the notion of one's body as one's own inviolable kingdom' (Kent, 2013, pp. 116–17). Our journey towards body acceptance must attend to the individualistic culture of Western societies. While the formation of an individual identity is a key process in adolescent psychosocial development, it has become vastly overemphasized within Western culture. So much so that 'be true to yourself' has become the best truth offered to adolescents and young adults.

This plays out in the pursuit of an ideal as an individual responsibility, in which self-determination and willpower of the individual are characteristics required for 'success'. 'I' am a self who has reign over *my* body, and 'I' will work to achieve the end goal. As a result, the individual pursuit of the thin body often breeds competition, comparison, envy and shame. A truly Christian view of the body is not marked by individualism, but instead by the belief that we are made for community with God, others and the whole creation. Theologically the ultimate purpose of the body is relationship with God through Jesus Christ, outworked in self-giving love to the other, as we await the final redemption of our bodies (Rom. 8.22–25) and eternal communion with God in the new creation (Rev. 21).

The Revd Charlie Shedd's assumption that fat can be named and measured as 'sin' is misguided and harmful, and the theology behind it must be critiqued. When our efforts to pursue a 'good' body cause harm to others (as we become 'superior' to those who have 'bad' bodies), or harm to ourselves, it is obvious that something has gone awry. We must recover a more biblical narrative of what human flourishing entails in holistic and communal terms. We are to take care of the vulnerable in our society – people prone to eating disorders, people in disabled bodies, people who are discriminated against because of their shape, size, race, class or gender. A focus on Jesus' Sermon on the Mount (Matt. 5—7) reorientates our moral compass towards the virtue of integrated human flourishing rather than fake morality that in fact causes harm to others. Jesus' teaching connects with greater social realities in a very practical and active way, pointing to an outworking of Christian virtue that is outward-focused, glorifying God through worship, mission and service to others. Human flourishing as envisioned in the Sermon on the Mount can only be realized through being focused on the common good of all human beings – being an active disciple of Jesus in the world, loving others and bearing witness to how Jesus responded in the world.

The integrated life: a vision for everyday living

> A beauty that is found in integrity of relationships; in a deep integration of who we are as individuals and as a community; a beauty that does not fear age and can look suffering in the face with courage. A beauty that finds its roots in the compassion of God and shines glory into the darkest crevices of our world. A beauty that is Christ shaped and marked by faith, hope and, most of all, love. (Gooder, 2016, p. 132)

I read Gooder's book a few years ago, but these words and the re-imagined definition of the 'body beautiful' have continued to replay in my mind. The image our culture imprints on our hearts and minds of what a beautiful female body 'should' look like can overshadow the true vision of what God has called us to live into. The fact that the Christian tradition (the worst parts of it) seems to back up our body hatred makes it difficult to see the form of culture's influence. A prophetic vision about our bodies radiating, as Gooder says, 'A beauty that is Christ shaped and marked by faith, hope and, most of all, love' makes me excited for the possibilities women hold to live free from the force of self-hatred and body shame.

However, it is difficult to move towards this vision without first understanding how practices and rituals work in our lives to draw us towards a certain vision or *telos*. Practices have the power to unconsciously lead us towards a certain end goal; as Foucault described: 'People know what they do; they frequently know why they do what they do; but what they don't know is what what they do does' (quoted in Dreyfus and Rabinow, 2013, p. 187). In our current Western society, it is probably more common for a woman to move towards the goal of cultural beauty instinctively, rather than consciously considering what body-shaping practices do to her self-understanding or how these practices affect other people. We saw an example of this in the opening quote from Knapp: 'I had no idea what any of this meant, where the compulsion to starve came from ... I just acted, reacted' (2003, pp. 1–2).

The anthropologist Roy Rappaport suggested ritual is *the* basic act of humanity, and characterized emotions as the stimulating force of many rituals. He said of emotions: 'It is not unreasonable, therefore, to take them to be a source of ritual's "power" or of the participants' ability to bring about the states of affairs for which they strive' (Rappaport, 1999, p. 49). The repetitive, embodied practices aimed at the goal of thinness can be likened to religious rituals such as habitual prayer, meditation, partaking of the Eucharist or worship through singing. In the same way daily prayer and worship connects our emotions to the presence of the sacred, the practices of weight loss and body shaping are empowered by the desire to achieve an 'ideal' body and an 'ideal' life. When we begin to view the rituals of body shaping as identity-forming practices, or liturgies, we can begin to do the process of 'cultural exegesis' – that is, a critical examination of how cultural practices shape our lives. The important questions to ask when interpreting culture, according to James Smith (2009), are not those related to what culture teaches us through film or policy and so on, but rather how culture forms us as people when we practise certain rituals. 'If culture works *on* anything,' Kathryn Tanner wrote, 'it works on bare animal or bodily based capacities with an extensive and indefinite range of possible outcomes' (1997, p. 28; her emphasis). I suggest that the everyday practices of shaping our bodies to match the cultural vision of beauty are what distract us from moving towards something more like Gooder's definition of beauty.

Everyday practices associated with attaining or maintaining the cultural ideal of the body beautiful are in many ways a normal or seemingly necessary part of life for many women in the postmodern privileged West. The lives of many women are organized around routines such as food restriction, calorie counting, excessive exercise, separating food as 'good' and 'bad', food diaries and weight monitoring. These practices may seem like superficial daily motions void of any 'religious' meaning – for example, stepping on the bathroom scales each morning does not seem like a religious activity. However, these routines are working at a deeper level, shaping our values and identity as we commit time, thought and energy to them. Like any other rituals 'secular' or sacred, the embodied practices aimed at thinness 'say' something about what is being done (Rappaport, 1999, p. 38). They say something about what it is we ultimately love; they say something about what we desire.

As Mary Douglas identified, interconnectedness of the 'two bodies' – the physical body and the social body – are continually at work in our daily lives. She wrote: 'There is a continual exchange of meanings between the two kinds of bodily experiences so that each reinforces the categories of the other. As a result of this interaction the body itself is a highly restricted medium of expression' (Douglas, 2003, p. 72). The physical body, according to Douglas, is a symbolic form on which the hierarchies, rules and metaphysical commitments of culture are impressed on and applied through language of the body. If Douglas's theory is right, the social demand for female bodies to be 'better' inevitably plays on the consciousness of women within Western culture. As women begin to restrict food and deny the appetite, the body 'knows' what is going on even when the conscious mind might not be aware (Smith, 2013).

The social body has already recruited many women through body rituals of slimming, toning and shaping to improve and repair the body. These rituals can bolster self-confidence in women and bring control where life is otherwise chaotic. The language of self-worth is used to recruit many women to the pursuit of self-improvement. For example, WeightWatchers set clients a '30-day Self Love Challenge'. But the self-esteem promised by such advertising (if it is ever delivered on) comes with a cost to true Christian discipleship. The social body has encoded in us a *habitus* (a second nature) by involving us in practices and move-ments with an 'ultimate concern' of an 'ideal' body (Smith, 2013, p. 95). These practices are ordered by messages of mass media and social expectations. The 'social body', as Smith explains, 'marshals *my* body to act as a kind of organ of that wider body – and so primes my action in ways that resonate with the vision of the social body well beyond the specific ritualized sites' (Smith, 2013, pp. 95–6; his emphasis).

For the many women who have dieted to lose weight or experienced an eating disorder, the body has a 'sense', a web of associations and understandings of what restricting food is all about within our culture (Smith, 2013, p. 95). Many also have a 'sense' of what it means to resist the social body and react with overindulgence and purging. To move past this 'sense', to understand our bodies as 'shaped and marked by faith, hope and, most of all, love' (Gooder, 2016, p. 132), requires a 'body-turn', a reimagining of what it means to be embodied within the community of believers. A new *habitus* needs to be formed by practices that are aimed at the kingdom of God as our *telos* or ultimate concern. Embodied Christian discipleship practices aim our love towards God, directing our attention to the truth about God: a God who chose to cre-ate human beings in his image; the restorer, redeemer and giver of life.

For Christians, desire for God remains the centre of identity. Even amid cultural desires and the allure of 'secular' goals, our hearts are still restless for God, as St Augustine wrote all those years ago. Sarah Coakley writes:

> desire is no less that which continuously animates us to God ... it allures us, liberates us, gives us the energy and ecstasy of participation in the divine life, makes us humans 'fully alive' for whom nothing in the created world – as also in the divine compassion – can be 'alien-ated' from the same God of love. (Coakley, 2015, p. 10)

As hearts are drawn towards God's love, we encounter approval and security – we find ourselves 'at home' in our own bodies and in the body of Christ. Christian identity is not, however, immediate or even instinctive to believers. Christian identity develops over time, through habits and practices performed with the intention of learning to desire the kingdom of God.

The way we live in the world as human beings is as embodied creatures of love and desire. As desiring creatures, our daily practices orientate our lives towards the *telos* we desire – and our desires are our perceived picture of what we consider to be human flourishing or the 'good life' (Smith, 2009, p. 52). Reorientating desires means considering our daily practices and the picture of the 'good life' they represent. In the context of women who desire the ideal body, the end goal or picture of the good life is tied up with an aesthetic ideal of feminine beauty. The desire for this ideal life connects our identity to the size and shape of our physical body. Yet the 'good life' supposedly promised by thinness is not guaranteed. The picture of happiness, health and a problem-free life portrayed by many weight-loss industries is an unrealistic and false picture of what a 'new' body can achieve for someone. In contrast, the picture of human flourishing presented in the Scriptures is an identity 'in Christ' (2 Cor. 5.16–17), a life defined by the love of God that remains secure (Rom. 8.31–39). Reorientating our desire towards the kingdom of God means intentionally practising rituals and embodied routines that remind us of our secure place in God's kingdom.

In practice, this means taking seriously embodied Christian practices such as prayer, communal worship, hospitality, baptism and partaking of the Eucharist. As Christians, we are people with a future hope – a hope in the coming kingdom of God. This eschatological hope is ignited and developed by embodied Christian practices that turn our body towards God and towards the common good. As Stanley Hauerwas rightly says, 'We are hardwired by our bodies to be people of hope' (2013, p. 175). Embodied practices that remind us of the incarnation of Jesus Christ, such as the Eucharist, are where women can journey into a space of body acceptance. Kent, in her research on the Church and eating disorders, looks at baptism and the Eucharist as key practices affirming identity. She argues that 'the central place of Eucharist as a consuming of bread and wine as a regular confirmation of baptismal identity cannot be underestimated' (Kent, 2013, p. 95). For the Church body, the Eucharist can be a moment to enter us into the dimension of the kingdom in new and formational ways as those called by God 'come together' around a practice 'in remembrance of' Christ's body and perfect love (1 Cor. 11.20–26). The body that was broken becomes the symbol of our wholeness and identity (Matt. 26.26–28). In Christ, *my* body is made whole, and the allure of self-improvement fades as the desire for true well-being is realized in Christ.

Conclusion

In the closing pages of her memoir, Knapp reflects on the long fight against her body and food:

> I no longer fear sliding back into the anorexic prison, but I am somewhat stunned, and a little rueful, at how arduous it all is, how long it can take a woman to achieve a degree of balance around appetites, to learn to feed herself and to understand and honor the body, and to hunger for things that are genuinely sustaining instead of hungering for decoys. (Knapp, 2003, pp. 190–1)

The journey towards body acceptance can be arduous, as it was for Knapp. It can also become a journey of wonder and surprise as we realize the beauty of our here-and-now bodies, and we learn to embrace the diversity that we are created with. The challenge for the Church is to provide flourishing and sustaining communities where the obsession to improve the body is met by life-giving opportunities for women to accept their bodies with delight and their call to true discipleship with joy. The Church has the potential to be the place where women practise and exemplify to the broader culture what true embodiment means. Rather than the body being perceived as something to hide, discipline and control, the body can become a sacred gift, through which the presence of the sacred is made alive.

Note

1 As recorded on https://www.nutrisystem.com/success-stories, accessed 10.05.2024.

Bibliography

Bell, Rudolph M., 1987, *Holy Anorexia*, Chicago, IL: University of Chicago Press.
Bordo, Susan, 2003, *Unbearable Weight: Feminism, Western Culture, and the Body*, 10th edn, Berkeley, CA: University of California Press.

Bovey, Shelley, 1989, *The Forbidden Body: Why Fat Is Not a Sin*, London: Pandora.

Bringle, Mary Louise, 1992, *The God of Thinness: Gluttony and Other Weighty Matters*, Nashville, TN: Abingdon Press.

Brumberg, Joan Jacobs, 2000, *Fasting Girls: The History of Anorexia Nervosa*, New York: Vintage Books.

Bynum, Caroline Walker, 1987, *Holy Feast and Holy Fast: The Religious Significance of Food to Medieval Women*, Berkeley, CA: University of California Press.

Cavanaugh, Joan and Forseth, Pat, 1976, *More of Jesus, Less of Me*, Plainfield, NJ: Logos International.

Chadwick, Owen (ed.), 1958, *Western Asceticism*, Philadelphia, PA: Westminster.

Chapian, Marie and Coyle, Neva, 1979, *Free to Be Thin*, Minneapolis, MN: Bethany House.

Coakley, Sarah, 2015, *The New Asceticism: Sexuality, Gender and the Quest for God*, London: Bloomsbury Publishing.

Douglas, Mary, 2003, *Natural Symbols*, London: Routledge.

Dreyfus, Hubert L. and Rabinow, Paul, 2013, *Michel Foucault: Beyond Structuralism and Hermeneutics*, London: Routledge.

Geertz, Clifford, 1973, *The Interpretation of Cultures*, New York: Basic Books.

Gerber, Lynne, 2011, *Seeking the Straight and Narrow: Weight Loss and Sexual Reorientation in Evangelical America*, Chicago and London: University of Chicago Press.

Gooder, Paula, 2016, *Body: Biblical Spirituality for the Whole Person*, Minneapolis, MN: Fortress Press.

Grimm, Veronika E., 1996, *From Feasting to Fasting: The Evolution of a Sin: Attitudes to Food in Late Antiquity*, London and New York: Routledge.

Hauerwas, Stanley, 2013, *Approaching the End: Eschatological Reflections on Church, Politics, and Life*, Grand Rapids, MI: William B. Eerdmans.

Hunter, Frances G., 1975, *God's Answer to Fat – Loøse It!*, Houston, TX: Hunter Ministries.

Kent, Elizabeth, 2013, 'Consuming the Body: The Church and Eating Disorders', Doctoral Thesis, Durham University, http://etheses.dur.ac.uk/6905/, accessed 21.08.2024.

Kite, Lindsay and Kite, Lexie, 2021, *More Than a Body: Your Body Is an Instrument, Not an Ornament*, Boston and New York: Marina Books.

Knapp, Caroline, 2003, *Appetites: Why Women Want*, Berkeley, CA: Counterpoint.

Lewis, Carole and Whalin, Terry, 2001, *First Place*, Venture, CA: Regal Books.

Lovett, C. S., 1977, *Help Lord – the Devil Wants Me Fat!*, Baldwin Park, CA: Personal Christianity.

Martin, Courtney E., 2007, *Perfect Girls, Starving Daughters: The Frightening New Normalcy of Hating Your Body*, London: Piatkus Books.

McDaniels, Evelyn, 1988, *Loving More, Eating Less*, Laramie, WY: Jelm Mountain.

Murphy, Nancey, 2006, *Bodies and Souls, or Spirited Bodies?*, Cambridge: Cambridge University Press.

O'Donnell, Gabriel, 1990, 'Monastic Life and the Search for God', in G. O'Donnell and R. Maas (eds), *Spiritual Traditions for Contemporary Church*, Nashville, TN: Abingdon Press, pp. 55–72.

Pattison, Stephen, 2000, *Shame: Theory, Therapy, Theology*, Cambridge: Cambridge University Press.

Peretti, Jacques, 2013, 'Fat Profits: How the Food Industry Cashed in on Obesity', *The Guardian*, 7 August, https://www.theguardian.com/lifeandstyle/2013/aug/07/fat-profits-food-industry-obesity, accessed 21.08.2024.

Rappaport, Roy A., 1999, *Ritual and Religion in the Making of Humanity*, Cambridge: Cambridge University Press.

Schaff, Philip and Wace, Henry (eds), 1978, *A Select Library of Nicene and Post-Nicene Fathers of the Christian Church*, 2nd edn, Grand Rapids, MI: William B. Eerdmans.

Shamblin, Gwen, 1997, *The Weigh Down Diet*, New York: Doubleday.

Shedd, C., 1957, *Pray Your Weight Away*, Philadelphia, PA: J. B. Lippincott & Co.

Smith, James K. A., 2009, *Desiring the Kingdom: Worship, Worldview, and Cultural Formation. Volume 1 of Cultural Liturgies*, Grand Rapids, MI: Baker Academic.

Smith, James K. A., 2013, *Imagining the Kingdom: How Worship Works. Volume 2 of Cultural Liturgies*, Grand Rapids, MI: Baker Academic.

Strings, Sabrina, 2019, *Fearing the Black Body: The Racial Origins of Fat Phobia*, New York: New York University Press.

Tanner, Kathryn, 1997, *Theories of Culture: A New Agenda for Theology*, Minneapolis, MN: Augsburg Fortress.

von Rad, Gerhard, 1972, *Wisdom in Israel*, Nashville, TN: Abingdon Press.

Questions for reflection and discussion

1 Do you tend to think of a person as being composed of a separate body and soul (anthropological dualism) or in a more unified way? What has shaped that understanding for you, and what implications does that have in terms of how you relate to your body and the bodies of others?

2 Can you identify practices in your everyday life that are aimed at the pursuit of a 'better' body? Can you identify how these practices are linked to certain desires?

3 Take a moment to image the kind of beauty that is found in genuine relationships. What new practices could you incorporate in your everyday life that are aimed at building an integrated life as an individual and a community? What practices might you choose to let go of?

6

Unspeakable Fat, Unspeakable Beauty: Fatness, Apophasis and the Overflowing of Excess

HANNAH BACON

'What kind of secret can the body of the fat woman keep?'
(Moon and Sedgwick, 2001, p. 305)

We think we know a lot about fat. We know that it is bad for our health and for the public purse and we know it is faulty and needs fixing, either through slimming or through medical interventions like surgery or weight-loss drugs. We also think we know a lot about fat people. We know people are fat because they indulge their appetites, are weak-willed and lack self-restraint. We know fat people need to move more and eat less and take responsibility as global citizens for fixing themselves. If people are fat, it is because they have 'let themselves go'.[1] Such is the Western neoliberal public 'knowingness' about fat.

According to Eve Kosofsky Sedgwick, Western culture is an 'economy' or 'culture of knowingness' in which certain discursive constructs are reified as truths by 'silent presumption' (Moon and Sedgwick, 2001, p. 300). Discussing the 'gay body', she notes how the public confidence that attests to know what homosexuality means leads to a 'dangerous consensus of knowingness about the unknown' (Sedgwick, 1990, p. 45). In a similar way, she suggests that when people see a fat woman, they think they know something about her straight away; there is a presumption to know her will, her history, her perception, her prognosis (i.e. she is killing herself) (Moon and Sedgwick, 2001, p. 306). This presumption is facilitated by capitalist consumer culture that frames anything that does not figure as compulsion as absolute choice. Thus, we know that the fat woman is fat because of her faulty food choices and that she can decide to be thin/ner by making wiser free-market choices. In this economy, Sedgwick suggests that 'coming out' of the closet as fat means women speaking their fatness on their own terms, uttering their own bodies to the people around them who claim to know; it is, she says, 'a way of staking one's claim to insist on, and participate actively in, a renegotiation of *the representational contract* between one's body and one's world' (Moon and Sedgwick, 2001, p. 306; Sedgwick's emphasis).

But for all we know about fat, our culture of knowingness continues to produce more and more about it. This is ironic when we consider that fat bodies are consistently read as excessive. Indeed, underpinning the Western economy of knowingness about fat is the cultural truth that fat bodies are always *too much* – they are too big, too greedy, too lazy, too appetitive, too heavy and too soft. Fat bodies exceed their imposed limits, whether spatially, temporally, socially or symbolically, and they even consume their own lives, since to be fat is to erase one's future and risk plunging oneself into an early grave. The feared excesses of fatness are matched, if not exceeded, by Western's culture's irrepressible obsession with fat: by a plethora of stories that spill over the pages of magazines and newspapers and which capaciously dominate news headlines, taking up seemingly more and more space; by yet more television documentaries and 'fattertainment'[2] game shows (Archer, 2016), by an overflowing of memes and social media threads. Our sayings and tellings about fat seem endless and seep into multiple areas of public discourse: medical, scientific, political, religious, educational and legal. Anti-fatness is, to quote the fat activist Aubrey Gordon, 'the waters we all swim in everyday' (Finlay, 2023). It would appear, then, that there are never enough words to capture the spectacle of fat, its abhorrence, its vastness, even its dangerous attraction.

Of course, if there is always more to say about fat then it is not known at all. Instead, the excessive nature of Western discourse about fat confronts us with the vast unsayability and unknowability of fatness. This, I suggest, begins to expose fat bodies as apophatic bodies: bodies that 'speak and unspeak volumes' (Boesel and Keller, 2010, p. 1). Sedgwick may be right that the economy of knowingness about fat can and must be challenged by fat women uttering their own flesh as a political performance, as a 'hearing to speech' of their own fat bodies, and I have certainly promoted this in my own feminist work on women's dieting culture (Bacon, 2019). But what of the *un*speakability of fat? What might it mean for women to *un*say their fatness?

In this chapter, I draw on the Christian tradition of *apophasis* to forward a theological appraisal of fat bodies as apophatic. Apophatic theology (or 'negative theology') is often described as the practice of negating all positive statements about God. It is glimpsed in Augustine's famous retort that if we have understood, then what we have understood is not God (*Sermons*, 52.16). According to Chris Boesel and Catherine Keller, the apophatic 'presses toward the pause and the silence within language' (2010, p. 1). They rightly reflect that most people would not consider bodies to be apophatic, given their materiality, familiarity and finitude. This is especially the case, I believe, when it comes to women's bodies, given the way Western thought has aligned them with materiality, death and excess. Indeed, there may be legitimate concerns about rendering women's fat bodies apophatic, given the lengths to which feminist theologians have gone to positively affirm materiality and bodiliness against a theological tradition that has often negated and been suspicious of them. Outside of the theological arena, the body positivity and fat pride movements have also made sizeable interventions into anti-fat discourse, emphasizing the political importance of positive constructs of fatness. Given this, the call towards *apophasis* – towards unsaying fat and the bodies of fat women – may seem wrongheaded and look suspicious, given it comes at a point when social movements and theologies are starting to 'materialize' the bodies of marginalized people (Keller, 2010, p. 26), including the bodies of fat women. It risks reversing this liberative process of en-fleshing by turning it into a process of de-fleshing, and thus into another type of compulsory weight loss.

With this challenge in mind, I draw on Augustine's theology of perfect heavenly bodies, including his theological rendering of beauty and fat, to consider what apophasis might mean for feminist theological thinking about fatness and women's fat. Routinely criticized for promoting a flight from the body and its excessive passions, and a vision of resurrection bodies as free from the imperfections of the material flesh, Augustine provides an interesting although perhaps unlikely dialogue partner for thinking about this. My claim is that there is much to glean from him, despite the difficulties he presents. There is also much to garner from feminist fat activism and from critical feminist reflections on the fluidity of fat embodiment. Both inform my feminist theological appraisal of fat bodies as unspeakable bodies.

Unmasking the economy of knowingness about fat

In the contemporary economy of knowingness about fat, women's fat is both said and unsaid, brought to speech but negated at the same time. This saying and unsaying of bodies is political because it concerns the way some get to speak while others do not. In Euro-American culture, fat women are denied speech, pictured in the commercial media as bodies without heads. According to the fat activist Charlotte Cooper, the image of the 'headless fatty' confirms the common assumption that fat women have no right to speak and nothing of value to say. 'We are there but we have no voice, not even a mouth in a head, no brain, no thoughts or opinions', she reflects. 'Instead we are reduced and dehumanized as symbols of cultural fear: the body, the belly, the arse, food' (Cooper, 2007). Fat bodies in Western culture, especially fat women, Cooper contends, are viewed as objects that are talked about rather than as subjects with a voice. Consequently, fat women are not only rendered unspeakable (beyond words in their revoltingness), but also denied their own words, feelings and opinions about what it is to be fat. And, of course, in a setting in which fatness is presumed to be already known, there is no need for fat women to speak. Instead, fatness is reduced to a site of disgust and horror, with fat bodies, and fat women especially, viewed as symbolic of physical and social death, identified with a body that is 'embarrassing and too much' (Farrell, 2023, p. 3).

Gender plays an important role in the cultural production of fatness as unspeakable. As Sedgwick acknowledges, fat women are charged with the task of 'concentrating and representing "a general sense of the body's offensiveness"' (Sedgwick, 1990, p. 2). In this culture of knowingness, fat women are positioned as 'hyper(in)visible', as people who are constantly on display as the target of a disproportionate amount of attention and judgement and as almost totally erased from sight at the same time, having their needs, lives and desires ignored (Gailey, 2023, p. 20). In this context, women's fatness is brought to speech or made visible only to be negated through a pathologizing discourse.

A BBC documentary, *Obesity: The Post Mortem* (BBC Three, 2018), shows just how the politics of negation and offence work to condemn fat women. The programme shows two pathologists dissecting the organs of an anonymous dead fat woman in a real-life autopsy. As viewers, we are encouraged to watch close up as one of the pathologists slices down the length of the woman's torso. 'There is a very large amount of fat here', she announces. So much fat makes the process of cutting very difficult, she says, because the fat is greasy 'like butter'. Shortly after, her colleague comments that the woman's liver feels 'like paté'. We are invited to gaze at the woman's body and to scrutinize her inners, but we are expected to recoil in disgust as these experts make connections between the woman's size and her premature death in her early sixties from heart disease.

That her fat is likened to food makes the disgust even more poignant – all the more disgusting – since as the feminist Sara Ahmed reminds us, food is 'the very stuff of disgust' (2014, p. 86).[3] Ahmed, however, also makes clear that disgust is dependent on contact. Disgust first fixes the object in its gaze, she explains, holding it fast with fascination. It is only as we move close to the object that this proximity is experienced as an offence, causing the body to pull away. The 'double movement' of 'towards, away', she argues, is however forgotten in the pulling away, 'as if the object moved towards the body, rather than the body having got close enough to the object' (Ahmed, 2014, pp. 85–6). So also in this documentary we are encouraged to fix our eyes on the spectacle of the woman's fat, only to recoil as the pathologists squeeze out the fluid in her lungs, slice through her liver and kidneys, and explain how her fatness penetrates through to her innermost parts. The desire and fascination that pulls viewers towards this woman is forgotten with the feeling of disgust. The intention is to leave those observing offended by the obscenity of her girth. The narrator helps to produce this disgust as she unmissably emphasizes the woman's weight: we don't know the woman's name, she says, but we do know that she was five foot five and weighed seventeen stone (can you believe it?). As we closely witness the unmasking of her fat we are left without any doubt that this woman was responsible for her own demise.

The programme demonstrates how women's fatness is only brought to speech as a site of abjection or disgust. The woman's fat body is presented as a deadly and revolting excess, and her fatness is cast as a terrain that can be breached and excavated by outsiders without any moral difficulty. While she is judged for not keeping her appetite in, we are invited and expected to join the pathologists in pulling her insides out. While she must be judged for not patrolling her borders, we are encouraged to cross them. The programme thus communicates that fat women are no-bodies. It does not afford the woman a name, she is just a collection of body parts. Ultimately, the documentary confirms that the only fitting response to women's fat is to drag it out into the open so it can be publicly shamed and established as an abject site of offence. Within this culture of knowingness, women's fat can never have positive signification because the only way for her fatness to be (said) is for it to be undone and unsaid, pathologized and collapsed into a negative field of meaning.

However, anti-fatness is not only a gendered discourse, it is also racialized and rooted in a long history of anti-Blackness. Sabrina Strings (2019) provides an excellent discussion of tracing this fatphobia in

America back to the racial and gendered assumptions about civilized bodies that gathered pace with colonialism and the transatlantic slave trade. The enslavement of Africans required a way to distinguish White colonizers as superior, and while the demonization of Black skin served that purpose, the association of fat with Black femininity provided an important way to identify Black bodies, and Black women especially, as inferior. Fatness was linked with the greedy appetites of Africans and came to be seen as evidence of the unevolved and uncivilized nature of Black people, and as confirmation of the insatiable sexualities and appetites of Black women in particular. As well as informing the racial scientific rhetoric of the seventeenth century, this manifested in Enlightenment rationalism, in which fatness was aligned with Blackness and stupidity, helping to secure the intellectual superiority of elite White (male) Europeans. By the eighteenth century, the White thin ideal fused in America with the post-Reformation emphasis on temperance, constructing fatness as 'immoral' and 'Black'. The early twentieth century saw thinness lauded as the only proper form of embodiment for elite White Protestant women, and it was only at this point, Strings argues, that medical establishments started to promote the eradication of fat as a matter of public health. This, she maintains, exposes anti-fatness as an ideology rooted much more in race, sex and class hierarchies than in scientific concerns about health. She concludes that anti-fatness is a racial discourse that works both to degrade Black women and to discipline the bodies of White women.[4]

The ongoing colonial effects of this racial discourse are seen by the way the Euro-American slender feminine ideal is marketed to women across the globe without concern for food insecurity or divergent cultural standards of beauty (Lelwica, 2017, p. 114). This image confronts us as a White symbol of civilization (Lelwica, 1999, p. 46), tasking White women with maintaining the boundaries of civilized culture and depicting a female body that is 'absolutely tight, contained, [and] "bolted down"' (Bordo, 1993, p. 190). This body knows its place and does not protrude. Her body is 'fixed', with its contours and appetites self-contained and any 'imperfections' digitally or cosmetically removed. Because the systems of ableism, heteronormativity, classism, racism and misogyny conspire to mark fatness as defective, the pursuit of thinness becomes a way for women who are not White, straight, young, middle-class or able-bodied to produce themselves as persons; that is, as civilized, responsible, and 'good'.

As a feminist committed to the politics of fat liberation,[5] I want to ask how this culture of knowingness that only makes fat women visible through their erasure and compliance with a neocolonial vision of bodily perfection might be troubled. As a theologian, I am especially keen to explore if Christian theology can help think otherwise about fat bodies that breech imposed borders, and whether there might be ways to positively unsay women's fatness and excess without automatically erasing their flesh or producing it as defective. To explore this, I turn to Augustine's body theology, specifically his presentation of remarkable mortal bodies and eschatological bodies, including his views on the future of fat. Attending to some of the conflicts and tensions in his work, I argue that Augustine's vision of apophatic bodies offers theological tools that can help challenge contemporary confidence in the knowability of fat.

Into the darkness: Augustine and bodies beyond words

In the mystical Christian tradition, the metaphor of darkness communicates that God transcends all knowledge and understanding. According to the fifth-/sixth-century-author Pseudo-Dionysius, the incomprehensible God is beyond language or cognition, plunging us into the 'mysterious darkness of unknowing' (Pseudo-Dionysius, 1987, p. 137). Through the stilling of reason and by negating all affirmations of God, we come into a fuller knowledge of the God who is 'intangible and invisible' and 'beyond everything' (p. 136).

Although Pseudo-Dionysius introduces the terminology of 'apophatic' and 'kataphatic' into Christian theology, the principle that anything we positively affirm of God (*kataphasis*) must be grounded in a negation of any claim to divine knowing (*apophasis*) is present throughout Christian history. It is glimpsed in the early theologies of Clement of Alexandria, in the Cappadocian theology of Basil of Caesarea, Gregory of Nyssa and Gregory of Nazianzus, in John Chrysostom and Augustine (Louth, 2012, pp. 137–8). Augustine, however, provides an especially interesting case, with his view of bodies serving as an extension to his wonder and astonishment at the limitless and boundless reality of God.

For Augustine, God is uncontainable and breaches his imagination.[6] In *Confessions*, he embarks on a journey towards God through an introspective journey into the self, shaped by a forensic process of self-examination and rhetorical questioning. The text overflows with his exuberant outbursts of praise towards a God he experiences as totally unfathomable and beyond all words. 'What does anyone who speaks of you really say?' (*Confessions*, 1.1) he asks when confronted with the shattering ineffability of God. This God created the heavens and the earth and yet cannot be confined to them. This God is wholly present everywhere yet nothing contains the divine reality wholly. Augustine is aghast at how such a colossal God could possibly be invoked and called into his self but is nevertheless convinced that God's irreducible transcendence should not prevent human creatures from kataphatic praise: 'Woe betide those who fail to speak, while the chatterboxes go on saying nothing', he cautions (1.4.4).

Augustine certainly does not stay silent! In this volume, he speaks at length – we might say excessively – about his own unquenchable passion for God and confesses his own insatiable sexual desires. He pleads that God would set him on fire and give him continence (10.29.40) so that he might quell the rampant fires of sexual passion that always threaten to scupper his commitment to chastity. For Virginia Burrus and Karmen Mackendrick, Augustine is thus, in this work, in a 'constant struggle with excess', with his passionate 'self-exceeding' desire of God, with his own excessive thoughts and behaviours, especially as they pertain to his carnal desires, all of which show up as eruptions of praise or pleading (Burrus and Mackendrick, 2010, p. 80). He is 'passionate about undoing passion' and this, according to Burrus, Jordan and Mackendrick, exposes *Confessions* as an 'irreducibly erotic text'. Some who read it will think it is a work full to bursting with too much excess, they reflect; with 'too much desire and too much renunciation' (Burrus, Jordan and Mackendrick, 2010, p. 2).

In his later work, *City of God*, Augustine continues to imagine the glorious unboundedness of the 'supreme and immutable' God (*City of God*, 22.1) and laments once more the excesses of carnal desire, impassioned now about the male body's inability to control the erect penis. He speaks too about remarkable bodies that are glorious in their excess, bodies in the Bible and those he knows about that breech normality by reaching epic sizes, incredible ages and by being unbelievably tall. He tells readers that he has seen a gigantic human molar in Utica so big that it could be cut up into a hundred pieces with each piece being the size of a standard human tooth (15.9)! Aided by his interpretation of Genesis 6.1–4, he talks about a time when giants walked the earth; 'specimens … of extraordinary stature' (15.9) who he claims also exist in his present day since he knows of a 'giantess' who lived in Rome just before the Gothic sack of Rome (15.23). Having argued that humans could control all aspects of their bodies before Adam and Eve's rebellion, Augustine extols that even now, in the present, there are remarkable examples of humans 'so unlike ordinary people' (14.24) who can make parts of their bodies move simply through choice. Some can make their ears move together or one at a time, others can swallow objects and then choose which to regurgitate. Others still can 'make musical notes issue from the rear of their anatomy, so that you would think they were singing' (14.24)! Such examples, Augustine claims, show that there are no grounds for disbelieving that, before the Fall, the sexual organs were controlled by the passionless need for procreation rather than by the 'lecherous promptings of lust' (14.26). It would seem that for Augustine, everyone would have been able to wiggle their ears and fart a tune of their choice had Adam and Eve not rebelled!

Through stories of incredible and peculiar past and present bodies, Augustine paints for us a picture of excess, of bodies that exceed necessity, that stretch out beyond the bounds of comprehension and normality. These mortal bodies, he says, offer a glimpse of an unfallen past – a past of giants and other remarkable bodies – and they also provide a glimpse into the unimaginable future of resurrection bodies, when the flesh will be remarkably transformed and most resemble the risen Christ. Heavenly bodies will be extraordinary, reflecting the extraordinary healings in the biblical past and the remarkableness of modern miracles, which he also details with great verbosity. These contemporary events are continuous too with the equally extraordinary bodily resurrection of Christ. He writes at length to argue that if the omnipotent God can perform such unbelievable things, there are scant grounds for disbelieving in the resurrection of the body (22.24).

In these works, Augustine presents bodies as apophatic: as uncontainable in their variety and as an excess he struggles to contain on the page and capture in words (Burrus and Mackendrick, 2010). Such boundless extraordinary bodies breach his imagination and reveal something of the unfathomable and unsayable God; a God who is known through body but who nevertheless exceeds it (Burrus and Mackendrick, 2010, p. 81). These bodies transgress the borders of normativity and they lead Augustine to his own excess, to eruptions of praise and to an overflow of emotion that he struggles to limit. The body's inability to contain its passions also leads him at times to bottomless shame. This is not unlike fat bodies in Western culture that give rise to comparable excess: to an overflow of words, emotions and shame. Like Augustine, the rhetorical exuberance of contemporary fat-talk produces its own *apophasis*. By saying more and more, such discourse says less and less. Augustine's obsessive treatment of bodies thus provides a useful theological lens for re-reading the rhetorical excess of Western anti-fatness, exposing fat as a multiplicity that exceeds words, as an unbounded site of fragmentation and indeterminacy. Read this way, women's fat meets us not as a known or as an abject site of disgust, but as a glorious 'vastness that cannot be comprehended' (Gordon in Finlay, 2023). The apophasis of fat signals women's fatness as a revolt-ing seepage that rebels against the dangerous presumption to know. If, as Augustine suggests, remarkable excessive bodies reveal something about glorious heavenly bodies and about the unbounded God, then the irreducible nature of women's fat offers a theological glimpse into a future in which the boundaries of our existing assumptions about bodies will be exceeded, and into 'a God bigger [fatter] than any we've imagined' (Slee, 2011, pp. 142–3).

Augustine's fat-free heaven?

Augustine's meticulous examination of bodies intensifies even more when he turns to a fuller discussion of resurrection bodies in Book 22 of *City of God*. At the centre of his discussion is a belief that all bodies will rise perfect and beautiful and that there will be no 'deformities', defects or ugliness in the heavenly City. Here, bodies will have the kind of 'unimaginable beauty', grace and poise that is fitting for a heavenly City where 'nothing unbecoming can be found' (22.30). The body that rises will be a spiritual body composed of flesh but without the lust that shames the body (22.24). Informed by Luke 21.18 that 'not a hair on your head will perish' (NIV), Augustine believes God will restore all parts of the body, even those bits that have been lost or cut off, ensuring that nothing of the body evades God's redemptive transformation. This leads to some rather strange and sometimes entertaining questions from Augustine – again, he seems unable to contain himself: 'Will all the hair cut off by the barbers be restored?' (22.12). What about the fingernails that have been clipped? Worried about the 'deformity' and 'unsightly excess' (22.19) that would result from getting back all the bits that have been lost, he laments, 'where will be the physical beauty which, in immortal life, should be greater than in this corruptible life?' (22.12).

He argues that just as Christ rose with the same body he had when he was alive, so resurrected bodies will rise as they were originally (22.15; 22.28), but without 'deformity', 'infirmity' or 'decrepitude' (22.20). Bodies will thus get back those bits they lost but were always designed to have, so that in the resurrection there will be no incompleteness. The fat body poses a similar predicament to Augustine as excess hair and fingernails, since if nothing that is original to the body is lost but fat-ness, like too much hair, is an excess that makes the resurrected body unsightly, then he is forced to ask what happens to fatness at the final resurrection. He responds by suggesting that these 'deformities' will be refashioned by God so that their excess is 'redistributed throughout the whole body' while leaving the substance of the body intact (22.19). Just as a potter can remake an object by remoulding the same clay, losing nothing of the original material, so God can remake fat bodies, reintegrating excess fatness into the whole body so that the ugliness is eliminated but nothing of the substance of the body is lost. At the resurrection, God will make fat bodies into perfectly proportioned beautiful specimens.

Although this at first sounds like the ideal support for anti-fatness, Augustine's imaginings here lead to some rather intriguing ramifications, for if resurrected bodies get back all the bits they have lost, then it seems that any fatness/excess lost through slimming will be restored and regained at the resurrection, even if it is magically redistributed. 'Must not everything be restored that was sacrificed to personal appearance?' (22.12), he asks. Dieting, it would seem, is pointless! Augustine also suggests that bodies will rise as the size they reached or would have reached at maturity (22.20), around 30 years old,[7] so if a person is fat at 30, this seems to trouble his vision of a fat-free heaven. Most poignantly, though, if fat bodies do not lose any of their corporeality but rise beautifully proportioned like all resurrected bodies, then fat bodies appear to rise thin/ner but without losing any of their heft or weight![8] Here, fatness is not lost or eradicated – it is not dragged 'out' of the body like in the autopsy previously discussed – it is kept 'in', albeit precariously. God's redemptive work appears to function here like body sculpting underwear, moving fat around without removing it! Fatness thus lingers in Augustine's imagining of heaven, invading the borders of perfection as an unwieldy materiality that seeps into the redemptive future, now disguised by the mystery of redistribution like rolls of fat skilfully hidden under a loose-fitting outfit. Augustine may insist that all bodies will rise weightless and with a 'wonderful lightness' (*Sermons*, 242.11), but because heavenly bodies get back all the bits they have lost and will also incorporate matter they would have accumulated by maturity, it is difficult not to imagine them as absolutely massive![9] As such, Augustine, cannot get rid of fatness in heaven despite his best efforts. His tidy vision of proportionate bodies bulges at the seams. Indeed, we might imagine that had Augustine not viewed fatness to be such a defect of proportion synonymous with imperfection, he may have concluded that all bodies would rise gloriously fat!

Exceeding Augustine

Of course, Augustine's concern is ultimately with aesthetics.[10] His views about the weightlessness of heavenly bodies take their place within his thinking about beauty and the way resurrected bodies will, in his view, exist for beauty's sake rather than for utility. His association of fatness with disfigurement and ugliness, of course, does nothing to challenge the contemporary economy of knowingness about fat previously outlined, whereby women are frequently body shamed for the unsightliness of their girth. His theology also disassociates fatness from the 'substance' of a person, and so follows contemporary weight-loss culture in presenting fatness as an outer shell separate from the 'real' thin/ner self. Augustine, though, does not destroy fatness in his imagining of heavenly perfection, and this creates an opening in his theology for a more positive reading of fat. It communicates the stubbornness and persistence of fat – the way fat always shows up despite the measures we might take (like Augustine) to get rid of it! – and signals towards a future from which fat women cannot be removed. This said, it is obviously the case that fatness only shows up in Augustine's heaven as an excess that God reassembles. It is true too that like other early Christian thinkers, he is concerned to eradicate any sign of disability from heaven. This informs his views about beauty and confirms Western knowingness about disabled bodies, constructing these bodies as incomplete and in need of fixing/healing (see also Moss, 2011). Augustine's infuriation with the way sexual desire refuses to be ruled by the rational will has also helped to craft, at the centre of Western Christianity, a suspicion of sex and a fixation on controlling bodily boundaries, especially the boundaries of bodies considered to be symbolic of excess.

Despite these difficulties, Augustine is not anti-body. He insists that the human body is a revelation of the goodness of God (*City of God*, 22.24) and encourages his readers to love the body and 'care for it wisely' (*On Christian Doctrine*, I.25.26). For him, it is not escape from the body per se that the faithful must seek but escape from mortality and decay (*City of God*, 14.3). In this sense, Augustine does not entirely fall into the trap of promoting body-transcendence, but he does display a revulsion for the material process of change, and this causes him to identify perfection with stasis and immutability (Bynum, 1995, pp. 99f.). Such a denigration of change has served to shame women's bodies for centuries, aligning women more closely with finitude, sin, death and decay. Augustine configures beauty, wholeness and perfection in opposition to material process, leading to a demonization of age, a suspicion of hunger and desire,[11] and to a vision of resurrected bodies as bodies hardened to change (Bynum, 1995, p. 104). Because of the way change has been theologically gendered, women's bodies thus come to be equated with the corruptible death-bound flesh that will be overcome at the final resurrection – a gendered discourse that mirrors the symbolization of fat as death.

However, there is a tension in Augustine here between the fixity of heavenly bodies and his conviction that it will continue to be impossible to capture their beauty. Even if these bodies are 'fixed' in the sense that they do not change and have been remade and perfected to remove all signs of 'deformity', they remain unfixed because they continue to exasperate speech and comprehension, both now and in heaven, and produce in Augustine (once more) an overspilling of words and praise. As such, they still ooze excess. When Augustine asks himself what the heavenly City will be like and queries what activities the saved will do, he admits that this breaches his mind:

> I have no real notion of what eternal life will be like, for the simple reason that I know of no sensible experience to which it can be related. Nor can I say that I have any mental conception of such an activity, for, at that height, what is intelligence or what can it do? (*City of God*, 22.29)

Augustine is happy to point out that his view of resurrected bodies is not founded on Scripture or experience. Instead, he exceeds both of these and offers what Margaret Miles describes as an 'excited and lyrical hypothetical description of resurrected bodies' that is 'profoundly counter-experiential, counter-cultural, and beautiful' (Miles, 2012, pp. 88–9). He imagines that the happiness of the blessed will be 'inexhaustible' (*City of God*, 22.30) and that they will have bodies capable of extraordinary things, including the ability to see God with their eyes shut (22.29). Heavenly bodies will move with 'unimaginable beauty' and will celebrate the beauty of God and of one another's bodies with 'unwearying praise' (22.30).

In these final reflections at the end of *City of God*, Augustine directs us once more into the glorious darkness. Resurrection bodies appear as extraordinary, unfathomable and limitless in their beauty and magnificence, and they produce once more in Augustine further excitable excess. This is not an unsaying of bodies that evacuates the human being from the flesh. We are not met here by Augustine's silence or by an assumption that defleshing (immateriality) is the ultimate end towards which the blessed are called. Not only does Augustine present a profoundly materialistic understanding of heavenly bodies confirming bodies as necessary in the resurrection (Bynum, 1995, p. 101), he also understands heavenly bodies as bodies that will enjoy the sight of one another's infinite beauty and as bodies that will respond to this wonderment with unending praise and thanksgiving. Thus, just as Augustine continues to intensely write about the bodies he cannot grasp in writing, the unfathomable heavenly bodies he imagines extol the bodies of others and God whose beauty they will not be able to say. In both cases, the apophatic unsaying of bodies leads to an excessive *kataphasis* that in turn leads back into *apophasis*.

It seems, then, that if fatness does exist in Augustine's heavenly future (despite his best efforts to remove it), and we follow Augustine in imagining this future as one in which boundaries of our existing assumptions about bodies will be breeched, motivating boundless praise and thanksgiving before a boundless God, then this hypothetical imagining has the potential to galvanize kataphatic praise and thanksgiving for fatness in the here and now.[12] Such praise will not be a saying of fatness that limits fat bodies but a theological affirmation of fatness that evades closure. This saying of fatness will be an unsaying of fatness because it extols fat as an open and indeterminate site of enfleshing, beautiful in its diversity and wondrous unknowability. Augustine does not consider in *City of God* how our human appraisal of one another's bodies in the resurrection might impact our treatment of bodies in the here and now, but if, as Letty Russell suggests, we should 'live *now as if*' – that is, as if 'the new creation is already present in our lives (1 Cor. 7.25–31)' (1974, p. 42; Russell's emphasis), and this future is a future when heavenly (fat) bodies, unimaginable in their beauty, will celebrate and delight in the beauty of God and one another's bodies – then reading back from this to the present resources alternative possibilities to the present misogynist and racialized politics of fat hatred. It not only incentivizes a hearty celebration of fat women as bodies *with* a future, it motivates an apophatic delight in fatness as a site of excess that is not always already known.[13] In this sense, fat liberation can be cast in Christian eschatological terms as a 'liberation of the future' that leads to 'a new opening up of history, with its alternative possibilities to the present' (Moltmann, 1999, p. 196).

Embracing body ambivalence

To end, I want to take a further step and suggest that the tension in Augustine's theology between allowing fat to continue in heaven while simultaneously attempting to remove it provides a useful theological lens for acknowledging the ambiguities of fat embodiment and for attending to body ambivalence. In contemporary fat politics the notion of fat pride signifies a delight in fat embodiment and a refusal to acquiesce in the thin feminine ideal. Women within the fat community who have chosen to pursue weight loss have thus often been criticized and accused of compromising their commitment to fat acceptance.[14] This exposes fat politics as susceptible to the same difficulties found within anti-fat politics: namely, constructing its own culture of knowingness, forging its own moral absolutes and patrolling its own narrow borders around which bodies count as acceptable and which do not (also see LeBesco, 2014).

Samantha Murray is one fat activist who has troubled the demonizing of weight loss in fat politics. While committed to size diversity she explains how her feelings of ambivalence towards her fatness and struggles with health difficulties (which included insulin resistance, polycystic ovarian syndrome and hormone imbalances) caused her to opt for bariatric surgery. Although at first feeling furious with her doctor's suggestion of surgical intervention, she notes that her lived experience of fat led to a messy troubling of the straightforward orthodoxies of fat politics (Murray, 2010, p. 44).

Murray is concerned that the notion of fat pride is entrenched in the liberal humanist project of individualism. She sees in it a repetition of the mind over body dualism wherein fat people are expected to change their minds about their fat and never look back. For Murray, this is too simplistic because it ignores the difficulty of discarding dominant anti-fat discourses and overlooks the lived experience of fat embodiment. It suggests the presence of a fixed autonomous disembodied self that is free to invest in fat pride and detach from the corporeal complexities of living as fat and from how other bodies impact how we feel about our flesh. What is needed, she argues, is a fat politics that recognizes the intersubjective nature of being embodied. This would acknowledge ambiguity as a feature of lived embodiment and would mean understanding ourselves as 'body-subjects that are multiple, unfixed and always in process' (Murray, 2008, p. 177).

It is, I believe, this sense of openness to the future, to change and to the complexities, diversities and relational meanings of fatness that is needed to expand fat politics beyond the mind-over-matter mentality that worryingly mimics dieting culture, and to rupture the economy of knowingness about fat. Kathleen LeBesco is right that fat politics can often fix bodies in space and time by insisting that fat bodies permanently remain fat and by imagining a perfect future when fat people do not change. This is out of kilter with a reality in which the lines between thinness and fatness are blurred and bodies frequently transition in size (LeBesco, 2014, p. 54). As a woman in my mid-forties, I have experienced my body expand with age and as I approach menopause. It has also shrunk at certain points through dieting, through illness and diagnosis with coeliac disease. I do not experience my size as entirely stable and this is punctuated by my queer identity since I will intentionally produce my body as thinner and more feminine through the clothes and make-up I wear in contexts in which I feel my queerness may be a site of challenge.[15]

This shows how fatness is materialized through normative discourses about gender and sexuality and how body size and shape can be 'un-fixed' and denaturalized (see also Longhurst, 2014). One feminist interpretation of what it means to unsay fat, then, is to hear to speech the complex and sometimes conflicting messy lived experiences of fat women committed to fat acceptance, giving space to the shifting and fluid ways in which fat women might perform their size as 'change agents' (LeBesco, 2014, p. 58).[16] It is also to acknowledge that bodies are shaped through relation to others and by discursive structures we cannot easily control. Unsaying fatness, then, is not a dream of detaching from these constraints nor is it a call for women to disappear or rise above their flesh. It is instead an invitation to negate the static economy of knowingness about fat, aware that there will always be more to say and that our experiences of fatness are always on the move.

As a feminist Christian praxis, unsaying fatness is a saying of fat intent on 'holding our bodies together', to borrow a phrase from the feminist disability theologian Nancy Eiesland (Eiesland, 1994, p. 95). For some women this will mean an unadulterated affirmation of fatness as a locus of delight and an unapologetic taking up of space and claiming of desire. For others, it may mean giving voice to the 'jumbled pleasure-pain that is our bodies' (Eiesland, 1994, p. 96), embracing the 'complexity and the "mixed blessing" of life and bodies' (p. 102). In this case, unsaying fatness is the Christian ethical praxis of living with the complex, sometimes tangled feelings we might embody about our size. Eiesland encourages us to hold such experiences of embodiment together as testament to our embodied wholeness. The apophasis of fatness read through this lens does not encourage women to punish themselves or judge those who experience being fat in a fat-hating world as too much. It calls instead for listening, openness and compassion. The obsessive quest for perfection in a weight-loss culture that fuels anti-fatness is an obsession with uniformity that our fat politics must avoid. To unsay fatness is to give voice to the tensions that can coexist alongside a commitment to fat pride. This means to embrace fatness as a wholeness found in the *continuing* unfolding of identity; to extol fatness as an expanse – an excess – that cannot be fixed in time, place, space or tidy politics.

Of course, if unsaying fatness is to positively affirm fat embodiment as unfixed, then fat liberation and size acceptance need not demand that fat bodies always stay the same. Indeed, fat politics may need to resist repeating Augustine's phobia of change and association of perfection with a static future. This will mean giving voice to women's lived experiences of body ambivalence, size fluidity, change and transition while not insisting that all fat women committed to fat liberation adhere to the same script. Such a strategy makes us better placed to challenge the narrow orthodoxies that work to shame people of a variety of sizes without obscuring the symbolic power thinness continues to wield in Western culture or the need to resist it. The future that fat politics may need to imagine is thus one a little closer to Augustine's, when fatness cannot be removed as a permanent feature, fat women and all fat bodies are extolled for their unspeakable beauty reflective of the unfathomable God who always occupies the space beyond, but when the uncomfortable desire to modify fat is also not rendered silent.

Conclusion

In conclusion, I have argued that the unsaying of fatness need not be a repetition of the politics of abjection whereby we obsessively fixate upon women's fat only to moments later balk in horror. Unsaying fat need not lend theological support to a retreat into intellectual abstraction or silence that rides roughshod over the real material experiences and bodies of fat women or the politics of fat pride. Instead, it can return us to a kataphatic affirmation of the uncertainty and indeterminacy of fatness and to a celebration of these features as marks of beauty that reflect the unfathomable and infinite beauty and vastness of God. This is, to borrow from Catherine Keller, an 'unsaying of the body in the name of the body' (Keller, 2010, p. 11), but it is also, more specifically, an unsaying of fat in praise of fat and in the name of fat women. Appraising fat bodies as apophatic means to relativize all we think we know about fat and fat women, interrupting the narrow orthodoxies that operate in our culture of knowingness but also inside the fat community. Augustine offers a reminder that for all we say about bodies – and so, by extension, about fat bodies, and fat women specifically – there is always *more* to say. This excess provides an opening into a theological future in which we are confronted with the wonderful indeterminacy of fatness and are better placed to hear to speech the embodied sayings of fat women, including those committed to fat acceptance who pursue weight loss and who experience themselves as change agents.

Notes

1 Cecilia Hartley suggests that this phrase is particularly levelled at fat women, exposing the patriarchal expectation that women should be bound and controlled (2001, pp. 63–4).

2 Helen Archer (2016) uses this term to describe entertainment game shows focused on fat people. UK examples include *The Biggest Loser*, *Lose Weight for Love*, *Fat Families* and *Secret Eaters*.

3 Ahmed explains that this is *because eating involves taking an object that is outside into the body, blurring the boundaries between inside and out*.

4 Discussing the way Black women were understood in the racial science of the seventeenth century, Strings draws on the specific case of Saartjie 'Sara' Baartman, who was famously exhibited as an exotic and scientific curiosity for the entertainment of British and other European men. Viewed as both grotesque and exotic, Sara's size and shape – in particular her ample bottom – became a lucrative attraction. When Sara died, the anatomist Georges Cuvier conducted an autopsy on her body, seeing the size of her hips and buttocks and the fat on her knees, thighs, stomach and breasts as proof of her defectivity. This carries some resonance with the BBC autopsy previously discussed, but here Baartman's fat is excavated as evidence of the barbarism of her 'race' (Strings, 2019, p. 97).

5 For me, fat liberation comprises an ethical, theological and political commitment to fat acceptance and to challenging size-based discrimination in its many forms.

6 My reading of Augustine in this section is influenced by Burrus and Mackendrick (2010), who make similar points about his excessive treatment of bodies.

7 This was the 'age to which we know that Christ had arrived' (22.15).

8 Burrus and Mackendrick thus ask, 'would we become unusually dense, excessive in weight but not in volume?' (2010, p. 86).

9 Augustine does indeed consider that when it comes to resurrection bodies, 'there may be some *increase in stature*, since beauty will demand a general distribution of what, in anyone member, would be an ugly excess' (emphasis mine) (*City of God*, 22.20). This, though, may indicate his musing that the saved could rise as giants.

10 For Augustine, the beards and nipples of men will not be removed in the resurrection. They exist and are intended by God to be beautiful and aesthetically pleasing, so to remove them would result in ugliness and there will be no ugliness in heaven (*City of God*, 22.24; *Sermons*, 243.6).

11 According to Augustine, the here-and-now body is subject to the 'calamities' of hunger, thirst, sickness and decay (*Sermons*, 240.3), but the resurrected body will enjoy changelessness. Augustine is sure that there will be no need for eating in heaven because eating is associated with the body's mutability.

12 For examples of this, see Slee's two poems, 'Fat Christa' and 'A Canticle in praise of large women' (2011, pp. 141–3).

13 In this sense, we would do well to embrace Marilyn Wann's point that 'The only thing anyone can diagnose by looking at a fat person is their own level of prejudice toward fat people' (Wann, 2005, p. 62).

14 Kathleen LeBesco cites the example of Marianne Kirby, who maintains that there is rightly a stigma attached to the decision taken by some fat activists to pursue weight loss: 'It runs counter to the very idea that fat activists are working so hard to promote: that being fat is not a statement of morality, is not a personal failing, is not a sign that a person doesn't care about their own body or the feelings of those around them. That being fat is, simply, being fat' (Kirby, cited by LeBesco, 2014, p. 49).

15 See also Robyn Longhurst's discussion of queering body size and shape (2014).

16 LeBesco identifies as a 'change agent' who has experienced her body change size at various points. She explains that 'Like a genderqueer person, I like presenting an incoherent identity' (LeBesco, 2014, p. 53).

Bibliography

Ahmed, Sara, 2014, *The Cultural Politics of Emotion*, Edinburgh: Edinburgh University Press.

Archer, Helen, 2016, '"So Much Fat!" – The Cruel Autopsy of a 17-stone Woman on the BBC', *The Guardian*, 13 September, https://www.theguardian.com/tv-and-radio/2016/sep/13/obesity-the-post-mortem-so-much-fat-the-cruel-autopsy-of-a-17-stone-woman-bbc, accessed 21.08.2024.

Augustine, 1979a, *City of God*, in Philip Schaff (ed.), *A Select Library of the Nicene and Post-Nicene Fathers of the Christian Church*, vol. 11, Grand Rapids, MI: William B. Eerdmans.

Augustine, 1979b, *On Christian Doctrine*, in Philip Schaff (ed.), *A Select Library of the Nicene and Post-Nicene Fathers of the Christian Church*, vol. 11, Grand Rapids, MI: William B. Eerdmans.

Augustine, 1990–7, *The Works of Saint Augustine: Sermons*, ed. John E. Rotelle, trans. Edmund Hill, Brooklyn, NY: New City Press.

Augustine, 1997, *Confessions*, trans. Maria Boulding, New York: New City Press.

Bacon, Hannah, 2019, *Feminist Theology and Contemporary Dieting Culture: Sin, Salvation and Women's Weight Loss Narratives*, London and New York: T&T Clark.

BBC Three, 2018, *Obesity: The Post Mortem, YouTube*, 22 April, https://www.youtube.com/watch?v=ZagG-rXrgPA, accessed 21.08.2024.

Boesel, Chris and Keller, Catherine, 2010, 'Introduction', in Chris Boesel and Catherine Keller (eds), *Apophatic Bodies: Negative Theology, Incarnation and Relationality*, New York: Fordham University Press, pp. 1–24.

Bordo, Susan, 1993, *Unbearable Weight: Feminism, Western Culture, and the Body*, Berkeley, CA; London: University of California Press.

Burrus, Virginia and Mackendrick, Karmen, 2010, 'Bodies without Wholes: Apophatic Excess and Fragmentation in Augustine's *City of God*', in Chris Boesel and Catherine Keller (eds), *Apophatic Bodies: Negative Theology, Incarnation and Relationality*, New York: Fordham University Press, pp. 79–93.

Burrus, Virginia, Jordan, Mark D. and Mackendrick, Karmen, 2010, *Seducing Augustine: Bodies, Desires, Confessions*, New York: Fordham University Press.

Bynum, Caroline Walker, 1995, *The Resurrection of the Body in Western Christianity, 200–1336*, New York: Columbia University Press.

Cooper, Charlotte, 2007, 'Headless Fatties', *Dr Charlotte Cooper*, https://charlottecooper.net/fat/headlessfatties/, accessed 21.08.2024.

Eiesland, Nancy, 1994, *The Disabled God: Toward a Liberatory Theology of Disability*, Nashville, TN: Abingdon Press.

Farrell, Amy Erdman, 2023, 'Connecting Gender and Fat', in Amy Erdman Farrell (ed.), *The Contemporary Reader of Gender and Fat Studies*, London and New York: Routledge, pp. 3–16.

Finlay, Jeanie, 2023, *Your Fat Friend*, https://www.yrfatfriendfilm.com/, accessed 21.08.2024.

Gailey, Jeannine A., 2023, 'Undesirably Different: Hyper(in)visibility and the Gendered Fat Body', in Amy Erdman Farrell (ed.), *The Contemporary Reader of Gender and Fat Studies*, London and New York: Routledge, pp. 19–29.

Hartley, Cecilia, 2001, 'Letting Ourselves Go: Making Room for the Fat Body in Feminist Scholarship', in Jana Evans Braziel and Kathleen LeBesco (eds), *Bodies out of Bounds: Fatness and Transgression*, Berkeley, CA and London: University of California Press, pp. 60–73.

Keller, Catherine, 2010, 'The Cloud of the Impossible: Embodiment and Apophasis', in Chris Boesel and Catherine Keller (eds), *Apophatic Bodies: Negative Theology, Incarnation and Relationality*, New York: Fordham University Press, pp. 25–44.

LeBesco, Kathleen, 2014, 'On Fatness and Fluidity', in Cat Pausé, Jackie Wykes and Samantha Murray (eds), *Queering Fat Embodiment*, London and New York: Routledge, pp. 49–59.

Lelwica, Michelle Mary, 1999, *Starving for Salvation: The Spiritual Dimensions of Eating Problems among American Girls and Women*, New York and Oxford: Oxford University Press.

Lelwica, Michelle Mary, 2017, *Shameful Bodies: Religion and the Culture of Physical Improvement*, London and New York: Bloomsbury Publishing.

Longhurst, Robyn, 2014, 'Queering Body Size and Shape: Performativity, the Closet, Shame and Orientation', in Cat Pausé, Jackie Wykes and Samantha Murray (eds), *Queering Fat Embodiment*, London and New York: Routledge, pp. 13–26.

Louth, Andrew, 2012, 'Apophatic and Cataphatic Theology', in Amy Hollywood and Patricia Z. Backman (eds), *The Cambridge Companion to Christian Mysticism*, Cambridge: Cambridge University Press, pp. 137–46.

Miles, Margaret, 2012, 'From Rape to Resurrection: Sin, Sexual Difference, and Politics', in J. Wetzel (ed.), *Augustine's City of God: A Critical Guide*, Cambridge: Cambridge University Press, pp. 75–92.

Moltmann, Jürgen, 1999, 'Liberating and Anticipating the Future', in Margaret Farley and Serene Jones (eds), *Liberating Eschatology: Essays in Honour of Letty M. Russell*, Louisville, KY: Westminster John Knox Press, pp. 189–208.

Moon, Michael and Sedgwick, Eve Kosofsky, 2001, 'Divinity: A Dossier, a Performance Piece, a Little-Understood Emotion', in J. E. Braziel and K. LeBesco (eds), *Bodies out of Bounds: Fatness and Transgression*, Berkeley, CA and London: University of California Press, pp. 292–328.

Moss, Candida R., 2011, 'Heavenly Healing: Eschatological Cleansing and the Resurrection of the Dead in the Early Church', *Journal of the American Academy of Religion*, vol. 79, no. 4, pp. 991–1017.

Murray, Samantha, 2008, *The 'Fat' Female Body*, London: Palgrave Macmillan.

Murray, Samantha, 2010, 'Women Under/In Control: Embodying Eating after Gastric Banding', in S. Vandamme, S. Van de Vathorst and I. De Beaufort (eds), *Whose Weight is it Anyway? Essays on Ethics and Eating*, Leuven: Acco, pp. 43–54.

Pseudo-Dionysius, 1987, *Pseudo-Dionysius: The Complete Works*, trans. Colm Luibheid, New York: Paulist Press.

Russell, Letty M., 1974, *Human Liberation in a Feminist Perspective – A Theology*, Philadelphia, PA: Westminster Press.

Sedgwick, Eve Kosofsky, 1990, *Epistemology of the Closet*, Berkeley, CA: University of California Press.

Slee, Nicola, 2011, *Seeking the Risen Christa*, London: SPCK.

Strings, Sabrina, 2019, *Fearing the Black Body: The Racial Origins of Fat Phobia*, New York: New York University Press.

Wann, Marilyn, 2005, 'Fat & Choice: A Personal Essay', 29 September, *MP: An Online Feminist Journal*, pp. 60–2, http://academinist.org/wp-content/uploads/2005/09/010308Wann_Fat.pdf, accessed 21.08.2024.

Questions for reflection and discussion

1 The author explains how fat women are 'viewed as objects that are talked about rather than as subjects with a voice … [and] denied their own words, feelings and opinions about what it is to be fat'. Do you think this is an accurate assessment of how fat people, and fat women in particular, are treated in Western culture? Are there examples you can draw on?

2 How have you experienced and/or expressed the prejudicial assumption of knowingness towards fat people? Maybe take some time to contemplate how you approach your own body or the fatness of others.

Are there steps you can take to challenge these assumptions? Consider how messages about fatness are transmitted – through families, medical institutions, education and religion. Are there ways we can disrupt these messages? What might be the role of faith in this?

3 The author explores 'an unsaying of fatness' that 'extols fat as an open and indeterminate site of enfleshing, beautiful in its diversity and wondrous unknowability'. As far as you consider this to apply to you, how might it look for you to positively '*un*say your fatness'?

4 How have your expectations for the nature of the resurrection body, particularly in terms of weight, been shaped by fatphobia? How does the author's proposal that fatness exists in our heavenly future (with or without Augustine's nuances) impact your eschatological imagination, and how might this impact your treatment of bodies in the here and now?

5 The author points to the ambiguities of fat positivity and the ambivalence of the lived experience of fatness. How do you feel about a commitment to fat acceptance coexisting with active interventions to lose weight?

7

Perfectly Able, Beautiful and Slim: Desired Bodies in the New Creation, Shamed Bodies in the Old

MAJA WHITAKER

As an academic it can be a struggle at times to explain your research to the lay person and to help them connect it with their lives and their context – often eyes glaze over and the conversation is quickly turned to more comfortable common ground. As a practical theologian, I am committed to this, however, and so during my doctoral study I worked hard at translation. When people asked me, 'So what's your PhD about?' I would often say something along the lines of 'I am imagining what the resurrection body might be like for a person with a disability.' One day a woman at my church responded with a curt, 'Well, perfect!' For her, this statement was the ultimate conclusion and the end to all speculation – it would have made for a short thesis! For me, however, it exposed the nub of why I was so interested in the topic I had chosen: this preoccupation with normality shapes our expectations of perfected human life and perfected human bodies, in ways that are inconsistent with the vision of glorious diversity and shameless vulnerability that we see in Scripture. In this chapter, I will explore how a vision of the new creation as populated by diverse bodies can provide a much-needed correction to this preoccupation with both normality and conventional aesthetic standards. These speculations around a disabled resurrection body confront deeply rooted issues that extend beyond disability into body shaming more generally. Note that my intention in reflecting on the intersections here is to draw on the growing literature in disability theology to sharpen our critique of fatphobia and beauty obsession, without diminishing attention to the persistent stigma and harms that people with disabilities have experienced and continue to experience.

My interlocuter's response was conditioned by assumptions deeply entrenched in modern culture and in the Christian tradition, which both presuppose that a perfect body is a 'healed' body, by which we usually mean a normalized body – that is, a body like ours, or at least the body that we would like to have. Along these lines, Bishop Otto of Friesing, from the twelfth century, wrote:

> We must not suppose that giants are brought back in such great stature, dwarfs in such extreme littleness, the lame or the weak in a state so feeble and afflicted, the Ethiopians in an affliction of colour so disagreeable, the fat or the thin in their superabundance or their lack of flesh, to a life which ought to be free from every blemish and every spot. (Otto of Friesing, 1928, p. 470)

I would like to think that most Christians today would recoil from Bishop Otto's proposal that the new creation is populated exclusively by White people, but his claims about overweight and disabled bodies probably sit more comfortably with many.

In contrast, an increasing number of people with disabilities have expressed the expectation that they will in their resurrection bodies retain some element of their disability (Betcher, 2004; Eiesland, 1994; Koks, 2015; see also Gosbell, 2021; Powell, 2023, pp. 115–37; Yong, 2007b). This hope for eschatological embodiment tends to emerge from the way these people relate to their disabilities: they do not see them as something that needs fixing or curing, and instead consider them to be an important, perhaps even essential, part of their identity. For example, consider Nancy Eiesland's reflection:

> Having been disabled from birth, I came to believe that in heaven I would be absolutely unknown to myself and perhaps to God. My disability has taught me who I am and who God is. What would it mean to be without this knowledge? (Eiesland, 1994, p. 2)

This is indeed a disorientating prospect. In response, Eiesland meditated on the wounds of the risen Christ as offering an alternative vision of humanity in which impaired bodies are flourishing and truly human bodies:

> In presenting his impaired hands and feet to his startled friends, the resurrected Jesus is revealed as the disabled God. Jesus, the resurrected Savior, calls for his frightened companions to recognize in the marks of impairment their own connection with God, their own salvation. In so doing, this disabled God is also the revealer of a new humanity.

> The disabled God is not only the One from heaven but the revelation of true personhood, underscoring the reality that full personhood is compatible with the expression of disability. (Eiesland, 1994, p. 100)

Christ presents his wounded hands, feet and side as proof of his identity and resurrection (Luke 24.38–40; John 20.20, 27), but also as a representative of resurrected humanity, thus implying that fulfilled humanity need not exclude impairment. More than this, eschatologically fulfilled human bodies are not free from flaws – Christ's skin is not smooth and unblemished, it is at best marked with scars or, at the more extreme reading that I advocate, still open and wounded (Whitaker, 2022). As I have argued elsewhere at length (Whitaker, 2023), this picture of the post-resurrection Christ suggests at the very least the possibility that people with disabilities might retain in their post-resurrection bodies features of their embodied existence that in the old creation contributed to the experience of disability and impairment.

To understand how this 'retention view' can allow for the full flourishing of human bodies while still retaining aspects of disability, we need to break down the factors that contribute to the lived experience of disability. It is common within the social model of disability to distinguish 'impairment' from 'disability': 'impairments' appear in the lived experience of a person as their body interacts with the physical world around them – pain, limited movement, altered locomotion and non-standard modes of communication. In addition to this, there are the negative social aspects that cause living with an 'impairment' to become a 'disability' – stigma, architectural obstacles, social exclusion, limited possibilities for communication and limited prospects for education and vocation. However, beneath both impairment and disability lie what I term 'diverse embodiment'. These are the physical characteristics that a person with a disability exhibits (whether an intellectual, sensory or physical disability). Eschatologically we can expect a thorough transformation of both the physical and social nature of the old creation, so much so that diverse embodiment need not produce the lived experience of impairment and disability in the new creation. This means that there is no requirement for the diverse embodiment of persons with disabilities to undergo special transformation for the consummation of human flourishing. Eschatological persons will flourish in the presence of God in every aspect of their personal identity, but this need not entail the normalization of their bodies – these bodies can remain flawed and limited, yet still be 'perfected'.

Thus, I argue that embodied features that currently contribute to disability might *in some cases* be retained in the resurrection body (see Whitaker, 2023). As Eiesland suggested, for some persons with disabilities their diverse embodiment is identify-forming. This means that the retention of those features is required to safeguard the continuity of identity through the transformation of resurrection. I base this claim on an account of personal identity over time in which threads within the biological, psychological, narrative and relational criteria of personal identity intertwine to create a continuous web that carries what I call 'personal self-recognition' over time (Whitaker, 2023, pp. 45–65). Personal self-recognition is the sense that 'I am me', and it is determinate but non-analysable from any other position than the first-person perspective at the time in question. That is, I do and will know that I am myself at any particular point in time, but I cannot from another point in time look at person X and say 'That is me' according to certain features that I recognize – I will have strong intuitions about which features of my self are identity-forming, but I cannot know for certain. In addition, a third human person cannot definitively make these claims about another person at any point in time, neither identifying a person nor their identity-forming features. Note that I say *human* person. Crucial to this account is the claim that while we cannot be completely confident about which features of ourselves are identity-forming, we are fully known by God, so much so that our 'real life is hidden with Christ in God' (Col. 3.3, NLT). This means that I may awaken (metaphorically) in the new creation and find myself surprised about which features of my self are continuous, but this will be paired with a recognition that, yes indeed, this is who I really am (even when I could not recognize this before). We can trust that God knows us better than we know ourselves, and we can trust in the goodness of God, so much so that while we might be surprised about the nature of the resurrection body, we will not be disappointed.

All this means that features of diverse embodiment are probably not identity-forming for all persons with disabilities, and so I am careful not to argue that disabling features of our bodies will always be retained in the resurrection body. Rather, their retention in some cases presents no threat to God's goodness nor to the eschatological flourishing of the person in question and the full realization of their humanity.

While this retention view has several proponents, particularly Amos Yong (2007a, 2007b, 2012), it also has many critics who insist that disabilities must be eliminated in the new creation. James Barton Gould, for example, writes:

God's will for us is wholeness, health, and species-typical functioning; dysfunction of body and mind is destructive – it does not come from God and is contrary to God's loving purpose in creation. To redefine disability as intrinsically good is to deny the created perfection, present brokenness, and future liberation of creation. (Gould, 2016, p. 321)

Both Yong and Gould are writing from the perspective not only of theologians, but also as family members of a person with an intellectual disability. How do they arrive at such differing conclusions? In large part, the difference lies in the underlying assumptions that each holds about what it means to be human, and whether limitation of physical and intellectual capacities is opposed to the *telos* of human life or compatible with it. Gould is working within the commonplace framework that defines disability as a 'bad-difference' rather than a 'mere-difference', to employ Elizabeth Barnes's terminology. She distinguishes bad-difference views of disability, whereby 'having a disability would still be a bad thing even if society was fully accommodating of disabled people', from mere-difference views of disability, where having 'a disability makes you physically non-standard, but it doesn't (by itself or automatically) make you worse off' (Barnes, 2016, p. 55).[1] Opponents to the retention view are often operating within a narrative of deficiency in which disability is the loss of certain goods and a hindrance to the form of flourishing that is determined to be essential to fullness of human life. However, this 'form' is usually determined by reference to statistical norms – what is normal has become normative. In contrast, Thomas Reynolds, reflecting on intellectual disability, writes:

Disability does not mark an incomplete humanity – a failure, defect, or sinful nature. It models one way of being human as vulnerable yet creative, relational, and available. Notice the absence of terms like 'reason,' 'productivity,' and 'independence.' Full personhood is neither diminished by a paucity of these nor confirmed by their abundance. Instead, personhood lies in being affirmed by God as a dependent creature loved into being with others. (Reynolds, 2008, p. 186)

Dependency, vulnerability and limitation do not sit easily within a conception of perfected human life developed with the modern Western definition of a person as a rational autonomous being. However, theologically these are aspects of what it means to be a human being; they are not a threat to our humanness but a condition of our relatedness (Brock, 2019; Creamer, 2009).

Renewing our understanding of perfection

As the short conversation that I opened this chapter with illustrated, at the heart of the conceptual opposition to the retention view is the question of what perfection entails. In 1 Corinthians 15, Paul describes the transformation of resurrection through a series of contrasts: from 'perishable' to 'imperishable', 'dishonour' to 'glory', 'weakness' to 'power' and 'natural' to 'spiritual' (vv. 42–44, NIV). That final contrast is sometimes translated as from 'physical' to 'spiritual' (as in the NRSVA), and this can be read to suggest that human life in the new creation will be non-physical – that is, somehow disembodied. However, this 'physical body' is the *soma psuchikon* and the 'spiritual body' the *soma pneumatikon* – more literally they describe the 'soulish' body and the 'spiritual' body. The distinction here is not between the material substance of the earthly human existence and the immaterial substance of heavenly human existence, as a substance dualist account of human ontology might insist. Paul here is not writing with ontological distinctions in mind; he instead describes what the human body will be animated by and orientated towards: the soulishness of a person pre-resurrection and the power of the Spirit post-resurrection. There is no inevitable connection between perishability, dishonour, weakness and soulishness, and diverse embodiment; these are instead descriptors of the earthly existence that all human creatures experience. 'Normal' bodies do not exhibit less perishability, dishonour, weakness or soulishness than disabled bodies (or at least they need not on their own merits); these metrics do not apply more or less to bodies that occupy the middle of the statistical bell curve than to those at either end of the range of normal biological variation.

The clearest picture of what we can expect of embodied life post-resurrection is provided by the accounts of the only body that has been truly resurrected: Christ's.[2] Yet here we have a confusing picture: he is sometimes recognizable and at other times not; at times he is solid enough to consume food but other-worldly enough to walk through walls and disappear from sight (see e.g. Luke 24.13–43). There is both continuity and discontinuity between the earthly and resurrection bodies, and we cannot be wholly confident of the legibility of Christ's post-resurrection body. With so little clarity provided in Scripture, a lot is left to the imagination. In general, I have no problem with the use of a sanctified and biblically informed imagination; however, the degree of sanctification is often in question: our biases shape our speculation, particularly when we are unconscious of them. Thus we find the speculation of Bishop Otto, who assumes the resurrected body will be of average size and weight, able-bodied and White – this is the kind of body his biases lead him to imagine. He is following Augustine's lead here, who speculates thus in his *Civitate Dei* (*City of God*):

> Therefore, let those who, on earth, are too thin or too fat take comfort. They would not choose to be that way now if they could avoid it. They will certainly not be that way in eternity. For, what makes a human body beautiful is an harmonious contour combined with a pleasing complexion ... Here, every deformity is transformed, and every part that is too small is readjusted as God knows how, and every part that is too large has its excess redistributed throughout the whole body. (Augustine, 1954, 22.19)

Moreover, Augustine asserts that those over the age of 33 are rewound in their transformation back to that peak of perfection, and those younger advanced (*Civitate Dei* 22.14–15). Men retain their beards as a core marker of ideal masculinity (*Civitate Dei* 22.24) – and, one assumes, grow them to a satisfactory degree of thickness if they could not before. Similarly, the mosaicists of Ravenna depict the female saints in the Basilica of Sant'Apollinare Nuovo as uniformly 'beautiful', their homogenous bodies featuring pale skin, fair hair and slender hands. The uniformity here is so uncanny and expresses such a narrow range of biological and aesthetic variation that Candida Moss (2011, p. 992) describes them as 'heavenly Stepford wives'.

These standards of beauty are not merely aesthetic. Conventional physiognomic assumptions pair moral standards with aesthetic standards: the beautiful body reveals a person of good character. The Gospel writers were steeped in this world view, which associated features such as dwarfism, lameness and malformed limbs with smallness or distortion of character, but on occasion they used these features to subvert the paradigm (Parsons, 2006). These physiognomic assumptions are not merely supported by entrenched prejudice, but also encoded in the neural systems that connect visceral disgust with moral disgust (Tybur et al., 2013). These prejudicial assumptions once provided an evolutionary advantage by helping us to avoid pathogens, ensure the fitness of our offspring and preserve in-group and out-group dynamics. Yet they are no longer fit for purpose, as the ancient concern for evolutionary advantage has been ameliorated by cultural developments and the range of assistive techniques and devices employed by all people. These unconscious biases are examples of the 'patterns of this world' that we must not conform to, and instead we are urged to participate in the trans-forming work of the Spirit who renews our minds (Rom. 12.2). This is deeply counter-cultural work, however, and must be confronted both at the level of cultural discourse and at the level of the neurally embedded habits of mind. We must resist the narrow and ableist conception of what perfected bodies and perfect life entails that lies at the heart of our inability to conceive of disabled bodies flourishing in the new creation.

In Matthew 5.48, Jesus sums up his teaching on the law with the command to be 'Be perfect, therefore, as your heavenly Father is perfect [τέλειος, *teleios*]' (NIV). The word 'perfect' here is easily read as entail-ing flawlessness of some kind, that a certain ideal standard – whether moral, biological or aesthetic – has been met. However, *teleios* denotes far more than flawlessness, and is used throughout the New Testament to refer to spiritual maturity.[3] In his study of the holistic understand-ing of health presented in the New Testament, John Wilkinson includes the word *teleios*, which he defines as perfection, maturity or the com-plete expression of the wholeness God intends for a human being (1998, pp. 24, 29). The person who is *teleios* is fully expressing their *telos* – that is, their end, purpose or goal; they have reached the ultimate result of the process towards that *telos*.

The *telos* of the human person involves the *imago Dei*, which we gradually grow into via the ongoing work of the Spirit in the trans-formation of theosis. This is a more dynamic view of the *imago Dei* than the structural, functional or relational views that have prevailed. Stanley Grenz describes it as the 'goal or destiny', 'a reality toward which we are moving ... what we are *en route* to becoming' that we will fully bear in the new creation (2000, p. 173). The process of theosis, in which we gradually come to full expression of our *telos* is, as Myk Habets writes, 'about becoming more fully human than we ever dreamed possible' (Habets, 2016, p. 227). However, contra Habets, I argue that theosis need not entail the correction of physical or intellectual limita-tions or the normalization of diverse embodiment. The image of God is not located in superior intellectual or physical capacity, and it is cer-tainly not located in bodies that fit the biological norm. In Genesis 1, we see a God of abundant creativity who creates living creatures of every kind, and declares them *all* to be good (vv. 20–25). It is almost hard to understand how we can move from this picture to expecting the normal-ization of biological variation in resurrected bodies, yet so strong is the hold that ableism and the cult of normality has on us.

James K. A. Smith describes human beings as 'desiring arrows' pri-mordially orientated towards our *telos* as agents of love (2009, p. 71).

Our *telos* can be 'misdirected' into 'very different visions of what "the kingdom" looks like' (p. 55) by the practices we engage in, but this leads to ultimate frustration as we find that the good life we thought we were heading towards is not good after all. Smith points to the cultural liturgies of the mall as an 'intensification of the wider web of practices and rituals associated with consumer capitalism' that exemplify this misdirected *telos* (p. 55). Along these lines, we can easily see how our desires might be misdirected towards a *telos* characterized by a certain biological and aesthetic ideal: the bodies we yearn for and expend ourselves on seeking.

In her book *Perfect Me*, Heather Widdows (2018) explains how in recent years local ideals of beauty have converged into a global beauty ideal, one that has moved from an aesthetic sense of taste to a totalizing ethical ideal. This beauty ideal is encapsulated by the descriptors 'thin, firm, smooth and youthful' – to which I would also add 'non-disabled'. This has become the goal for all women everywhere, and it is a mandatory goal that we are obliged to pursue as a kind of moral responsibility that subsumes all other values. If we are not, we are 'letting ourselves go', or failing to 'take care of ourselves'. Thinness, firmness, smoothness and youthfulness thus characterize the ideal female body, and this is the *telos* towards which an unreasonably vast proportion of a woman's time, energy and finance are to be directed. Yet in focusing our attentions on this literally superficial goal, we have taken our eyes off the *imago Dei*, off human flourishing and off the kind of rich experience of humanness that allows for diversity and weakness within abundant community.

Shaping our bodies to shape our selves

The body has become a worksite. We ignore the humble invitation to receive the bodies that we ourselves are given. Instead, we attempt to alter and transform our bodies, sometimes in subtle and gentle ways and at other times in more violent and overt ways – from a variety of dress and fashions, to body-building, dieting, cosmetic surgery and body modification. This approach is characteristic of Western modernity, where the body is conceived of as a project that can and should be worked on. This project is aimed in part at expressing a person's self-identity, ensuring that the outer self authentically externalizes the inner self, but also at reflexively shaping that inner self. That is, we try to make ourselves into someone different by working on our outer selves (Öberg and Tornstam, 1999). Anthony Giddens writes: 'What might appear as a wholesale movement towards the narcissistic cultivation of bodily appearance is in fact an expression of a concern lying much deeper actively to "construct" and control the body' (1991, p. 7). Sarah Coakley describes this as a kind of 'sweaty Pelagianism' whereby 'our only hope seems to reside in keeping [the body] alive, youthful, consuming, sexually active, and jogging on (literally), for as long as possible' (Coakley, 2002, p. 155). As she describes, this project is about more than self-improvement or maintaining a certain look, it is an expression of our deepest longings for meaning and for freedom from death and decay. However, this liberation and the consummation of our *telos* is promised only in the redemption of our bodies, for which we eagerly long with all creation (Rom. 8.19–23).

Thus, this modern project is inevitably flawed: bodies are simply not as malleable as we might like to believe, and even if they were they could not address the deeper needs that only the eschatological redemption of our bodies can meet. Even when the routinized control of bodily regimes can design the body with some success, the success is short-lived – for those fortunate to live long enough, the process of ageing cannot be interminably delayed, and illness and disability often come with it.

In many cases, the lives of people with disabilities confound the modern project to shape the body to express and shape the self. The goals of the culturally determined aesthetic ideals are often, to some degree, unattainable for the disabled body, and so the opportunity to opt out of this serious game may become more readily apparent and can often be experienced as empowerment rather than defeat. Eiesland wrote:

> Instead of flagellating ourselves and aspiring to well-behaved 'perfect' bodies, we savor the jumbled pleasure-pain that is our bodies. In a society where denial of our particular bodies and questing for a better body is 'normal,' respect for our own bodies is an act of resistance and liberation. (Eiesland, 1994, p. 96)

This does not mean that persons with disabilities do not and should not enjoy making themselves beautiful, and certainly not that they are not beautiful. Though conventional aesthetic standards tend to exclude bodies with markers of both intellectual and physical disability, the definition of beauty as that which is attractive to the senses has been distorted by the implications of sin, and is often at odds with a more theologically resonant definition of beauty as that which rightly pleases. It is only in recent years that advertising has employed models of diverse body types (whether mature, fat or disabled), and there is certainly a measure of joy in seeing diverse bodies celebrated. However, as Widdows (2018, pp. 118–19, 220) notes, this is a limited revolution: the 'diverse' models in body-positive beauty promotions only diverge on one of the features of the beauty ideal. If they are not thin, they are still firm, smooth and youthful. Similarly, when a model with a disability is featured, she is usually thin, firm, smooth and youthful. These attempts at body positivity are a step in the right direction, yet they can also be critiqued as a 'naïve integration' (Heiss, 2011) that reinforces the ideology of normate bodies and the beauty ideal.

Desiring bodies, shaming bodies

This simmering discontentment with the body characterizes modern Western culture: we are simultaneously body denying and body obsessed. The obsession is fuelled by media messaging financed by the burgeoning cosmetic, fashion and health industries, and by more localized phenomena, as women comment on clothes in the changing room or 'encourage' one another with comments about weight loss. Yet still we deny the bodies that we are in, seeking to discipline and control them, contradicting natural diversity and fluidity over time. All this is built on and builds the assumption that our bodies are not good enough as they are, and we must want our bodies to be better – where 'better' is defined in narrow cultural prescriptions of beauty and even, at times, of health. The undercurrent of shame is destructive in a range of ways, both obvious and hidden. Brené Brown (2015) claims that feeling physically unattractive or inadequate is the number one 'shame trigger' for women across cultures (p. 86).

Both the disabled and the heavy body are commonly experienced as 'ugly' – by the self and by the other. Basic aversive emotional responses, including fear, pity and disgust, are elicited by disabled bodies. Bill Hughes describes these as 'the major – though not exclusive – building blocks of the emotional infrastructure of ableism. It is these emotions that settle as sediment in the non-disabled imaginary' (Hughes, 2012, p. 91). Similarly, when asked to image their feelings around ugly, disgusting and dreaded bodies, most women reveal a fear of fatness which, along with ageing and disability, exemplifies 'failed femininity' (Fahs, 2018). As we have seen, this perception is embedded not only in cultural discourse, it is also encoded in the human psyche. In addition, not only do we tend to be disgusted by diverse or overweight bodies in an aesthetic or visceral sense, but the neural phenomenon flows over into our moral perceptions via physiognomic assumptions. Our ways of thinking and perceiving, both individually and communally, are greatly in need of renewal!

In contrast to these reactions, Brian Brock notes that the degree to which we find others repellent is the degree to which our view of beauty is distorted. In the context of the resurrection, he notes: 'Bodies and minds that today some find repulsive will be gloriously visible to all in the beauty that God's eyes behold in them' (2021, p. 132). The transformation of resurrection is not only corporeal; our moral perceptions, social relations and cultural discourses will be radically reconstructed. Our values both aesthetic and moral will be renewed, and the aim of our *telos*-driven desire redirected towards God's will – that which is good, pleasing and perfect (Rom. 12.2).

The subversive power of a vision of eschatological diversity

The Church has not only done a poor job of protecting Christians from these body-related cultural ills, in some ways it has contributed to them in both theology and practice. Ragan Sutterfield describes how a theology of salvation bereft of embodiment led him not only to ill-health but also to an atrophied spirituality:

> A church where the soul alone and not the body is saved becomes a place where the body is left to other stories or no story at all. Because the body doesn't matter to our eternal salvation in this view, Christians tend to adopt secular views of the body or simply ignore it and its health altogether. (Sutterfield, 2015, p. 13)

Historically, the body in general, and the female body in particular, has been viewed as something to be tamed, feared and ultimately escaped. This, coupled with the Cartesian assumption that the body as a separate component can be successfully controlled by an autonomous self, has led to the expectation that not only the body should be controlled in line with a normalized ideal, but that it *can* be controlled as such.

The Church's concern with embodiment has often been preoccupied with questions about 'personal holiness' rather than communal, let alone ecological, considerations. In the twentieth century there was an overwhelming flood of attention to sexuality and the reproductive capacities of women's bodies. However, very little attention was given, for example, to the Christian approach to food – whether relating to disordered eating, food insecurity or methods of food production.

In American evangelicalism in particular, the pursuit of embodied holiness has turned into a pursuit for bodily perfection, uncritically embracing diet culture and sprinkling it with Christianese and Christian celebrity endorsements (Griffith, 2004). This does not mean that we should not be exhorting our congregations towards good health, but in doing so we must define health accurately and holistically, and proclaim all bodies – including fat, disabled and chronically ill bodies – as good bodies. Too often, theological motifs are co-opted into a cultural framework of self-improvement. Body shaming is actively practised and preached within the body of Christ.

As a corrective, I propose that we consider the possibility of embodied diversity in the new creation, as proposed by the retention view of disability in the resurrection. That is, as we sit with the possibility that the new creation might be populated by bodies still exhibiting markers of disability, we find ourselves more able to entertain all kinds of post-resurrection diversity. Our post-resurrection bodies will probably not conform to the beauty ideal that Widdows (2018) has named: instead of thin, firm, smooth and youthful, they may be fat, flabby, hairy, aged and disabled – yet glorious and perfected. Offering a picture of post-resurrection persons expressing a variety of embodied forms in the new creation extends affirmation of diverse bodies to all persons in the present time, and provides a corrective to prevailing culture. Our bodies may not fit the dominant aesthetic ideal, but they are still beautiful, potent and fit for eternity; and so we must behave accordingly towards our own bodies and the bodies of others.

I suggest that the retention view – in which persons with disabilities might retain their features of diverse embodiment in the new creation – can function as a kind of eschatological parable that provokes a re-examination of our attitudes to bodies in the here and now, in relation to both disability and body aesthetics.[4] Scholars of disability studies have long been active in critiquing the value systems deployed by the dominant culture; the lived experience of bodies that do not fit these systems offers an epistemological advantage in questioning the assumptions that undergird them. The ideal body that much of Western modern culture is bent on pursuing is always assumed to be *non*-disabled – and so the possibility of perfected *disabled* bodies undermines both the goal and assumptions of that pursuit.

A picture of resurrection bodies flourishing in all their glorious diversities prompts an expansion of our imagination about what kinds of bodies are desirable to God, and what kinds of embodied lived experience can be described as flourishing. My hope is that this could contribute to the transformation of both our self-talk and communal ethic about the beautiful bodies that we all possess – disabled and non-disabled.

Notes

1 Note that the 'mere-difference' view still allows that disability might entail the loss of intrinsic goods, such as the ability to hear or see, but it also asserts that disability is more than the lack of these goods as it may allow participation in other goods that might be unique to the experience of disability (Barnes, 2016, pp. 57, 16–20). See also Colgrove (2020).

2 We must distinguish the resurrection of Christ from the raising or revivification of people such as Lazarus (John 11.38–44), Jairus' daughter (Mark 5.35–43), the widow's son at Nain (Luke 7.11–17), or the widow's son at Zarephath (1 Kings 17.17–24).

3 For example, in 1 Corinthians 14.20, 'Brothers and sisters, do not be children in your thinking; rather, be infants in evil, but in thinking be adults [*teleioi*]' (NRSVA). See also 1 Corinthians 2.6; Ephesians 4.13; Philippians 3.15; Colossians 1.28; James 3.2.

4 Here I am working with John Dominic Crossan's delineation of a parable as that which subverts our received expectations about how things should or will work out (Crossan, 1988).

Bibliography

Augustine, 1954, *The City of God, Books XVII–XXII*, Catholic University of America Press.

Barnes, E., 2016, *The Minority Body: A Theory of Disability*, Oxford: Oxford University Press.

Betcher, S., 2004, 'Monstrosities, Miracles, and Mission: Religion and the Politics of Disablement', in C. Keller, M. Nausner and M. Rivera (eds), *Postcolonial Theologies: Divinity and Empire*, St Louis, MO: Chalice Press, pp. 79–99.

Brock, B., 2019, *Wondrously Wounded: Theology, Disability, and the Body of Christ*, Waco, TX: Baylor University Press.

Brock, B., 2021, *Disability: Living into the Diversity of Christ's Body*, Grand Rapids, MI: Baker Academic.

Brown, B., 2015, *Daring Greatly: How the Courage to Be Vulnerable Transforms the Way We Live, Love, Parent, and Lead*, New York: Penguin.

Coakley, S., 2002, *Powers and Submissions: Spirituality, Philosophy and Gender*, Oxford: Blackwell.

Colgrove, N., 2020, 'The (In)Compatibility of the Privation Theory of Evil and the Mere-Difference View of Disability', *National Catholic Bioethics Quarterly*, vol. 20, no. 2, pp. 329–48.

Creamer, D., 2009, *Disability and Christian Theology: Embodied Limits and Constructive Possibilities*, Oxford: Oxford University Press.

Crossan, J. D., 1988, *The Dark Interval: Towards a Theology of Story*, Santa Rosa, CA: Polebridge Press.

Eiesland, N., 1994, *The Disabled God: Toward a Liberatory Theology of Disability*, Nashville, TN: Abingdon Press.

Fahs, B., 2018, 'Imagining Ugliness: Failed Femininities, Shame, and Disgust Written onto the "Other" Body', in S. Rodrigues and E. Przybylo (eds), *On the Politics of Ugliness*, Palgrave Macmillan, pp. 237–58.

Giddens, A., 1991, *Modernity and Self-Identity: Self and Society in the Late Modern Age*, Cambridge: Polity Books.

Gosbell, L., 2021, 'Space, Place, and the Ordering of Materiality in Disability Theology: Locating Disability in the Resurrection and the Body of Christ', *Journal of Disability & Religion*, vol. 26, no. 2, pp. 149–61.

Gould, J. B., 2016, 'The Hope of Heavenly Healing of Disability Part 1: Theological Issues', *Journal of Disability & Religion*, vol. 20, no. 4, pp. 317–34.

Grenz, S. J., 2000, *Theology for the Community of God*, Grand Rapids, MI: William B. Eerdmans.

Griffith, R. M., 2004, *Born Again Bodies: Flesh and Spirit in American Christianity*, Berkeley, CA: University of California Press.

Habets, M., 2016, 'Disability and Divinization: Eschatological Parables and Allegations', in A. Picard and M. Habets (eds), *Theology and the Experience of Disability: Interdisciplinary Perspectives from Voices Down Under*, Abingdon: Routledge, pp. 212–34.

Heiss, S., 2011, 'Locating the Bodies of Women and Disability in Definitions of Beauty: An Analysis of Dove's Campaign for Real Beauty', *Disability Studies Quarterly*, vol. 31, no. 1.

Hughes, B., 2012, 'Fear, Pity and Disgust: Emotions and the Non-Disabled Imaginary', in N. Watson, A. Roulstone and C. Thomas (eds), *Routledge Handbook of Disability Studies*, London: Routledge, pp. 89–101.

Koks, S. J. I., 2015, 'On the Journey to New Creation: Mission with People with Disabilities', in R. Dewerse and D. Cronshaw (eds), *We Are Pilgrims: Mission from, in and with the Margins of Our Diverse World*, Dandenong, Australia: UNOH Publications, pp. 165–76.

Moss, C. R., 2011, 'Heavenly Healing: Eschatological Cleansing and the Resurrection of the Dead in the Early Church', *Journal of the American Academy of Religion*, vol. 79, no. 4, pp. 991–1017.

Öberg, P. and Tornstam, L., 1999, 'Body Images among Men and Women of Different Ages', *Ageing and Society*, vol. 19, no. 5, pp. 629–44.

Otto of Friesing, 1928, *The Two Cities: A Chronicle of Universal History to the Year 1146 A.D.*, in A. P. Evans and C. Knapp (eds), trans. C. C. Mierow, New York: Columbia University Press.

Parsons, M. C., 2006, *Body and Character in Luke and Acts: The Subversion of Physiognomy in Early Christianity*, Grand Rapids, MI: Baker Academic.

Powell, L. D., 2023, *The Disabled God Revisited: Trinity, Christology, and Liberation*, London: Bloomsbury Publishing.

Reynolds, T. E., 2008, *Vulnerable Communion: A Theology of Disability and Hospitality*, Grand Rapids, MI: Brazos Press.

Smith, J. K., 2009, *Desiring the Kingdom: Worship, Worldview, and Cultural Formation*, Grand Rapids, MI: Baker Academic.

Sutterfield, R., 2015, *This Is My Body: From Obesity to Ironman, My Journey into the True Meaning of Flesh, Spirit, and Deeper Faith*, Charlotte, NC: Baker & Taylor.

Tybur, J. M. et al., 2013, 'Disgust: Evolved Function and Structure', *Psychological Review*, vol. 120, no. 1, pp. 65–84.

Whitaker, M. I., 2022, 'The Wounds of the Risen Christ: Evidence for the Retention of Disabling Conditions in the Resurrection Body', *Journal of Disability & Religion*, vol. 26, no. 3, pp. 280–93.

Whitaker, M. I., 2023, *Perfect in Weakness: Disability and Human Flourishing in the New Creation*, Waco, TX: Baylor University Press.

Widdows, H., 2018, *Perfect Me: Beauty as an Ethical Ideal*, Princeton, NJ: Princeton University Press.

Wilkinson, J., 1998, *The Bible and Healing: A Medical and Theological Commentary*, Edinburgh: Handsel Press.

Yong, A., 2007a, 'Disability, the Human Condition, and the Spirit of the Eschatological Long Run: Toward a Pneumatological Theology of Disability', *Journal of Religion, Disability & Health*, vol. 11, no. 1, pp. 5–25.

Yong, A., 2007b, *Theology and Down Syndrome: Reimagining Disability in Late Modernity*, Waco, TX: Baylor University Press.

Yong, A., 2012, 'Disability Theology of the Resurrection: Persisting Questions and Additional Considerations – a Response to Ryan Mullins', *Ars Disputandi*, vol. 12, no. 1, pp. 4–10.

Questions for reflection and discussion

1 Take some time to quietly imagine your own resurrection body, and then that of others. How might you describe the images that arise, and what do these intuitions reveal about your assumptions regarding perfected bodies?

2 Consider the role and function of disgust and dread in our perception of bodies. How does this play out in your thinking and behavioural responses? It can be difficult to confront these biases that are deeply embedded in the brokenness of our humanity, so endeavour to do so with compassion.

3 How do you see the beauty ideal of 'thin, firm, smooth and youthful' play out in your context? How do you feel about the amount of time, energy and finance that you and others spend on pursuing this ideal?

4 Can you imagine the new creation populated with diverse bodies? How does this vision impact how you perceive and relate to diverse bodies – both your own and those of others?

8

Are We Having Great Sex Yet? Women, Their Bodies and Their Pleasure

LISA ISHERWOOD

While the sexual revolution supposedly set us all free from shame and guilt, many feminists are wondering what it actually propelled women into. Once upon a time not so very long ago, a 'good girl' said 'NO' to most sexual activity before marriage, but now it seems the 'good girl' who is the right shape and size says 'yes' to everything even if it is distasteful to her. In the 1990s, the WRAP Report (Women, Risk and AIDS Project) described how large numbers of women of all ages were going along with high-risk behaviour that gave them no sexual pleasure but enabled them to keep their man (Holland et al., 1998). Reports these days seem to suggest that things have not got better for many women; sexual performance is the sign of a good woman and this can, in many cases, involve risk, abuse, humiliation and, crucially, no sexual pleasure. We should perhaps not be surprised, as Victoria Smith (2023) reports that most men will have watched a huge amount of porn before they even touch another human being. She says that porn is changing what is regarded as normal, and while we once thought that removing stigmas and overarching restrictions would make things better, it has actually made things worse. The new frigid is seen as those who just want vanilla sex and the pleasure that can go with it. Many Gen X women report that it is far from unusual for their partners to choke them, spit at them, pull out their hair, verbally abuse them, and simply assume anal sex with no conversations about whether that activity is desired by their partners. All of this behaviour men would have seen in porn videos, and the end result is that violence to women has become eroticized. What has gone wrong? Reading the great sex gurus of the last 20 years has not made my feminist heart gladden. With Smith and others, I am convinced that the sexual revolution has indeed, from a woman's point of view, been an anticlimax. Women are more sexually available, but the male agenda remains largely unchanged and this is ultimately very limiting and unsatisfactory for women. Indeed, Slavoj Žižek (2022) goes further – he says sex researchers have shown that while women are expected to clearly and confidently state their desires, the reality is that women's desire is often slow to emerge while men are keen to insist they know what women want. Žižek says that this presumption is violence, yet many young women who are naïve about how sex should be are unaware that in this scenario they have been sexually assaulted.

As a theologian who believes we are all part of divine incarnation, this becomes a question concerning the fullness of abundant life, not simply satisfactory sex.

'I did not know the background and so I have often missed the meaning of the foreground' (Hoffman, 1998, p. 190)

This chapter will be an exercise in sexual theology, which for me relies heavily on an understanding of radical incarnation. For centuries, the Christian churches operated with what can be called a theology of sexuality; that is to say, they dictated what acceptable sexual behaviour was. This approach was based in a dualistic understanding of a person formed by the way they conceived of God and the world. God was above, and a human being was to be controlled, particularly when it came to sex, as these desires were viewed as destructive. The female body, associated with Eve, came off very badly under this approach; it is seen as the most unruly and likely to be led astray.

My starting point as a feminist liberation theologian is rooted in the potential of radical incarnation. By this I mean that the incarnation, the passionate and promiscuous love of God made flesh, changes the world. It changes the world because, as feminist theologians have shown, it is our power as much as that of the man Jesus that is our inborn heritage. Carter Heyward (1982) and others have demonstrated that the Gospels do not hold incarnational potential for the man Jesus alone, rather he alerts his followers to their own process of becoming. This radical shift in understanding Christology means that our bodies are human/divine incarnations, and this should change everything. However, sadly, the world has not essentially changed, and so I ask: What has gone wrong? My conclusion is that we have not taken seriously the power of our own incarnation, our own flesh (Isherwood, 1999). I am not then a body-denying and spirit-embracing theologian like many of my predecessors and peers. Rather, I assume that we explore the depths of that which we call divine through an engagement with that which the divine called holy – human flesh. Christianity has declared that the fullness of the divine vision could only be revealed through incarnation, through the flesh, and this is what feminist body theology seeks to explore: the fullness of our divine potential, the fullness of our incarnation. As such, all 'matters of the flesh' are of importance and sex is central to this, as we are dealing with one of the most fundamental of all human experiences. Radical incarnation means that sexual activity, no less than feeding the poor, is a place in which redemptive praxis is embodied; it is a place in which we are drawn into mutuality and empowerment or crushed and denied our incarnational potential.

Feminist theorists have argued over the years that the battle rages most intensely in the arena of sex: the actions involved as well as the rhetoric about it. The common language associated with intercourse gives a clue as to the symbolic power it is thought to have. A woman is fucked, poked, given one, screwed, had, taken – the list is endless and the words do not describe an act filled with mutuality and empowerment. From this we see that intercourse takes place in the context of socially constructed power relations, whatever the intentions of the individuals.

Theology, rooted as it is in a story of an unequal model of complementarity and a wayward woman, makes it hard to develop a positive theological anthropology and almost impossible to believe that the body has been socially constructed. Rather, it has its origins in the divine plan in which Eve is the second creation taken from the body of a man. Although the divine plan went astray it still has the seeds of redemption within it, but men need to be cautious around women and to exert God-given power over them. These ingredients, when passed through the ages and the lenses of Greek metaphysics, parousial anxiety and patriarchy, make a powerful cocktail in the normalizing and divinizing of neurosis, fear and a will to power exercised on and through the female body. This female body becomes the 'other' and bears all the weight of guilt and distrust that men are unable to carry themselves. At times in Christian history the female body becomes the demonic body and everything about it seems charged with evil and corruption. In this way, it loses its personhood and becomes the carrier of many societal fears as well as expectations, while the woman in that body is totally lost within the discourses about it. Theology and religion, once aware of their part in the denigration of the female, should then have as a priority the honouring and fostering of the autonomy of women.

But do they? While I am not suggesting that all Christians are damaging their girls through a patriarchal rhetoric, it is still surprising to me how many Christian parents hope their daughters will be virgins before marriage. I am sure many parents see this as just a personal wish, but is it that simple? It has always been the case that when it comes to males marking cultural territory, the bodies of women are good sites to choose for that enactment. The Christian abstinence programme True Love Waits is bounded by women's bodies and the weight they are required to bear for group purity. It is of course true that men are also expected to be pure, but the vast majority of the literature in this programme is dominated by women. The narrower the Christian interpretation of Scripture and tradition, the more we see that sex is tightly regulated; not only does it become confined to marriage, but missionary-position sex is then seen as the only holy act. The reasoning behind it is that it symbolizes the position of men and women in creation: man first and on top, and woman on the receiving end of sexual power enacted as divine will, one of the curses poured down on women after Eve's excursion with the snake and the fruit being that woman would desire her husband and he would rule over her.

Many of the women involved in the True Love Waits campaign write excitedly about the advantages of celibacy and the moral high ground they are able to occupy due to it. Cassie, an 18-year-old with her own website writes: 'I encourage you all to keep yourselves sexually pure.' Why? Well, because 'God will greatly reward you!' (Isherwood, 2006, p. 79). The reward of course will be heaven, but it is also understood to be a well-off man who will keep the woman in luxury. There is a prosperity gospel running through much of the celibacy programme. Cassie does not wish people to kiss either, as it is unnecessary and tests willpower. Sadly, self-loathing and distrust of the self are aspects that the preachers in the True Love Waits programme work very hard on. A constant message is of disaster associated with sex outside marriage, which is likened to fire that will burn your house down and ruin your life. Indeed, it will mean you do not have a fine house at all, as you will become unusable – a word that I have chosen deliberately.

We begin to see the double standards in the programme, as masturbation is allowed for boys, since it makes sure they are fit for marriage. Many of the boys questioned about abstinence and the place of masturbation said it was a rehearsal for marriage in which they could 'have sex 24/7'. The truth of these statements can be observed in another True Love Waits documentary (Isherwood, 2006, p. 80), which followed a young couple through the final days of marriage preparation and to the day after their wedding. They were in their early twenties and neither had had sex, but they were hopeful, saying that God will be watching and approving. The young woman was saying she had heard that sex in marriage is when you hear the angels sing. Their pastor prepared them with a diagram of sexual intensity marked 0–100 and time 0–2 minutes marked as a graph; he warned the man that women become easily distracted during sex. It is therefore not surprising that when interviewed the next day the woman looked in shock, which somewhat bears out the remarks of Žižek at the beginning of the chapter. The man could not stop grinning while his wife said she had not heard the angels and was not keen to repeat the exercise. However, her husband was relieved to hear that his wife felt that when they had sex, and how often, was up to her husband. Given that all the pre-marriage advice about the body has focused on the male body, and particularly the penis, I am not too hopeful that women who received counselling within this programme will naturally experience a happy sex life.

The purity agenda was dealt a blow when Peter Bearman and Hannah Bruckner (Isherwood, 2006, p. 81), from Columbia and Yale Universities respectively, conducted a survey of 12,000 teenagers. They found that while those who took the purity pledge had sex on average 18 months later than others, they had similar rates of STIs. The difference in high-risk sexual behaviour was significant, with 2 per cent of non-pledgers engaging in anal sex while 13 per cent of pledgers did engage in it. Those who had pledged were of course less likely to use condoms or to have tests for STIs. The report concluded that pledging and abstinence-only education actually increases the risk of STIs. So far from keeping their children safe and well, those who advocate the True Love Waits campaign are placing them at some risk.

Regardless, those involved in the campaign continue to claim it is God-given and that the women's movement, which they say declares that sexual freedom is a right, has brought endless harm and pain into the lives of young girls. Further, they question the moral fortitude of feminist mothers and assert with vigour the passive role of women in marriage, society and church. Of course, those who are advocating virginity have the problem to face of at least 50 per cent of high school children being sexually active, and so they have introduced the idea of secondary virginity. This is, of course, a ludicrous idea and helps to expose some of the real agendas behind this whole programme. The difference speaks for itself, as the girls are anointed as virgins and the boys as warriors. Far from being a statement of reclaiming, it is a way of realigning women with the dominant ideology: they are clean again and can be delivered into patriarchy through the inevitable stereotypical marriage. Evangelical religion rests on the Christological idea of exchange and ransom and it is highly likely that all social interactions will also have that regime behind them. Sexuality is simply another social interaction and so is not immune from the more elaborate metanarratives. My concern is that women are being given a script that has at first glance some credibility, but actually uses them as conveyors of a larger and much more destructive script: that of global patriarchy and the politics and economics it underpins. It should also not be forgotten that for some involved in this movement, producing as many White children as possible is part of the agenda. This sits well with a fundamentalist notion of Manifest Destiny, which has come down the generations and underpins the justification for White colonizers to commit genocide on the original inhabitants and to continue to believe that the United States is a White nation granted by God.

The Male in the Head

In case we think that it is just Christianity that has it wrong in relation to female sexuality, a report conducted across a wide range of young women from varying backgrounds is a worrying read. Although the study was carried out in 1998, if we are to believe Victoria Smith, then things have not changed – indeed, they may have got worse.

When I first read the report I dared to hope that the young women of today, as daughters of feminist mothers, may not be playing the same old tune of inequality in sexual relationships. It was a nice thought but it did not appear to be true. The findings of the WRAP (Women, Risk and AIDS) and MRAP (Men, Risk and AIDS) projects (Holland et al., 1998) make very depressing reading. Their research was carried out over nine years, involved young people from the ages of 16 to 21, and focused on Manchester and London. It covered a range of class, ethnic and educational backgrounds and aimed to see if heterosexual relations are becoming more equalitarian. Have women, after generations of trying, become subjects in the heterosexual discourse? The answer is not encouraging.

The researchers were themselves struck by the discrepancies between expectations and experience, between intention and practice, and between different discourses of femininity. They found that young women's ability to choose safer sex practices, or to refuse unsafe (or any other) sexual activity, was not an issue of free choice between equals, but was one of negotiation within structurally unequal social relationships (Holland et al., 1998, pp. 5–6). The title of the book, *The Male in the Head*, gives a clue to just how difficult this negotiation can be. The authors conclude that heterosexuality is not just male-dominated and male-defined, but instead it is masculinity itself projected as the whole sexual experience, thus leaving to one side the female experience. Young women are taught not just about sex, but about their place in heterosexuality, and of course this is a place that is most pleasing to men and places them as 'other' in the discourse of masculinity. The authors suggest that masculinity and femininity are not two opposites within the heterosexual framework, but are rather locations within the same male-dominated framework: they both reproduce male dominance. Therefore, female desires that may lead to resistance are viewed as unruly forces which have to be kept under control – by violence if necessary (Holland et al., 1998, p. 11). Indeed, female desire does not seem to play a large part in the sex education of girls either at home or in school. The young women questioned reported being told a great deal about reproductive capacity in conjunction with warnings about men who are only after one thing, with the latter serving to express a strong message of female passivity and the strength of male desire and dominance. The girls reported that physical pleasure and the clitoris were totally absent from both formal and home-based conversations about sex. Young men, on the other hand, were being told how good sex is and how real men are knowing agents in pursuit of sexual pleasure (Holland et al., 1998, p. 7).

Beginning with the idea that intercourse is something enacted on women by men, and that this implicitly holds power, is not the best place to start in search of a discourse of mutuality. It was found that girls tend to distance themselves from the ways in which boys talk about sex, and this has meant that they do not have a language of their own. They do have a language to do with relationship, but not to do with sex, which places them in limbo. Instead, young women learn 'the boundaries of feminine identity and the social mechanisms of sexual reputation' (Holland et al., 1998, p. 68). Heterosexuality, then, is more than a set of sexual practices, it actually grounds and embodies a range of gender relations, which in turn underpin patriarchal society. Making the power of heterosexuality visible is very difficult because it is so embedded in the fabric of everyday life that it becomes natural and invisible – it is the way things are and are meant to be!

The researchers did find that young women were having sex with some pleasure, but this notion was gender defined. They note that 'young women are drawn into their own disempowerment through their conception of what sexual encounters are about' (Holland et al., 1998,

p. 9). Sadly, these encounters are often understood as his orgasm and her part in it. Many of the women felt that if they made their desires known this could lead to the end of the relationship or it could reinforce the man's idea of control. The language used was that of gift and pleasing, with nothing about desire and pleasure. Often women reported that their pleasure was in giving the man what he wanted. Some women reported having to curb their desire as men found it too threatening. In some cases, the women are simply cast aside as nymphomaniacs and whores.

The project findings are no more encouraging when it comes to who defines what sex is. Many of the women enjoyed non-penetrative sex the most but gave in to male definitions of this as merely foreplay and consented to penetration, which they enjoyed much less. Further, the question of consent was found to be a tricky one. In some cases, women consented for fear of violence and in others because they believed they were responsible for male arousal, and therefore responsible for satisfying this in the way the man wanted – the latter being an example of the power of the cultural construction of male desire as a driving need. All of the young women reported that they received, in one way or another, undue pressure to have penetrative sex. This was not the end of the story. Once they had agreed to 'sex', they had to be mindful of how much pleasure they could show without falling into the nymphomaniac trap. Most said that they faked orgasms, and generally suggested more pleasure than they were actually experiencing. The vast majority reported that his orgasm signalled the end of sex for them both, and most agreed that sex for them was judged as good or bad according to closeness and not physical pleasure. A small number of women in the study did report actively asserting their desire, and this was found to link with questioning the way they understood femininity. The report suggests that while women are capable of expressing their desires and receiving satisfaction within certain relationships, this is not really a form of empowered embodiment that they can carry with them to other relationships; it really does depend on the man.

The study found that young women had great difficulty, despite their wishes, in getting partners to use condoms. Once again, it was found to be an area of gender-related power games: the girl who carries them is a slag, and the one who insists on their use is a killjoy. Men were more amenable to using condoms if they thought of the girl as a slag, as they wished to protect themselves from disease; however, they felt that once there was trust in a relationship they should not have to bother. Women often gave in under those circumstances, as they felt a condom might diminish their partner's pleasure. Men, on the other hand, had no idea how a condom affected the pleasure of their partner.

The study seems to suggest that women's sexuality is disembodied. Indeed, it shows that women:

> are under pressure to construct their bodies into a model of femininity which is both inscribed on the surface, through such skills as dress, make-up and dietary regimes, and disembodied, in the sense of detachment from their sensuality and alienation from their material bodies. (Holland et al., 1998, p. 109)

The result of this is that women are made into passive and fragmented sexual objects, both of which are necessary if they are to be eroticized in cultures that see sexual relations as power relations. Women are encouraged to gain control over the surfaces of their bodies but to give away all control in social relations, intercourse and pleasure. It is a grim picture, and while young women are aware of what they see as double standards in the sexual arena they are, for the most part, resigned to acceptance. In reality, they have very little choice.

This is the stuff of feminist theological reflection. How do we grasp liberation, mutuality and our divine essence from the many-layered oppressions that are as intimate to us as our own thoughts and our body-touching? To speak of women's experience as liberative in the light of the WRAP study is indeed a leap of faith, since it is asserting that there is enough in their body-knowing for women to find and hold as their own in order to resist the dominant discourse. The question remains as to whether there are sufficient theological and secular resources to aid women in this struggle or whether sexual relations as lived are rooted in original religious suspicions of, and desires to control, the female body that are far from purged.

Sex, capital and cheap meat

If the picture so far was not bleak enough, we know that sex in the twentieth and twenty-first centuries has turned into an industry whose advertisers encourage the notion that sex is a recreational pursuit that is surpassed by none. As a result, pharmaceutical companies that provide oral contraceptives – and the remedies for the problems they did not warn women of from these contraceptives, such as strokes, heart problems and breast cancer – do very well from the industry. Recent research shows that the leather industry is experiencing a boom, as sado-masochism becomes the fastest-growing sexual recreation of the middle-aged and middle class (Isherwood, 2000, p. 157).

Of course, in order to partake in this sexual recreation, people, particularly women, have to look the part: the figure, the face and the clothes all have to be just right. This creates a great deal of money for those who propagate the patriarchal myths of youth and beauty. The cosmetics industry is worth $20 billion a year while the diet industry tops that at $30 billion (Cline, 1994, p. 136). More worrying still is the boom of genital cosmetic surgery in the United States. Women are being encouraged to have 'designer genitals', vaginas 'tidied up' in order to give their men more pleasure. One American surgeon was proud to have carried out over 4,000 such operations, saying that vaginal orgasm would now be more of a possibility for these women (Cline, 1994, p. 138). This is body colonization in the extreme, being physically moulded to increase pleasure for your partner (and perhaps for yourself) but certainly made to 'fit' the penetrative requirement. No question here that a woman's pleasure can be sought through a more imaginative and explorative range of sexual activities; the knife fixes the 'problem'. All these recreational, sex-as-industry 'products' place women in danger and many lose their lives, be it through servicing hardcore porn, Western tourists, the diet industry or the surgeon's knife. The jury is still out about the number of deaths from the use of oral contraception, but it already looks alarming.

These are not just events that 'happen' as if we are simply living out some inevitable reality. They are ingrained as much through our Christian sex education as through any other servant of patriarchy. Christianity has played a major part in laying these foundations through an overemphasis on spirit and a denigration of the body. Dualistic thinking that has been part of Western Christianity makes it easy to commodify ourselves and others because we have a schizophrenic understanding of our incarnation. This splitting off makes us able to sit in judgement on parts of ourselves and others and dispassionately sacrifice them to those things/parts of us/others we consider more worthy. It is one manifestation of this thinking that allows women to give away their autonomy to men. When women no longer understand themselves as consumable goods for the delight of men it should not only change the way they think about themselves and their bodies, but also have an effect on the way they consume. Many of the trappings of the mating game can then be discarded, which will have both economic and ecological benefits. Radical incarnation demands that we shout out how beautifully and awesomely we are made in the body we have.

Feminist body theology does not end at the edges of our own skin and the relationship we have with ourselves, but rather it places us in relationship that is beyond the individual and is global. This is easily demonstrated in matters of employment and human rights, but I hope to show it is also relevant in the area of sex education. Our sexuality, like all aspects of us, is part of an advanced capitalist system that thrives on division, feelings of inadequacy and the desire to have more and be better, as well as a nuanced system of exclusion.

If we look globally we see that some economies only barely survive because of the sex tourist trade. Horrifying facts are emerging regarding the setting-up of such economies. Rita Brock and Susan Thistlethwaite (1996) illustrate how the sex industry was planned as a strategy of development in Asia, backed by the World Bank, the IMF and the United States Aid for International Development Fund. Women and children are provided on the cheap in Asia for Western men who often believe they are making life better for those they abuse in this way. The unquestioned dominant/submissive agenda in sex education sits well with a racist ideology that views Asian women and children as cheap meat – as barely human. Chung Hyun Kyung reminds us that colonialism is not dead; it is alive and well in development programmes and GATT, MTV and CNN, as well as in peace-keeping forces and tourism. This colonialism combined with capitalism results in the commodification of everything, including women and children who are referred to as 'little brown fucking machines fuelled by rice' by the tourists and the soldiers alike (Chung, 1996, p. 134). This naming graphically highlights the depth of objectification that becomes possible when racism and sexism are combined. The cost in human suffering that such a mindset unleashes is immeasurable, and many Asian feminist theologians are calling on their Western sisters to think about the global cost of our personal freedom. By this they mean a culture that, rather than thinking the whole sexual agenda anew, simply allows certain women to take on the male privilege within it. Asian feminists are claiming that Western women who want it all are alienating their men, who are turning to the bride market or the sex industry in Asia to reassert their masculinity and find the traditional 'feminine females' that this type of masculinity requires to be legitimized (Chung, 1996, pp. 136–7).

This argument is no reason for Western women to return to submissive femininity, but rather is an urgent call for women to realize that no woman is liberated from the yoke of patriarchy until we all are. In addition, it is an overdue call for the reassessment of the type of masculinity that underpins such exploitation. While the sexes are constructed in opposition to one another, masculinity will always be seen as dominant in a patriarchal culture. We have to theoretically remove ourselves from such binary thinking if we are to provide a base from which mutuality can be achieved. While masculinity has the privilege of defining women as the other and the discourse in which we find ourselves is phallic, there is little hope for a femaleness that is authentic since it is at best a projection of male desire and at worst a complete alienation from self and embodiment.

A new sexual ethic?

Marvin Ellison sets out to create an ethic of sexuality that is not body denying and, in Christian circles, not dependent on marriage as the justification or the end point. His reason for doing this is to give an alternative to repression of sexual desire that will challenge the rhetoric of social control. He writes: 'Repression of sexual desire keeps people in doubt and uncertainty about their feelings and values ... when people lose touch with feelings they are likely to lose their inner compass and become more readily susceptible to social control and exploitation' (Ellison, 1996, p. 42). He believes that our sexuality embodies the injustice in our society and he is concerned with providing ways out of that situation. He suggests that there are three dimensions to sexual injustice within the Western Christian world that have to be overcome if we are to be free within our bodies and enabled to live justice-seeking lives. These dimensions are sex negativity, heterocentrism and the eroticization of non-mutual relations.

For Ellison, sex negativity takes several forms, from the obvious viewing of the genitals and sex itself as unruly and dirty to creating a male hierarchy. The body is seen to be inferior and not part of who we essentially are, thus it can be exploited and it is here that we find the heart of extended forms of capitalist exploitation: if the body is not important, then it can be used for things that are important – like money-making. Desire, of course, threatens to disrupt everything and so has to be strictly monitored since it has the power to break down all boundaries. The dualism and distancing that such an approach encourages also lends itself to a male hierarchy, as male and female are also divided into opposites and someone has to take the lead. The role of the woman then becomes one of support and wifely duties that range from sex to child-rearing. Ellison comments: 'Heterosexual marriage is therefore far from being a free and voluntary choice; it is a political requirement for normative status in this culture' (1996, p. 84). It acts as the glue for a hierarchical system that is based on ownership and lends itself to the generation of wealth – just the kind of thing the Jesus movement seemed to disapprove of. One of the most pressing aspects of this arrangement for Ellison is the power that is eroticized in patriarchal sexual relations. Ellison thinks that Christian sex ethics have failed to address the issue of power precisely because they have always concentrated on marriage, a system that is based on power. While 'compulsory coupling', as he calls marriage, may fit the dominant capitalist ethos, it does not lend itself to our full becoming as humans. It makes us dependent on one other for the fulfilment of our needs, limits our range and the importance that we place on friendship, and weakens our ties with the wider community. Within some fundamentalist circles, marriage is referred to as the boot camp for citizenship, and in our context as in that of Jesus, citizenship means serving the father's house, the dominant system. Marx and Engels were not the first to realize that the division of labour and the assigned roles of men and women have political and economic origins and are not in any way based in what is natural. Patriarchy is fundamental to capitalism's exploitation not just of human relations, but also of human desire and labour. Therefore, there is no better way to ensure that these roles are lived out than through the dividing of the genders, the romantic myth, and marriage as the staple of a good Christian life. In 1996 the United States passed the Defence of Marriage Act, which considered rewarding states that showed a decrease in single mothers on their welfare benefits. This Act also encouraged states to offer financial benefits to middle-class couples if they were married; these benefits included property tax exemptions and beneficial healthcare coverage. None of this is surprising since marriage is the dense transfer point for land and inheritance. It is also, as we have seen, the point at which the next generation of labour power is nurtured. A wife under these circumstances spends a great deal of free time ensuring that the present and future labour force is well cared for, which is just what aids capitalism since the accumulation of profit relies on cheap labour in the home and outside it. The family is not only the reproducer of the next generation of those to serve capitalism, it is also the 'legal arrangement concerned with consumption' (Hennessey, 2000, p. 50).

For theologians, Audre Lorde, although not a theologian herself, stands out as the provider of the essential canon on the erotic. That is to say, much of the work by feminist theologians on the erotic refers to her. Both Heyward (1982) and I (Isherwood, 1999) have developed Christology based on understandings of the erotic using her work. This has, in both our cases, placed the erotic as found in human flesh at the centre of ethical understanding. For Lorde, the erotic is the intense kernel of our being that, when released, 'flows through and colours my life with a kind of energy that heightens and sensitizes and strengthens all my experience' (Lorde, 1984, p. 57). It is a form of outreaching joy that connects us to all things and transforms all experiences into delight. This kind of joy is of course alien to any form of powerlessness, self-denial or self-effacement and is the outreach that overcomes all forms of isolation, even the more communal aspects of alienation. This erotic joy is physical, intellectual, psychic and emotional, and forms a solid bridge between people that continues to allow difference but lessens the threat that difference is often perceived to contain. It is a profound teacher, as it allows the kind of closeness that produces our deepest knowledge, which in turn leads to the transformation of the world. Lorde claims that recognizing the power of the erotic within our lives can give us the energy to pursue genuine change within our world, rather than merely settling for a shift of characters in the same weary drama. It is, then, deeply ethical in both its nature and the effect it strives to have. Lorde makes extremely bold claims for the erotic as located in the female body, and so it is not really surprising that theologians have been so taken with her stance; after all, we are attempting to recover from centuries of suspicion of the erotic in any form – let alone the female form.

And so … how was it for you?

Sex is a complex issue and, as we have seen, it throws into question many other related issues. It would be foolish in the extreme to think that we can wave a magic wand and guarantee that every woman will have great, satisfying sex.

There is nothing new in declaring that the individual body is central in any social or political construction of reality. The Greeks conceived of citizens, cities and the cosmos as constructed on the same principles. From Plato through to Irigaray, the body and the restrictions placed upon it have been understood as more than personal. Therefore, the moulding and control of bodies is a political act. What is relatively new in this debate is the feminist gaze, which sees that even this control is gendered, racialized and sexualized – with some gaining more from it than others. This is, unfortunately, as true in the realm of sexuality as any other to do with the body and there seems to be no way out, because people are led to believe that the way things are is natural and, from a certain Christian perspective, divinely ordained. The early feminist rhetoric calls us to be suspicious of anything that is deemed 'natural', as this places it beyond examination and criticism – 'You may not like it but that's the way it is' poses as a statement of empathy yet resignation, but is in fact a power-laden status quo utterance.

As Christian educators, we should be examining our praxis and creating an environment in which young women may claim their own embodied empowerment and autonomy. In this claiming they pose a challenge to patriarchy, a system that, while sitting well with Christianity as it is, does not align with its radical incarnational core. The WRAP report and the True Love Waits campaign, let alone everyday understandings of sex, do not describe some inner compulsion or divine essence; rather, they highlight how sex has become based on inequality and domination. We need to enable women to free themselves from enacted dominant/ submissive relationships, which ultimately extend far beyond the edges of their skins.

As Christian educators, these are the issues that should concern us, not those that *seem* to, such as loving and mutual relationships that are not sanctioned through the Church – for example, gay relationships, unmarried relationships, one-night stands and so on. We should be putting forward a set of values that enable people to revel in the beauty and exquisite pleasure of bodies, including their own. We become pawns of patriarchy when our own self-love and respect are damaged through distrust, caution and, at times, hatred of the embodied self that is our true reality.

So what could we be teaching? Certainly not disgust of the body and alienation from the divine. My starting point is to change our Christological understanding, which means doing away with a dualistic view of reality and claiming our own divine embodiment. This is a biblical demand as much as, if not more than, virginal marriage and racist breeding. Jesus, as understood in Mark's Gospel (Heyward, 1982), gives us the same potential as he has for 'becoming divine'. We are made of the same stuff but, to date, have failed to embrace it fully. This is a serious commission and involves understanding who we are in our humanity and embodiment as much as understanding who Jesus was, or who we are, in our divinity.

Feminist theologians would argue that sex education within a Christian context becomes a radical interconnection of bodies, politics and economics, a way in which our private acts of intimacy connect with wider aspects of justice-seeking in the world. This is not to say that attraction will become unimportant but rather that it will be face-to-face, not image-to-image. The planet cannot sustain the present rate of consumption, and while not all consumption is to do with enhancing ourselves, a large amount is, and the reduction of this would have major benefits not only on the environment but also in individual lives.

Sex education within a Christian context, then, needs to take into account the exploitation of the self and others through the consumerization of desire. It needs a global and an ecological awareness framing female sexuality as autonomous and broader than the procreative. Of course, masculinity also has to be reframed if we are simply not going to export the worst problems of heteropatriarchy. The agenda has to go far beyond the Christian legitimacy or otherwise of certain acts with certain people. Through the way that Christians understand their embodiment and incarnation, they can offer real resistance to the genocidal realities of capitalism and consumer racism. Understanding that one does not have to live on starvation rations, submit to the knife or hide behind the many masks of modern fashion to be a passionate, sexual and fulfilled person is the kind of realization that is a real body blow to a repressive system (Isherwood, 2007). Our bodies do not need to be polluted and manipulated in order for us to have a satisfying sex life. In a world where so many ills rest on the model of dominance and submission, it seems that the churches have a duty to incarnate opposition to such a crushing reality, and what better way than through the bodies of believers?

Christian sex education has to go beyond the edges of the skin and offer a radical alternative in a discourse that is alienating us in our most intimate relating. As a feminist theologian, I would like to see sex education in church schools that positively addresses 'the personal as political' and engages with the negative effects of the Christian tradition while at the same time tackling fundamental and interconnected issues: issues of sexual pleasure for women and the embodied empowerment that this enables; rhetoric about the 'right body' that makes women victims of capitalist exploitation and causes them, in the worst cases, to harm themselves; and the global implications of a patriarchal sexual agenda. Theologies need to endorse these views and not make the body the enemy or – at best – the worst-kept secret in the world. Liturgies can run in conjunction with sex education programmes and celebrate the joy of awakening sexuality and the changing of bodies. I would like to see women's bodies in all their changing aspects celebrated within Christian liturgy, not simply those of young girls. Of course, the ways women's bodies change have over the years been viewed with suspicion by a theology that advocates a God who is the same yesterday, today and tomorrow and in which scheme change is potentially threatening. The liturgies I would love to see for women of all ages should be sensuous and empowering, engaging the whole body in celebration of itself. They should not just celebrate the procreative nature of women, rather they should revel in the capacity for pleasure that a woman has and the vast potential that pleasure has to change the world.

This encouragement of real self-love, acceptance and the self-esteem that flows from it is the first step towards women not becoming the 'objects' of male desire. Young women need to understand that they are women and that this looks as they wish it to; they are not made into women by the gaze of others. Placing women's sexual pleasure at the centre of theological reflection and the sex education programmes that spring from it provide a very strong embodied base for challenging consumerism and poor ecological awareness as well as domestic violence, rape and other acts of female objectification. While masculinity has the privilege of defining women as the other, and the discourse in which we find ourselves is phallic, there is little hope for a femaleness that is authentic since it is at best a projection of male desire and at worst a complete alienation from self and embodiment.

Christian sex education that prioritizes female pleasure opens up an agenda that has not been explored by 'male stream' theology. It encourages women and men to move beyond the prescribed and power-laden narratives that have been the sexual world for centuries and, in so doing, to open ourselves to the possibility of mutual relation. This will not just mean that our sex lives will improve, it will also place the personal in the global political arena. But what is the purpose of this? Well, as Rosemary Radford Ruether tells us, a good fuck is no excuse for getting fucked, nor does it excuse the fucking of 80 per cent of the world's population who struggle on the underbelly of advanced capitalism (1996, p. 6). Pleasure and pain are not purely private matters; they link us with a world that is bigger than ourselves and one that suffers from a lack of justice. Justice-making begins in our most private acts and extends far beyond. Sex education in a Christian context has the duty of encouraging passionate lovers and justice-makers; if it continues to try and control passion, it will kill justice. Christianity proclaims the gloriously passionate, promiscuous love affair that is the incarnation, and it is time that Christian sex education followed suit!

Bibliography

Brock, Rita and Thistlethwaite, Susan, 1996, *Casting Stones: Prostitution and Liberation in Asia and the United States*, Minneapolis, MN: Fortress Press.

Chung, H. K., 1996, 'Your Comfort vs My Death', in M. J. Mananzan et al. (eds), *Women Resisting Violence: Spirituality For Life*, Maryknoll, NY: Orbis Books, pp. 129–41.

Cline, Sally, 1994, *Women, Celibacy and Passion*, London: Optima Publishing.

Ellison, Marvin, 1996, *Erotic Justice: A Liberating Ethic of Sexuality*, Louisville, KY: Westminster John Knox Press.

Hennessey, Rosemary, 2000, *Profit and Pleasure in Late Capitalism*, London: Routledge.

Heyward, Carter, 1982, *The Redemption of God: A Theology of Mutual Relation*, New York: University of America Press.

Hoffman, Eva, 1998, *Lost in Translation*, London: Vintage Books.

Holland, J. et al., 1998, *The Male in the Head: Young People, Heterosexuality and Power*, London: Tufnell Press.

Isherwood, Lisa, 1999, *Liberating Christ*, Cleveland, OH: Pilgrim Press.

Isherwood, Lisa, 2000, *The Good News of the Body: Sexual Theology and Feminism*, Sheffield: Sheffield Academic Press.

Isherwood, Lisa, 2006, *The Power of Erotic Celibacy: Queering Heteropatriarchy*, London: T&T Clark.

Isherwood, Lisa, 2007, *The Fat Jesus: Feminist Explorations in Boundaries and Transgressions*, London: Darton, Longman & Todd.

Lorde, Audre, 1984, 'Uses of the Erotic', in *Sister/Outsider: Essays and Speeches*, Berkeley, CA: Crossing Press.

Ruether, Rosemary Radford, 1996, *Women Healing Earth*, London: SCM Press.

Smith, Victoria, 2023, *Hags: The Demonisation of Middle-aged Women*, London: Fleet.

Žižek, Slavoj, 2022, *Surplus Enjoyment: A Guide for the Non-Perplexed*, London: Bloomsbury Academic.

Questions for reflection and discussion

1 The author names unequal power structures as being at the root of how we think about, experience and engage in sexual activity. How does this resonate for you?

2 How have purity culture and programmes such as True Love Waits influenced your life and the way you feel about sex, relationships and your body?

3 'When women no longer understand themselves as consumable goods for the delight of men it should not only change the way they think about themselves and their bodies, but also have an effect on the way they consume.' How might your patterns of consumption be affected by an altered understanding of yourself?

4 'Radical incarnation demands that we shout out how beautifully and awesomely we are made in the body we have.' What might it look like for you to shout this out in your own life?

9

'How Is Your Beloved Better Than Others, Most Beautiful of Women?': Song of Songs 5.9–16 and the Primary Prevention of Domestic Abuse

ERIN MARTINE HUTTON

The Church has a biblical text from which to espouse respect and equality in relationship: Song of Songs. In Song 5.9–16, the woman of the Song models mutual respect and gender equality through her panegyric-like praise-poem on her beloved. Throughout the poem, imagery and metaphor most often associated with the woman (the lover) is used to extol the man (the beloved), blurring and blending gender roles and subverting (ancient and modern) assumptions about how the 'most beautiful of women' and a man who is 'better than others' might look or behave. As Moore (2001, p. 41) enthuses, the 'gender-blurring imagery of the Song overruns the margins of the page' in this poem, giving us a biblical representation of gender that resists 'binary absolutes' (Spencer, 2017, p. 139). A poetic portrait emerges of two young lovers who exemplify mutuality, respect, healthy sexuality and gender equality. Social research indicates that gender inequality is the largest driver and predictor of gender-based violence. To prevent violence such as domestic abuse, we must work to address its gender-inequal drivers. In this chapter, I argue one of the ways we can contribute to domestic abuse primary prevention is exploring how the Song, particularly the waṣf at 5.9–16, exhibits gender equality. The Song blurs and blends gender roles through reversing the typical male gaze to a loving looking and describing from an autonomous woman. Rather than demanding perfection, the lover lauds her beloved – indeed, the lovers are in awe of each other – precisely because of his personhood, not because he is a perfect male specimen. Through her encomium, the Song provides an alternative to gender roles, hierarchies and stereotyped masculinities, thus contributing to domestic abuse primary prevention.

Domestic abuse

Before we scale the mountainous metaphors of Songs of Songs, admiring doves and cedars along the way, we must pause and parse some of the terminology used in the domestic abuse primary prevention framework. Australia's National Research Organisation for Women's Safety (ANROWS), in their research report 'Attitudes Matter: The 2021 National Community Attitudes towards Violence against Women Survey (NCAS)', defines domestic abuse as:

> Violence within current or past intimate partner relationships, which causes physical, sexual or psychological harm. Domestic violence can include physical, sexual, emotional, psychological and financial abuse, and often occurs as a pattern of behaviour involving coercive control. (Coumarelos et al., 2023, p. 13)

To prevent domestic abuse, we must address the 'underlying causes that create the necessary conditions in which violence against women occurs' (Respect Victoria, 2023, p. 20). There is a growing body of evidence that attests that it is gender inequality that drives and indicates violence against women, including domestic abuse.

Primary prevention

Primary prevention is part of a proven public health prevention framework and the first stage of the prevention continuum. In terms of domestic abuse, primary prevention is aimed at preventing this gendered violence before it occurs, through confronting gender inequality at a community level. Secondary intervention addresses where there is risk of, or a known context for, domestic abuse. Tertiary postvention appropriately responds to domestic abuse that has already occurred, seeking to minimize its impact and prevent recurrence (Pidgeon, 2021, p. 566). According to Australia's *National Plan to Reduce Violence against Women and their Children*, domestic abuse primary prevention means acknowledging, addressing and challenging its gendered drivers, such as rigid gender norms and hierarchies; masculinities emphasizing aggression, dominance and control; condoning men's violence; limits to women's independence and decision-making; and other gendered and intersectional power imbalances (Commonwealth of Australia, 2022, p. 34).

Both the NCAS and the report *National Plan* indicate that initiatives such as 'education about respectful relationships' (Coumarelos et al., 2023, p. 24) that 'influence … the practices and behaviours of organisations, groups and individuals' (Commonwealth of Australia, 2022, p. 79) contribute to the kind of integrated and mutually reinforcing whole-of-population prevention work required to stop domestic abuse before it starts. Gender-transformative approaches 'that challenge and attempt to change problematic gender stereotypes, scripts, norms, the gender binary and the gender hierarchy' (Coumarelos et al., 2023, p. 14) flip the script on the roles and behaviours imputed to gender and the way these are enacted and reinforced in society. My research is devoted to primary prevention within the Church, focusing on education about consensual, equal, healthy, mutual relationships through a feminist interpretation of Song of Songs. The Church needs to work to change the attitudes, beliefs and behaviours that drive domestic abuse and gendered violence, and we can do this by looking to the Song.

The Song and primary prevention

In this chapter, I employ an interdisciplinary approach, integrating a feminist biblical hermeneutic and social research on domestic abuse primary prevention, paying particular attention to imagistic representations of the man's body (compared with the woman's body), and the often-gendered interpretation of concepts evoked and associated with 'masculinity' or 'femininity'. I work my way through the *waṣf* and, using ANROWS' NCAS report specifically, and domestic abuse primary prevention more generally, I show how this poem challenges rigid gender roles and stereotypes, promotes women's independence and decision-making and supports positive masculinities. So my gender-transformative approach is to explore the Song's 'own propensity to blur gender boundaries' (Moore, 2001, p. 41). That is, the way it 'masculinizes' the female body and 'feminizes' the male body, and the way it frequently employs similar or even 'the same images for both bodies' (Moore, 2001, p. 41). Carr (1984, p. 139) provides a comparison-at-a-glance for this *waṣf* and Song 7.1–6, presenting their common features: animal comparisons; geographic comparisons; flowers and spices; springs and pools; the work of architects, goldsmiths and jewellers, and states that the emphases are 'colour, form, beauty and strength'. I would add that this is true of each *waṣf* – regardless of the subject's gender – along with other common *waṣf* elements (e.g. verticality and sensory experience); their personhood and sexuality are also emphasized.

Waṣfs

Before diving into the details, we should understand what the genre is and does. A *waṣf* is a poem from the Arabic lyric genre that describes and celebrates its subject piece by piece, appreciating the beauty and integrity of the whole. The four *waṣfs* in the Song are highly suggestive and erotically charged. Song 5.9–16 is unique in its celebration of the man's beautiful body. The woman looks upon and poetically details her beloved, subverting the genre and expectation of a male poet gazing upon and exalting a woman. Examining this *waṣf* entails considering cultural gender, biological sex and where they intersect in human sexuality in what Moore (2001, p. 13) cheekily calls 'a kind of epistemic *ménage à trois*'. Moreover, gendered interpretation of the Song – and the ways this perpetuates the gender stereotypes driving and indicating gendered violence – must also be examined.

The *waṣf* at 5.9–16

I may be the first academic arguing for the Song's use in domestic abuse primary prevention, but I am certainly not the first scholar to notice its subversion of ancient and modern concepts of gender. Falk (1982, p. 85) referred to this *waṣf* when she argued that the lovers do not conform to gender roles and stereotypes. In fact, interpretations that are skewed towards gender roles and stereotypes (ancient or modern) miss both the point of the *waṣf* and the similarities between the lovers. The *waṣfs* that laud the woman do so for her whole embodied incomparability, and this *waṣf* praises the man for his holistic worth and value beyond compare.

Gendered commentary and gendered violence

To illustrate what is missed when commentators import gendered assumptions on to the text, and following Falk's lead, I begin my exegesis with a representative sample of gendered interpretation:

> The poetic imagination at work in 5:10–16 where the maiden speaks of her lover is less sensuous and imaginative than in the *waṣfs* of chapters 4 and 7. This is due in part to the limited subject matter and may even be due to the difference in erotic imagination between poet and poetess. (Soulen, 1967, p. 184, n. 6)

Even a cursory glance at this *waṣf* proves that it is no less sensuous or imaginative than any of the others (Falk, 1982, p. 85). 'The woman's figurative depiction of the various parts of her lover's body is intimate and erotically suggestive, just as his descriptions of her are' (Exum, 2005, p. 202). And neither is the subject matter limited. In fact, the woman uses many of the very same images that the man uses to describe her body: 'flowing hair, dove-like eyes, wet and fragrant lips, along with a familiar descriptive repertoire of water springs, milk, lilies, Lebanon cedars, and various jewels and spices' (Spencer, 2017, p. 139). And I can only assume, in claiming a difference in erotic imagination between poet and poetess, Soulen had not read Sappho.

Falk argues this kind of 'bias was hardly embedded in the text' and, unfortunately, such interpretative bias continues to be 'representative of much modern scholarship' (Falk, 1982, pp. 85–6). No matter how prevalent the (mal)practice of imposing our own cultural values on the text, 'we should recognize that it derives from specific, culture-bound prejudices which are incompatible with the cultural sensibility that created the Song' (Falk, 1982, p. 86). Modern Australia's specific, culture-bound prejudices have contributed to a society marked by gender inequality, gendered violence and, on average, one woman a week murdered by her (ex-)partner.

In fact, as I wrote this chapter, in just one of Australia's eight states and territories, there have been four alleged domestic homicides in one week (Leckie and Mason, 2023). Furthermore, there is 40 years of research indicating domestic abuse is a problem in and for Australian churches (Sessions, 2023, p. 95). Such gendered violence is not unique to Australia; domestic abuse is rampant the world over. So we must work to transform the attitudes, beliefs and prejudices undergirding Australia's – and the Church universal's – problem with gendered violence. This includes promoting biblical interpretation that does not adhere to dominant gendered scripts or perpetuate gender stereotypes through poor exegesis. Or as Falk (1982, p. 87) stated over four decades ago (her words remaining equally true and urgent today): 'It may even turn out that this ancient text has something new to teach us about how to redeem sexuality and love in our fallen world.' The Song can teach our church communities about respectful relationships. It is not an exaggeration to say that gendered interpretation contributes to cultures that drive and indicate domestic abuse, and good exegesis saves lives.

With that in mind, let's look at this *waṣf* in more detail:

> How is your beloved better than others,
>   most beautiful of women?
> How is your beloved better than others,
>   that you so charge us?
> My beloved is radiant and ruddy,
>   awe-striking among ten thousand.
> His head is purest gold;
>   his locks are wavy
>   and black as a raven.
> His eyes are like doves
>   by the water streams,
> washed in milk,
>   mounted like jewels.
> His cheeks are like beds of spice
>   yielding perfume.
> His lips are like lilies
>   dripping with myrrh.
> His arms are rods of gold
>   set with topaz.
> His loins like polished ivory
>   decorated with lapis lazuli.
> His legs are pillars of marble
>   set on bases of pure gold.
> His appearance is like Lebanon,
>   choice as its cedars.
> His mouth is sweetness itself;
>   he is altogether lovely.
> This is my beloved, this is my friend,
>   daughters of Jerusalem.
> (Author's paraphrasing of Song of Songs 5.9–16)

5.9–16 and domestic abuse primary prevention

The woman extols the beloved's 'matchless beauty' (Duguid, 2015, p. 130). He is 'the epitome of male physical beauty, just as [she ...] preserves the ideal of female beauty' (Carr, 1984, p. 139). However, it is important to understand that beauty is here used 'in its broadest form, as encompassing the character and virtues of embodied persons' (Spencer, 2017, p. 138). The lover's ode to her beloved's body incorporates more than physical appearance. Just as the final line of the first *waṣf* (4.7) lauds the lover as 'altogether beautiful', praising the whole embodied woman, the final line of this *waṣf* (5.16) proclaims that the beloved is 'altogether lovely'. This *waṣf* is 'extravagant and lush in its metaphorical description' (Gledhill, 1994, p. 183) and, as we shall see, 'the bodies of the woman and the man beautifully flow together in a common pool of natural delights' (Spencer, 2017, p. 139), using imagery for the man that is usually availed for the woman.

Following the Daughters of Jerusalem's questions (v. 9), the woman is primed to paint a poetic portrait – or, perhaps better, songfully sculpt a statue of her paramount paramour. Gazing upon and 'under the literary guise of ... describing her beloved ... the woman actually reminds herself of all the things that she finds extraordinary about him' (Garrett and House, 2004, p. 220). She begins by exclaiming 'my beloved is radiant and ruddy.' The use of the epithet 'my beloved' in verse 10 and verse 16 'provides an *inclusio* for the section' (Duguid, 2015, p. 130). 'Radiant' could be in reference to his clear complexion since the *waṣf* begins at his head. However, it is more likely evocative of his comprehensive radiance. The translation of *tsach* (צַח), 'dazzling, glowing, clear', as 'radiant' is informed by its usage at Isaiah 18.4 and Jeremiah 4.11 describing heat (Hess, 2005, p. 181), with scholars also offering 'shimmering' like the sun's heat rising from a road (Fredericks and Estes, 2010, p. 372) or reflecting off a statue (Snaith, 1993, p. 79). The lover is also dazzling (her eyes 'dazzle', *hirhibuni* הִרְהִיבֻנִי at 6.5), and shimmering mirage – even awe-inspiring aurora – have been used to describe both the woman (6.4, 10) and the man (Hutton, 2024). Yet until recently, scholarship had missed that the man and the woman find each other equally awe-striking, dazzlingly pure and shimmering (Andruska, 2018). More conservative scholarship has tended to find gendered differences rather than similarities.[1] Overemphasizing perceived differences between women and men – text-based or otherwise – undermines our common humanity. And as ANROWS explains: 'Rigid gender roles and stereotypes impact the ways people relate to each other in their relationships, as well as in organisational and institutional contexts' (Coumarelos et al., 2023, p. 109). Espousing such gendered differences and adhering to gender stereotypes drives and indicates domestic abuse.

Moreover, the concept of 'purity' – a radiant wholeness associated with *tsach* and then evoked throughout the *wasf* – attracts succinct (or no) comment (e.g. Alter, 2011, p. 604) whereas, curiously, the woman's bright 'purity' generates commentary linked to beauty, sexuality and/or virginity (e.g. Snaith, 1993, p. 92). Keel (1994, p. 219) deems commentary along these lines 'an example of puritanism totally foreign to the Song'.[2] And as I have argued elsewhere, the Madonna–whore dichotomy persists in Australia, with polarized perceptions of women as either 'pure' (meaning chaste) and good, or promiscuous and bad (Hutton, 2024). ANROWS' research indicates that endorsement of this false dichotomy correlates with 'patriarchy-supporting ideologies, confirming the role of stereotypes in controlling women and limiting their sexual freedom' (Coumarelos et al., 2023, p. 109). A reading that realizes that the Song's lovers – that women and men – are not so different, and pays particular attention to gendered interpretation, prevents domestic abuse.

Completing the first line of verse 10, 'ruddy' *adom* (אָדוֹם) is compared 'to David's appearance in his youth' (e.g. Spencer, 2017, p. 140). The connection that *should* be made is both the beloved and David are handsome and healthy. However, commentators have made the reverse of Goliath's mistake, and focus on the man's 'physical prowess' (Spencer, 2017, pp. 140–1), missing or minimalizing his beauty. David's rubicund complexion (and beautiful eyes) 'suggests that his features were "pretty" (יפה), an outward appearance normally indicative of femininity according to aesthetic conventions in the ancient Near East (ANE)' (Schaser, 2022).[3] Many male scholars have avoided 'feminine' interpretations, that the beloved is glowingly gorgeous, offering 'masculine' interpretations instead. Carr (1984, p. 140) writes 'her lover is "manly"'. Gledhill (1994, p. 184) offers: 'the word for ruddy could also imply manliness.' Garrett and House (2004, p. 220) state: 'Tan skin apparently was considered masculine'. And Hess (2005, p. 181) evokes Esau's hunting skill. The beloved may be 'manly' – whatever that implies – but there are better, more obvious and less unnecessarily masculinized interpretations. This is especially important as we consider the Song's contribution to domestic abuse primary prevention. It is well established that most existing gender systems – and that includes within the Church – are 'deeply hierarchical, privileging that which is male or masculine over that which is female or feminine' (Cislaghi and Heise, 2020, p. 410). Gender norms are nested in our beliefs and embedded in our institutions (Cislaghi and Heise, 2020, p. 407), permeating even exegesis of the Song, despite its long-established position as a counter-text to biblical and modern patriarchy (Sun, 2021, p. 11). Until we examine and address our societal, ecclesial and exegetical discomfort with that which is 'feminine' – particularly as it applies to someone expected to be 'masculine' – we will not be able to effectively prevent domestic abuse. 'Radiant and ruddy' – literally 'white and red' and symbolically 'milk and wine', as the Bible epitomizes (Bloch and Bloch, 2006, p. 185) – are primarily used to illustrate health, vitality and youthfulness (e.g. Longman, 2001, p. 170). We may read 'radiant and ruddy' as a beautiful man 'glowing with the full flush of his youthful prime energized by love' and his 'contentment radiates through his shining face' (Gledhill, 1994, p. 184), which makes sense in the Song's immediate context of a loving, equal, mutual and respectful, sexual relationship.

The second colon of verse 10 is variously translated 'outstanding among' (Murphy, 1990, p. 164), 'pre-eminent' (Fox, 1985, p. 140) or 'distinguished beyond' (Longman, 2001, p. 163) 10,000. The Hebrew word *dagul* (דָּגוּל) is probably related to the noun 'banner', meaning her bronzed beloved 'stands out like a banner' (Keel, 1994, p. 198) or a bright star (Carr, 1984, p. 140), in what is probably an intentional melange of martial and celestial imagery, much as it is for the woman at 6.4 and 6.10. The man is probably 'conspicuous, easily visible, identifiable' (Gledhill, 1994, p. 184) due to his dazzling appearance. However, these translations are lacking. Andruska (2018, p. 1) argues the usage of the root *dgl* (in *kanidgalot*) at 6.4 and 6.10 illuminates its meaning here. Translations of *dgl* at 5.10 usually differ from the varied interpretative offerings for 6.4 and 6.10, and this has given the 'impression that the lovers view each other differently', but 'they actually use the same word to describe one another and express similar feelings' (Andruska, 2018, p. 2). This means interpretation has missed the element of mutually awe-inspired reverence. To Andruska's argument I would add that the rare and particular word choice of *dgl* matches the meaning the poet wishes to convey. The beloved is distinctively, outstandingly daunting and the lover is uniquely, overwhelmingly intimidating, requiring a singularly compelling translation. Moreover, this rare and remarkable *waṣf*, eschewing the male gaze and empowering the female gaze, provides a biblical example of 'positive masculinity' and a woman who makes her own decisions – two elements of domestic abuse primary prevention. The point of this verse – like the woman's incomparability in Song 6.4–10 – is that he is awe-strikingly matchless among men. The lover and the beloved are *equally* awestruck.

'His head is purest gold' makes a shiny connection between verse 11 and verse 10, as the 'finest gold reflects the dazzling radiance of his complexion' (Duguid, 2015, p. 131). The use of extravagant materials and language coalesces to create a perception of the beloved as not only bronzed in appearance, but also 'beyond price' (Gledhill, 1994, p. 184). 'Comparing the head to smelted gold, gold that is proved and refined' (Keel, 1994, p. 199) signifies that the beloved is worth his weight in gold. This is the first of three golden metaphors for his head, arms and legs. So gold 'constitutes the essence of his exquisite frame from head to base' (Spencer, 2017, p. 139). Spencer (p. 139) takes this to mean the beloved provides a sense of stability. When the woman is likened to precious materials (7.1–2, 4) she is not described as 'stable'. ANROWS reports that the pressure on men to provide stability for their partner (and family) creates 'masculine role stress', especially when they are 'unable to meet perceived standards of masculinity, including self-reliance and the capacity to be the main income earner', which contributes to domestic abuse (Coumarelos et al., 2023, p. 270). Though it may be the case the beloved provides stability for his lover – since a healthy, mutual relationship is likely to be a source of stability for both partners – 'the concentration on colours and precious materials (gold, ivory, jewels) give[s] the impression of unexpected, colourful, and precious … splendor' (Keel, 1994, p. 198). Throughout the Song, royalty and divinity are evoked for both lovers, and here it underscores that the beloved is prized for his personhood. To prevent domestic abuse in our churches, we can emphasize (respect for) a person's individual humanity, made in the image of God.

The woman continues: 'his hair is wavy, black as a raven' (v. 11). The Hebrew word for his hair (קְוֻּצּוֹתָיו) is the 'relatively rare word locks' (Longman, 2001, p. 171). The next word, often translated as 'wavy' (תַּלְתַּלִּים) *taltallim*, is linguistically difficult. Akkadian and Arabic cognates indicate that the word means either date panicles or palm spathes (Exum, 2005, p. 204). Carr (1984, p. 141) reasoned the 'precision of the image is unimportant', but word choice is powerful in poetry, and Hebrew poetry is no exception. The word was carefully, intentionally chosen and I think Pope (1977, p. 536) has identified – at least in part – why: he points to Rabbinical use of the word to mean 'curly'. Among the similarities between the lovers are their curly black locks and dark skin. Since I have discussed hair with coils and curls, skin colour and the intersections of gendered and racial violence elsewhere (Hutton, 2024), here I argue the lovers' natural hair synecdochally signifies their freedom. Theirs is a relationship characterized by equality without hierarchy or control.

The verse concludes with the only poetic usage of 'raven' (כָּעוֹרֵב) in the Hebrew Bible. Spencer (2017, p. 141) wonders if it carries 'overtones of the ominous and the macabre associated with this predatory "unclean" creature'. Though it is offered that 'the black raven belongs to the realm of the hairy goat-spirits and the wild demons' (Keel, 1994, p. 199), scholarship is more likely to emphasize the beauty of the woman's goat-like hair (e.g. Hess, 2005, p. 129) than connect it to said goat-demons. And when the man's hair is compared to the shiny, luminescent raven, the simile tends not to be interpreted as handsome hair for this lauded and beautiful man. Much like his radiant, ruddy complexion, 'black hair implies youth and vigour' since he is 'neither bald nor gray' (Garrett and House, 2004, p. 220). Exum (2005, p. 162) is in the minority when she notices the man's hair 'is one of his arresting features'.[4] Commentary that misses the man's beauty (though a key feature of the *waṣf* genre) does disservice to interpretation and to men. Men can be beautiful too. And dominant norms of masculinity and patriarchal gender roles are harmful not only to women but for men and non-binary people too. ANROWS reports 'mental health, wellbeing and reluctance to seek help; suicide; their proclivity for risk-taking behaviours (such as alcohol use); and their risk of perpetrating or experiencing violence' among the harms (Coumarelos et al., 2023, p. 109). In this simile, and its counterpart at 4.1, the lovers' black, wavy, attractive hair is likened to free-ranging animals (sometimes with unpropitious undercurrents). In the Song, the lovers are beautiful, equal and make their own decisions, free from the strictures of gendered roles. Perhaps we may interpret the lovers, via the goat and the raven, as having vitality, freedom, lust for life and for each other (Keel, 1994, p. 142). These similarities pave the way for the next verse; a metaphor that is applied to both lovers.

It begins, 'his eyes are like doves, by the water streams, washed in milk', and then the unclear 'mounted', 'sitting' or 'fitly set' is intended to evoke either 'pellucid pools' (Exum, 2005, p. 204) or bezel-set jewels. While trying to work out the meaning of יֹשְׁבוֹת (followed by עַל-מִלֵּאת, which is hapax and probably signifies abundance) is fascinating, I am more interested in how the dove-eyes metaphor/simile is interpreted along gender lines. Though some scholars see the usual emphases of the *waṣf* in dove eyes – for example, Hess (2005, p. 96) notes 'form, beauty, and love' for the woman's dove eyes and colour, form and beauty for the man's (pp. 182–3), with Spencer (2017, pp. 92, 141) and Carr (1984, p. 141) adding movement and vibrancy – others do not. Gledhill (1994, p. 184) states: 'It is hardly likely that she has the same qualities in mind as he perceived when he described her eyes as doves.' But why not? This is a 'stock metaphor' (Garrett and House, 2004, p. 220) and the 'twinning of common imagery for the eyes of the man and the woman binds the two of them together as a matched pair' (Duguid, 2015, p. 131). Gledhill does not say why the man and woman could not possibly have alike eyes or common qualities, but Polaski offers the following interpretation:

> the lover and the beloved portray each other in identical terms. They describe each other's eyes as doves (1:15; 4:1; 5:12). The feminine figure considers her lover to be a gazelle (2:9; 2:17; 8:14); the masculine figure applies the same term (*'oper*) to her breasts (4:5; 7:3) ... there is a degree of mutuality in the relationship here that may tend to blur the edges of the descriptions. In other places, however, the Song of Songs blurs the gender lines only to reiterate them in some way, expressing a certain anxiety about maintaining clear distinctions. This is frequently the case when the feminine figure asserts some kind of power, a control over the world of the Song. (Polaski, 2008, p. 440)

There is a crucial difference between power and control. There is a difference between a powerful woman (Hess, 2005, p. 121) and how men respond to her (and her power). Note Polaski gives chapter and verse references for 'identical terms' used, but no citations are supplied here – biblical or otherwise – to support his claim that the Song expresses 'anxiety about maintaining clear [gender] distinctions'. It is not the Song that is anxious about blending and blurring gender 'lines'; rather, it is the Song's interpreters. The discomfort displayed, when gendered boundaries are not maintained, resembles resistance to gender equality. ANROWS explains: 'resistance and backlash exist on a continuum and may manifest in diverse ways within an organisational or institutional context' (Coumarelos et al., 2023, p. 45). More passive forms of resistance, such as discomfort with gender 'blurring' and reasserting stereotypical gender roles, 'can appear in a diverse range of organisational behaviours and attitudes, practices, structures and systems' (Coumarelos et al., 2023, p. 45). This includes churches, seminaries and, as we have seen, exegesis. Further along the continuum is when men actively 'become antagonistic and violent towards women partners (or women in general), as they are convinced that improving women's rights must inevitably come at the expense of their own' (Coumarelos et al., 2023, p. 45). The text loses nothing, and we have everything to gain, by recognizing, for example, that the man is beautiful (like the woman), the woman is powerful yet not controlling (like the man), and both they and their dove eyes need not be interpreted and defined in terms of gender roles or hierarchy. Thankfully, Keel (1994, p. 201) makes no such gendered distinction: 'the dove metaphor emphasize[s] the freshness, radiance, and happiness characteristic of eyes that proclaim love.' Each of these attributes could just as easily apply to the woman and, in the context of a *waṣf*, what should be emphasized is they each have beautiful, dazzlingly deep (whatever their colour) eyes for each other.

Continuing with verse 13, his cheeks are 'like beds of spice yielding perfume'. When the woman is compared to fragrances, it must be because she smells sweet (e.g. Munro, 1995, p. 49). This seems a good translation choice in poetry that engages our senses. However, when the same fragrances are evoked for the man, some scholars reassert his hardness and strength along with his sweet, spicy scent. This leads to a curious excursus through towers: the word translated as 'yielding' is arguably from the noun 'tower' (see Fox, 1985, p. 148). Translating 'towers' points out that 'the element of stone-built strength associated with the towers could nicely fit the woman's construction of the man's hard body if it suggests his chiselled cheek-bones and strong jaw' (Spencer, 2017, p. 142). We know she finds him attractive, so perhaps he *does* have great bone structure, and he probably *is* strong and healthy. However, we would do well to remember two things. First, a *waṣf* is hardly an identikit description. Second, though the towers are *implicit*, strength is linked to the man's handsome, fragrant cheeks, but when the woman is *explicitly* compared to a tower (e.g. 4.4; 7.5) there is a tendency to comment on, for example, necklaces rather than seeing her as a tower of strength (Sessions, 2021, pp. 115–16). The word 'spice' or 'perfume', *merqaḥim* (hapax) is from the verb *raqaḥ*, which is the art of mixing ointments and perfumes (Carr, 1984, p. 142). The alliteration and word-play[5] is pleasing and is 'reminiscent of the mountain of myrrh and hill of frankincense' (Keel, 1994, p. 201) used to describe the woman in 4.6d. Though there is plenty of evidence from the Ancient Near East, and the Song itself (1.3) attests to pleasingly redolent, perfumed men, it is not surprising some scholars shy away from 'feminine' fragrances for the man. Studies indicate scents can alter perceptions of masculinity or femininity (Hovis, Sheehe and White, 2021). 'Feminine' fragrances may be floral, and 'masculine' deodorants are 'Cool Kick', 'Hero' or 'Victory' (Lennox, 2023). A spice tower is not exactly structurally strong and stable, so perhaps the primary meaning is, in fact, as simple as: the man smells sweet (e.g. Hess, 2005, p. 184). Respectful lovers will endeavour to smell nice for each other and, we know from elsewhere in the Song (e.g. 4.10–11), scents are 'sensually pleasurable' (Garrett and

House, 2004, p. 220) and 'were associated with kissing' (Duguid, 2015, p. 131). So the point is that her nose is so close to his cheek that she can smell his scent, and her lips are 'able to graze among the lilies of his lips' (Duguid, 2015, p. 132), leading beautifully to the second half of verse 13: 'His lips are like lilies, dripping with myrrh.'

Lilies and myrrh usually apply to the woman (2.1–2; 4.10–11; 5.5; 6.2–3; 7.2), 'making this the point in the present *waṣf* where gender most blurs and blends together in one flesh' (Spencer, 2017, p. 142). That this occurs at the middle of the seven-part structure is not accidental – the lovers are most similar when their lips meet:

> In her beloved, the woman recognizes herself. The same myrrh that drips from her hands, drips from his lips, and in his eyes she recognizes the same flame of love ('dove') which shines in hers. Love ... makes out of the two only one flesh. (Barbiero, 2011, p. 283)

The metaphors point to his 'personality and individuality ... put another way, it is not simply his anatomy she loves; it is the man himself' (Garrett and House, 2004, p. 220). The lovers model for us what it is like to love and be loved, to be chosen over and again, for the intricate mix of qualities that make us who we are.

Next, verse 14 – 'His hands [arms] are rods [?] of gold set with topaz [or beryl, chrysolite or ...]' – is the volta of the *waṣf* where 'the metaphors change from predominantly natural images to images drawn from the world of sculpture and architecture' (Duguid, 2015, p. 132). Interpretative offerings for his golden hands include: 'cylinders' (Fox, 1985, p. 148; Hess, 2005, p. 184), 'bars' (Longman, 2001, p. 173), door pivots and curtain rings (Keel, 1994, p. 204), 'bracelets' (Carr, 1984, p. 142), and Spencer (2017, p. 142) offers 'jewel-studded gold ramrods' for the man's 'solid and powerful hands/arms'; however, 'the object with which the arms of the beloved are compared cannot be identified with certainty' (Keel, 1994, p. 204). Describing golden and jewel-encrusted arms with terms like 'muscular physique', 'substances of strength' and 'sinews' (Hess, 2005, p. 185) is questionable, when the metaphor more obviously expresses 'the infinite value of his person' (Duguid, 2015, p. 132). The emphasis is probably not on strength, since gold is not a strong metal, nor on the 'artistry of these materials', but on 'their value' (Keel, 1994, p. 204). The Song's modern scholarship appears to have been influenced by contemporary cultural ideas of how men's bodies should look (and how men should behave). 'Muscular masculinity' prizes a muscular physique as a 'primary sign of manhood associated with male success, intimidation, and status' (Cranswick et al., 2020). 'Research suggests a spectrum of socially acceptable and contextual muscular masculine physiques, ranging from a lean, athletic, physique to a hypermuscular body' (Cranswick et al., 2020). ANROWS' research shows that condoning such stereotyped masculinity 'ultimately contributes to and reinforces gendered oppressions, thereby maintaining a context that enables gender-based violence to occur' (Coumarelos et al., 2023, pp. 109–11). Body stereotypes harm everyone. Men need not have hard, musclebound, sinewy, 'strong' bodies to be 'manly'. The Song's man is metaphorically made of precious, malleable metal and beautifully bejewelled. I think the application here is less about (culturally relativized, idealized) musculature and more about uniquely embodied persons, made in God's image, having value regardless of physical appearance or ability.

The lover enthuses: 'His loins are like polished ivory decorated with lapis lazuli [or sapphire].' Some scholars have tended to, once again, focus more on the man being 'strong and powerful' (Hess, 2005, p. 185), with less attention paid to (metaphorical meaning from) ivory's colour, sheen, smoothness and worth. Glickman (1976, p. 67) asserts the man 'had rippling stomach muscles', Duguid (2015, p. 132) wonders if the simile 'indicates that his abdominal muscles were flat and hard', and Spencer (2017, p. 143) suggests 'we might modernize this into six-pack abs or a strong solid core'. That ivory (statuary) is hard and solid is not in doubt, but we can also equate this image with a 'luxurious object of carefully polished, dully gleaming ivory' (Keel, 1994, p. 205), which is more in keeping with the beloved's prized and dazzling description thus far. Interestingly, the word translated as 'loins' can mean bowels/intestines and has been translated as 'body', 'belly', 'stomach', 'abdomen', 'lumbar' (Hess, 2005, p. 185) and even 'compassion' (Keel, 1994, p. 204). I am inclined to agree with scholars who carefully reason 'loins' poetically, euphemistically refers to the man's penis (e.g. Longman, 2001, p. 173). Elsewhere, I have argued that 'navel' (7.2) refers to the woman's vulva, and understanding anatomy and sexuality helps to prevent domestic abuse (Sessions, 2020, pp. 80–1). The presence of genitalia in a Song about lovemaking, in *waṣfs* concerned with verticality, makes sense. As does teaching from the Song, exploring gender equality – including sexuality – and addressing the key driver of domestic abuse.

Moving to 'lapis lazuli', Gledhill (1994, p. 184) is unsure if it does more than 'heighten the extravagance of the description'. And according to Carr (1984, p. 143), literalizing will 'only result in ludicrous pictures, as Delitzsch's "branching blue veins under white skin"' or, according to

Murphy (1990, p. 172), Rudolph's tattoo argument. However, I think the (overall) point is that what *waṣfs* emphasize (e.g. colour, beauty and sexuality), taken together, connote royalty and precious worth, and perhaps even divinity, since the place where God's feet rest and God's throne (Exod. 24.10; Ezek. 1.26) were both made of lapis (Keel, 1994, p. 205). The woman respectfully refers to her beloved as 'the king' (1.4; 1.12; 7.5), along with other, mutual evocations of royalty (e.g. 1.9; 3.7; 4.4; 6.8–9), and it was common in the Ancient Near East to liken kings and queens to gods. Such awe and respect for one's partner should be encouraged! The research is clear that domestic abuse is steeped in disrespect for women, and respectful relationship education prevents domestic abuse (Coumarelos et al., 2023, p. 242).

This next verse (15) – 'his legs are pillars of marble/alabaster set on bases/pedestals of pure gold' – connects with the former through sound resonances between the words for ivory, (שֵׁן) *shen*, and marble/alabaster, (שֵׁשׁ) *shesh*. By now there should be no doubt that these are prized materials. Though statues are the image that most easily comes to mind (e.g. Longman, 2001, p. 171), Munro (1995, p. 63) has linked the legs to 'architectural components of Israel's most prominent buildings' (Spencer, 2017, p. 143) – the tabernacle, Solomon's palace and the temple in Jerusalem – further emphasizing the beloved's preciousness and his connection to divinity. Regardless of whether he is compared to statuary or architecture, the man's 'strength' (and the 'stability' and 'security' it provides) continues to stress (stereotyped) masculinity. For example, Hess (2005, p. 186) writes: 'the thighs of the male could be the most muscular part of the leg, revealing his strength and endurance.' Along with 'masculine role stress' comes 'masculine contest culture', which emphasizes aggression, competition, control, dominance and toughness (Coumarelos et al., 2023, p. 191). Healthy, unstereotyped, positive masculinity sees men as multidimensional. Interestingly, Hess (2005, p. 186) goes on to note this metaphor also applies to the feet of a beautiful 'ideal woman' in Sirach 26.18: 'Like golden pillars on silver bases, so are shapely legs and steadfast feet.' Let us also not forget the connection between feet and lovemaking (Sessions, 2020, p. 79). Legs and feet may be sexy, shapely, strong and steadfast regardless of gender.

'His appearance is like Lebanon, choice as its cedars' completes verse 15. Perhaps it is not surprising, since the image refers to the man's 'appearance', that much of the scholarship is focused on his height and strength – to the detriment of the simile's synaesthetic possibilities, and with little consideration for how the same imagery is applied to the woman. The beloved is described by commentators as 'stately' (Carr,

1984, p. 144); like 'majestically tall and straight cedars, to which she compares his noble bearing' (Duguid, 2015, p. 133); like 'the cedars of Lebanon, the strongest and tallest of living things' (Hess, 2005, p. 186); and 'His whole appearance is solid, immovable, firm and steadfast, like the range of the Lebanon mountains, imposing in their permanence' (Gledhill, 1994, p. 184). This may be true, but olfaction indicates he smells like the rich aroma of cedarwood. And the Song often invokes 'this sylvan region as a site of mysterious grandeur and a source of enticing odors' (Spencer, 2017, p. 143). When the woman is compared to Lebanon, she is both fragrant (4.11) and a tower (7.4); she is strong-soft.[6] This causes less consternation than a strong-soft man: 'the trees of the forest are both strong and beautiful (yet without excessive floral colouring) and so are an appropriate symbol of male beauty' (Garrett and House, 2004, p. 224). Rather than binding interpretation with gendered boundary markers, perhaps Lebanon's 'resin-rich forests, flowers, and fragrant plants make it seem a garden of the gods' (Keel, 1994, p. 206) regardless of gender.

Since the final verse is itself a summary conclusion, it will also serve as my conclusion. Along with the obvious meaning of the man's sweet smell and taste, and the woman wanting to partake of them, his mouth may be 'metonymic for speech or voice' (Spencer, 2017, p. 144), and this intensive reference to his sweetnesses anticipates the next line: 'he is altogether lovely'. This is also the only time she uses 'my friend', which is usually the man's term of endearment for her. Carr (1984, p. 144) writes that there is 'a refreshing candour in her identifying her lover as also her "friend" – friendship goes far deeper than mere sexual compatibility and excitement'. So how is the woman of the Song's friend and beloved better than others? The woman composes a score that includes positive masculinity and: 'From top to bottom he is magnificent, pure, costly, divine – like gold. He is superior to all others' (Keel, 1994, pp. 206–7). She eschews the ubiquitous male gaze, and her own female gaze is empowered as she decides to laud (the beautiful body of) her beloved. The lovers' counter-textual and counter-cultural verse descriptions of each other flip the tables on gendered expectations, challenging the gender inequality that drives domestic abuse. A *wasf* 'normally ends with a decision to enjoy the splendors that have been portrayed' (Keel, 1994, p. 206), and now the Daughters of Jerusalem – and we – know exactly who the woman enjoys: '*This* is my beloved, *this* is my friend.' Just as the woman is 'overwhelming' throughout the *wasf* at 6.4–10, 'her triumphant verbal description has overwhelmed both herself and her ... companions' (Gledhill, 1994, p. 185). *This* is how her beloved is better than others and *this* is how we break down gender roles – through an ancient text and in contemporary society – to prevent domestic abuse. *This* is God's given example of beautiful, mutual, equal love, free from gender stereotypes.

Notes

1 See, for example, Polaski (2008), Garrett and House (2004) or Soulen (1967).

2 Keel's comment is specifically in reference to Delitzsch's ridiculous use of 'stable of wenches' to refer to the women of the royal court; however, the point stands.

3 Compare Genesis 12.12–14; Deuteronomy 21.11; 1 Samuel 25.3; 2 Samuel 13.1; 14.27; 1 Kings 1.3–4; Esther 2.7; Job 42.15; Proverbs 11.22; Song of Songs 1.8; 5.9; 6.1; 7.1; Amos 8.13.

4 Longman (2001, p. 171) comes close with 'compliment'.

5 There is a fun interplay between the word *raqqah*, temple or cheekbone, and *raqah/merqahim*. Have we been so concerned with gender-boundary maintenance that we missed this glorious sound play and the beauty of the image?

6 My thanks to Safina Stewart for this phrasing.

Bibliography

Alter, Robert, 2011, *The Art of Biblical Poetry*, revised edn, New York: Basic Books.

Andruska, Jennifer L., 2018, 'The Strange Use of לגד in Song of Songs 5:10', *Vetus Testamentum*, vol. 68, no. 1, pp. 1–7.

Barbiero, Gianni, 2011, *Song of Songs: A Close Reading*, SVT 144, trans. M. Tait, Leiden: Brill.

Bloch, Ariel and Bloch, Chana, 2006, *The Song of Songs: A New Translation with an Introduction and Commentary*, Berkeley, CA: University of California Press.

Carr, G. Lloyd, 1984, *The Song of Solomon*, Tyndale Old Testament Commentaries, Westmont, IL: InterVarsity Press.

Cislaghi, Beniamino and Heise, Lori, 2020, 'Gender Norms and Social Norms: Differences, Similarities and Why They Matter in Prevention Science', *Sociology of Health & Illness*, vol. 42, no. 2, pp. 407–22.

Commonwealth of Australia (Department of Social Services), 2022, *The National Plan to Reduce Violence against Women and their Children 2022–2032*, https://www.dss.gov.au/sites/default/files/documents/10_2023/national-plan-end-violence-against-women-and-children-2022-2032.pdf, accessed 28.11.2024.

Coumarelos, C. et al., 2023, 'Attitudes Matter: The 2021 National Community Attitudes towards Violence against Women Survey (NCAS), Findings for Australia', Research report 02/2023, ANROWS.

Cranswick, Ieuan et al., 2020, '"Oh Take some Man-up Pills": A Life-history Study of Muscles, Masculinity, and the Threat of Injury', *Performance Enhancement & Health*, vol. 8, nos 2–3, article 100176.

Duguid, Iain M., 2015, *The Song of Songs: An Introduction and Commentary*, Tyndale Old Testament Commentaries, Downers Grove, IL: InterVarsity Press.

Exum, J. Cheryl, 2005, *Song of Songs: A Commentary*, Louisville, KY: Westminster John Knox.

Falk, Marcia, 1982, *Love Lyrics from the Bible: A Translation and Literary Study of The Song of Songs*, Sheffield: Almond Press.

Fox, Michael V., 1985, *The Song of Songs and Ancient Egyptian Love Songs*, Madison, WI: University of Wisconsin Press.

Fredericks, Daniel C. and Estes, Daniel J., 2010, *Ecclesiastes and the Song of Songs*, Apollos Old Testament Commentary Series, Downers Grove, IL: InterVarsity Press.

Garrett, Duane and House, Paul R., 2004, *Song of Songs/Lamentations*, Word Biblical Commentary 23B, Nashville, TN: Thomas Nelson.

Gledhill, Tom, 1994, *The Message of the Song of Songs*, The Bible Speaks Today, Leicester: InterVarsity Press.

Glickman, S. Craig, 1976, *A Song for Lovers*, Downers Grove, IL: InterVarsity Press.

Hess, Richard S., 2005, *Song of Songs*, Baker Commentary on the Old Testament Wisdom and Psalms, Grand Rapids, MI: Baker Academic.

Hovis, Nicole L., Sheehe, Paul R. and White, Theresa L., 2021, 'Scent of a Woman – Or Man: Odors Influence Person Knowledge', *Brain Science*, vol. 11, no. 7, p. 955.

Hutton, Erin Martine, 2024, 'Striking Like the Morning Star: How Can Song of Songs 6:4–10 Prevent Domestic Abuse?', in C. Greenough et al. (eds), *Bible and Violence Project*, London: T&T Clark.

Keel, Othmar, 1994, *The Song of Songs: A Continental Commentary*, Minneapolis, MN: Fortress Press.

Leckie, Evelyn and Mason, Olivia, 2023, 'Four Alleged Domestic Homicides Occurred in South Australia this Week and Advocates are Calling for Urgent Change', ABC News, 23 November, https://www.abc.net.au/news/2023-11-23/four-alleged-domestic-homicides-in-sa-this-week/103137634, accessed 31.08.2024.

Lennox, Will, 2023, 'The Smell of Success: These are the Best Deodorants According to GQ', https://www.gq.com.au/shopping/best-buys/mens-deodorants/image-gallery/dc3dda91493b64d8d40f72293cb7c881, accessed 28.11.2024.

Longman III, Tremper, 2001, *Song of Songs*, NICOT, Grand Rapids, MI: William B. Eerdmans.

Moore, Stephen D., 2001, *God's Beauty Parlor: And other Queer Spaces in and around the Bible*, Stanford, CA: Stanford University Press.

Munro, Jill, 1995, *Spikenard and Saffron: The Imagery of the Song of Songs*, London: T&T Clark.

Murphy, Roland E., 1990, *The Song of Songs: A Commentary on the Book of Canticles or the Song of Songs*, Minneapolis, MN: Fortress Press.

Pidgeon, Kylie Maddox, 2021, 'Complementarianism and Domestic Abuse: A Social-Scientific Perspective on Whether "Equal but Different" is Really Equal at All', in R. W. Pierce, C. L. Westfall and C. K. McKirland (eds), *Discovering Biblical Equality: Biblical, Theological, Cultural, and Practical Perspectives*, 3rd edn, Downers Grove, IL: InterVarsity Press Academic, pp. 551–73.

Polaski, Donald, 2008, 'Where Men are Men and Women are Women? The Song of Songs and Gender', *Review and Expositor*, vol. 105, no. 3, pp. 435–51.

Pope, Marvin H., 1977, *Song of Songs*, Anchor Bible 7C, New York: Doubleday.

Respect Victoria, 2023, 'Our Strategic Plan', https://www.respectvictoria.vic.gov.au/2023-2028-respect-victoria-strategic-plan-full-version-word, accessed 31.08.2024.

Schaser, Nicholas J., 2022, 'Do Appearances Matter to God?' *Israel Bible Centre*, 11 December, https://weekly.israelbiblecenter.com/does-god-regard-appearances/, accessed 31.08.2024.

Sessions, Erin Martine, 2020, 'Can the Bible Close the Orgasm Gap? How Song of Songs 7:1–6 Handles Anatomy and Sexuality, and How That's Good News for Women', *St Mark's Review*, vol. 251, pp. 75–88.

Sessions, Erin Martine, 2021, '"Descending from the Hills of Gilead": Undressing Descriptions of the Lover's Body and how Australian Women Can Reclaim and Embrace their Embodiment', in J. Firth and D. Cooper-Clarke (eds), *Grounded in the Body, in Time and Place, in Scripture*, Eugene, OR: Wipf & Stock, pp. 107–20.

Sessions, Erin Martine, 2023, '"Stay and Submit": What Have We Learned from the Domestic and Family Violence Body of Evidence, and Can Christians Redeem Our Communities?', in K. Beilharz, M. Miner and J. Fernandez (eds), *Redeeming Truth and Community in the Age of Individualism*, Cooranbong, Australia: Avondale Academic Press, pp. 79–102.

Snaith, John G., 1993, *Song of Songs*, The New Century Bible Commentary, Grand Rapids, MI: William B. Eerdmans.

Soulen, Richard N., 1967, 'The Waṣfs of the Song of Songs and Hermeneutic', *Journal of Biblical Literature*, vol. 86, no. 2, pp. 183–90.

Spencer, F. Scott, 2017, *Song of Songs*, Wisdom Commentary, Collegeville, MN: Liturgical Press.

Sun, Chloe T., 2021, *Conspicuous in His Absence: Studies in the Song of Songs and Esther*, Downers Grove, IL: InterVarsity Press Academic.

Questions for reflection and discussion

1 What has your experience been with reading Song of Songs, both personally and in community? What comes up for you as you consider the way the author presents the erotic imagination of the poetess here?

2 Have you experienced gender inequality in your church community? Have you or someone you know experienced gendered violence, such as domestic abuse?

3 In what ways do you think you could use or discuss Song of Songs in your context to prevent domestic abuse?

10

A Shameful Perfection: Racism and the Religion of Thinness

MICHELLE MARY LELWICA

Trigger warning: This chapter discusses eating disorders and body image problems.

The first time I made myself throw up, I didn't have a name for what I was doing. It was 1978, long before anorexia and bulimia were part of Westerners' shared lexicon. My ninth-grade cheerleading squad and I were in the upstairs bathroom at my parents' house. The smell of hot curling irons filled the air. One of the girls suggested we try a new 'diet trick' to get rid of the calories from the pizza we'd just devoured. All six of us lined up behind the toilet and took turns bending, fingers down our throat. Only two of us had any success. Little did I know how much this 'success' would consume my body, mind and spirit for years to come.

Looking back, I see that bathroom experience as a rite of passage, a tragic initiation into something I now call the 'Religion of Thinness': a network of toxic beliefs, rituals, images and moral codes that encourage girls and women to find meaning and pursue 'salvation' through the physical 'perfection' of thinness.

The Religion of Thinness

Some 15 years ago, I coined the term 'Religion of Thinness' based on five observations:

- For many girls and women in Western cultures today, devotion to thinness serves what has historically been a religious function, providing a profound sense of meaning and purpose and a strategy for dealing with suffering and uncertainty.

- Important features of this cultural devotion – for example, beliefs, rituals, images, moral codes, sense of community, salvation myth – resemble certain aspects of Christianity, which is the religion that's had the most power to shape Western gender/body ideals and expectations.
- Girls' and women's devotion to the thin ideal recycles specific norms and narratives of patriarchal religion, including Christianity's other-worldly, exclusionary, misogynistic tendencies.
- The misguided belief that you not only should – but can – perfect your body by controlling it fuses historical Christianity's moralizing teachings about 'the flesh' with the modern Cartesian understanding of 'self' as an unencumbered, autonomous individual. (Descartes's error is evident in our bodies' intelligent refusal to comply with the commands of our supposedly sovereign will.)
- The popularity of the Religion of Thinness is rooted in the genuine spiritual (or existential) needs to which it appeals (though ultimately fails to satisfy), including the need for belonging, creativity, structure, meaning, connection, empowerment and recognition.

Thanks to its deep ties to commercial culture, the Religion of Thinness has a missionizing orientation. With so many women already converted, marketers have increasingly sought to persuade boys, men and non-binary people to worry about their physical appearance and transfigure their bodies to a tight and lean ideal. No one should underestimate the suffering many of them experience when they perceive themselves to fall short of physical perfection. My research and writing, however, have focused on how the Religion of Thinness impacts the lives of girls and women in the United States (Lelwica, 1999, 2010, 2011, 2017a, 2017b; Lelwica, Hoglund and McNallie, 2009). And while gender and systemic sexism have been the primary lenses through which I've critically analysed this secular faith, the quest for the holy grail of bodily perfection is also shaped by race and systemic racism, in conjunction with class, sexuality, (dis)ability and other vectors of 'difference'. This chapter focuses on the racist underpinnings of the pursuit of salvation through thinness by examining the cultural associations between slender bodies, moral perfection and White supremacy. Drawing on both academic research and my own history of disordered eating, White privilege and agonizing perfectionism, I argue that White girls' and women's quasi-religious devotion to thinness is deeply entangled with racism.

Body hatred as a spiritual crisis

Indoctrination into the Religion of Thinness starts early. This is me when I was nine years old:

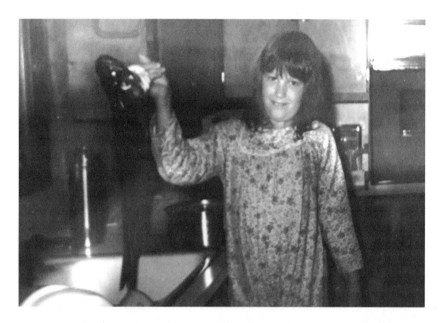

I'm proudly holding a large walleye fish that I caught on a family fishing trip. When I look at this photo, I can't help but notice how unselfconscious – how *unashamed* – I was about my body. No worries about my double chin. No attempt to 'suck it in' to make my belly look flatter.

By the next year, I was on my first diet.

Research suggests that I wasn't alone. By the mid-1980s in the United States, 80 per cent of ten-year-old girls surveyed said they had dieted (Brumberg, 2000, p. 32). More recent studies suggest that women's obsessive concerns about weight are part of a much broader epidemic of body dissatisfaction. Some 83 per cent of women surveyed say they don't like the way they look (Jackson and Lemay, 2018). According to some reports, as many as 90 per cent of women in Western and Western-influenced cultures are unhappy with our bodies.[1] More often than not, this unhappiness centres on weight and body size. Anxiety about being (or becoming) 'too fat' still starts young. Between 40 per cent and 60 per cent of elementary school girls say they worry about gaining weight, and 66 per cent of girls say they want to lose weight (National Organization for Women, 2024). Forty-five per cent of girls aged 16 to 19 said they had actively tried to lose weight during the past year (McDow et al., 2019). This desire to reduce shadows many women for decades. A study of females over 50 found that 70 per cent were trying to shed pounds, with 62 per cent saying their weight or shape negatively impacted their lives (Gagne et al., 2012). Although some minoritized racial and ethnic communities offer greater appreciation for diversely sized female bodies, studies show very little difference between White women and women of colour when it comes to body satisfaction (Grabe and Hyde, 2006).[2] As many Black and Brown women know, the relatively wider acceptance of women-of-size in some racially minoritized communities does not make them immune to the omnipresent pressure to convert their bodies to the supposedly superior, slender ideal (Bordo, 2009). In White-majority Western societies, slenderness has become the hallmark not only of physical perfection, but of everything that somatic perfection is seen to embody: happiness, health, beauty, belonging, safety, moral virtue *and* social privilege.

If the pervasiveness of girls' and women's body discontent suggests that this problem is far from personal, the depth of this unhappiness indicates that the problem is far from trivial. As a feminist religion scholar, I see the self-loathing that images of the 'perfect body' induce in many girls and women as a kind of spiritual crisis. The shame so many of us carry in and about our flesh funnels our moral and creative energies into the narrow project of 'perfecting' our bodies, rather than the prophetic work of repairing the world. Moreover, the sense that there's something wrong with our bodies – something that stands in the way of our happiness and freedom, something that needs to be eradicated or fixed in order for us to feel worthy and whole – distorts our divine humanity: the sacred goodness in every*body* that cannot be erased.

Cultural indoctrination into the legacy of Eve

By age 14, my relationship with my body was infused with a mistrust and shame I wasn't born with. Whereas the moral codes surrounding my Catholic upbringing centred largely on the virtue of controlling my bodily desires, my White, middle-class socialization taught me that, as a girl, my worth depended on being physically *attractive* (to boys), and everything in my cultural environment told – and showed – me that 'attractive' meant skinny. Controlling and perfecting my body were religiously and socially sanctioned strategies for gaining love and feeling a sense of virtue and belonging that all of us so deeply crave and need.

The problem, though, was that my body-policing and punishing behaviours exacerbated the very painful feelings – unhappiness, disconnection and unworthiness – they were supposed to eliminate. These feelings are evident on my face in this picture of me, taken when I was 15, not long after my bulimia began.

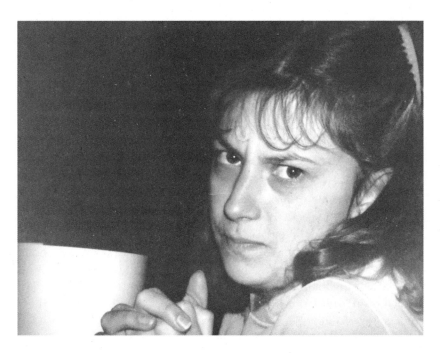

Fast-forward from the smell of hot curling irons in an upstairs bathroom to the scent of old books at Harvard Divinity School's library, where I was a graduate student doing research on what the early Church Fathers had to say about the mythical first lady: Eve. It wasn't pretty. These influential men kept blaming Adam's 'helpmate' for humanity's downfall. If only she hadn't eaten the forbidden fruit, there'd be no suffering, sin or death. If only Eve hadn't given in to her unruly body. If only she had controlled her appetite …

Wait a minute, I thought. *What does it mean that one of the most influential stories of Western culture depicts sin and shame entering the world through a woman's disobedient appetite?* Well, minimally, it meant that my girlhood obsession with conquering my hunger didn't originate with me.

The racist roots of fatphobia

The legacy of Eve lives on in the Religion of Thinness and in the pressure so many women feel to eradicate their shame by taming their appetites and perfecting their bodies. In fact, Eve's shame echoes throughout the history of fatphobia in the West, which is the flip side of the ascendency of the slender ideal. While the sexism embedded in this history becomes fairly obvious once you recognize how the story of the Fall associates female appetite with sin, shame and danger, the racist roots are less well known.

In her brilliant book *Fearing the Black Body* (2019), the sociologist Sabrina Strings examines these roots, highlighting their intersection with economic, ethnic and religious superiority complexes. The book is chock-full of examples from the worlds of art, literature, philosophy, history, self-help and medical discourses that document how thinness became increasingly associated with spiritual perfection and White supremacy. Starting in the early modern era and continuing during the colonial period, a select group of White Western elites began celebrating the virtues of slender bodies, which they viewed as more morally refined and superior to the supposedly 'uncivilized' Black and Brown bodies of 'heathens', which they deemed indecently voracious and voluptuous. Even a few highlights from Strings's analysis illustrate the historical trajectory in which the supposed perfection of thinness was indelibly shaped by a White superiority complex.

For much of Western history prior to the modern era, fat was largely seen as a sign of social privilege. Whereas bodily 'excess' signified wealth and status among White men, ample-bodied White women were considered beautiful. As early as the 1600s, however, European body standards started gradually shifting. That's when a small but influential group of elite White men, including scientists and philosophers, began seeing fat as evidence of an irrational mind, laziness, greed and lack of control. By contrast, thinness was deemed a sign of mastery over humans' vulgar 'animal' instincts. Based on this interpretation, these privileged men constructed a narrative that vilified Black women's appetites as overindulgent and their bodies as unsightly. From the late seventeenth century through to the nineteenth, they identified corpulence as a common physical feature of 'primitive' people, especially Black women, who they deemed incapable of controlling their carnal cravings (Farrell, 2011; Strings, 2019).[3] In the context of colonialism, robust appetites belonged to 'savages', while slenderness came to represent self-control, intelligence, spiritual virtue and high social rank, all of which economically privileged White Christians claimed for themselves. As the sociologist Amina Mire reminds us:

> Throughout western colonial history ... the dark body has been represented [by the dominant culture] as the least virtuous and aesthetically least appealing ... Constructing colonized people's cultures and body images as pathological, backward and ... ugly has been central to ... white supremacy. (Quoted in Clare, 2017, p. 77)

In the United States, the tall and lean form also came to represent *freedom*, a value that, according to Thomas Jefferson, Anglo-Saxons were more naturally inclined to embody and possess (Strings, 2019). Powerful politicians like Jefferson, who owned over 600 slaves, invented new ways to classify and rank human differences – namely, according to 'race' – to justify the brutalities of slavery. According to Eddie Glaude (2017), Jefferson expressed fear that either God or Blacks themselves would eventually take revenge on Whites for this brutality. This historic fear echoes in contemporary Whites' stereotypical perceptions of Black people as dangerous – and of their bodies as 'unruly'.

During the eighteenth and nineteenth centuries in the United States, body size became an indicator of religious, national and racial identity. Prominent Protestant ministers preached that fatness was evidence of sinful eating, that slenderness embodied a righteous soul and that Black bodies were intrinsically ravenous and greedy. In the eyes of these learned White men, it wasn't just people of African descent who were less civilized than their masters. Catholic immigrants from Ireland and from eastern and southern European countries were also seen to live at the mercy of their base appetites. In the minds of Anglo-Saxon Protestant elites, these ethnic and religious 'others' could not really be considered White. Their generally larger, stouter, rounder, 'gluttonous' bodies were sufficient evidence that these American newcomers were closer to people of African descent, and that, in the words of a prominent eugenicist of the time, they were 'only civilized on the surface' (Strings, 2019, p. 150).

By the turn of the twentieth century, a bourgeois, White, Protestant supremacist ideology prompted a growing number of affluent, White women to try to lose weight. Trimming their bodies became a way to embrace and showcase their superior status as White ladies. Motivated to eliminate the alleged 'unsightliness and discomfort' of their fat, high-class White women purchased weight-reducing products and followed diets prescribed by White Christian ministers, female beauty writers, and medical doctors alike (Strings, 2019). By the early twentieth century

in the United States, race, gender, cultural, religious and body-size hierarchies intersected as the slender ideal became increasingly associated
with upper-class, Anglo-Saxon, Protestant privilege, and the plump
form was identified with poor, working-class, and/or ethnic immigrants
– especially Jewish and Catholic women, whose bodies were considered
constitutionally weaker and who were encouraged to Americanize themselves by shedding pounds (Schwartz, 1986).[4]

Meanwhile, a growing number of powerful men praised the lean,
elongated female figure as the embodiment of American exceptionalism
– a form that represented a perfect mix of Western and central European
features. In different ways, the athletic-looking 'Gibson Girl' and the
boyishly-lean-yet-feminine 'Flappers' embodied this perfection in the
early decades of the twentieth century. Positioned at the feminine apex
of national, racial and religious identity, the tall, slender, Anglo-Saxon
woman triumphed not only over the bodies of 'primitive' females with
African ancestry, but also over the not-quite-White-enough bodies of
ethnic and religious 'others', who occupied the purgatorial space between
the 'top' and 'bottom' of the social hierarchy of femininity (Strings, 2019).

Initially, as Strings (2019) and other historians point out, some health
professionals were concerned about enticements for women to lose
weight. Several decades into the twentieth century, some medical men
feared that reducing adipose tissue would jeopardize the reproductive
health of elite White women – that is, the females they most wanted to
reproduce. By the mid-twentieth century, however, the preference for
feminine slenderness had gained widespread buy-in, thanks in part to
standards created by the Metropolitan Life Insurance Company that
ranked people's health based on a height/weight ratio. Using data from
middle-class White men, these metrics helped usher the United States
into a new era in which health = thinness, a simplistic equation that
gained traction with the help of already existing cultural associations
between thinness, moral perfection, beauty and social privilege.

The 'science' behind the quest for physical perfection

I remember studying the insurance standards in the years leading up to
my full-blown eating disorder. They were conveniently posted next to
the large scales in the hallway of the clinic where I had my annual check-
ups, and they were user-friendly. With heights listed in one column and
weights in another, it was easy to discover your health status based on
where the numbers converged. I remember hating the 'fact' (who can

argue with numbers?) that, every year, a mere five or ten pounds disqualified me from being in the 'ideal weight' category – and thus from being 'perfect'. Over the years, Metropolitan Life Insurance modified the language on its charts: from 'ideal weight', to 'desired weight', to 'healthy weight'. Yet even as the 'medical' vocabulary shifted, I understood clearly that words like 'ideal', 'desirable' and 'healthy' all pointed in the same direction: towards the superiority of perfection. Physical flawlessness was the only valid destination for any White, middle-class girl who wanted to prove herself worthy of others' attention, approval and admiration. I was just a girl, but I understood perfectly well that designations like 'desirable' and 'healthy' were code for moral virtue.

Around the world today, the Body Mass Index (BMI) is the most common standard for gauging 'healthy weight', 'overweight' and 'obesity' status. Even the World Health Organization relies on it. The BMI uses a weight-to-height ratio to determine the amount of fat on your body, which in turn supposedly determines your health status. By the time this measurement had replaced insurance company benchmarks for health and fitness, I was out of high school. Thus, I managed to avoid the unique humiliation of having to step on the scales in front of my peers during gym class – a practice that became common in the United States during the early 2000s – following the US government's declaration of a 'war on obesity'. For many teens today, this school-based ritual functions as an unwitting exercise in producing public shame that some youth internalize for years to come.

Internalized shame is a common thread in the personal narratives of diverse college students that Susan Greenhalgh features in her book *Fat-Talk Nation* (2015). In these narratives, Greenhalgh's students describe the evolution of their relationships with their bodies. One of them, a Mexican American young woman named Annemarie, describes how the seeming clarity of numbers and authority of science surrounding the BMI distorted her self-perception: 'I can easily pinpoint one specific moment in my life when the knowledge of BMI warped the image of my existence in society.' That moment happened in seventh grade when, after stepping on the scales during gym class, a nurse informed Annemarie that her BMI number was 'too high':

> [T]he nurse's words were news to me, and when she sternly looked at me and told me that I absolutely had to get my weight down, I was stunned ... I had never seen myself as fat, but from that moment on, I started comparing myself to the thin, beautiful eighth-grade girls who wore short skirts and a size 0. (Greenhalgh, 2015, p. 116)

Although Annemarie was a muscular athlete who, at age 12, stood 5'7" and could run a mile in under eight minutes, she came to believe that the BMI was, as she puts it, 'the word of God, unwavering and immovable' (Greenhalgh, 2015, p. 125).

The dogmatic assumption that health = thinness has played a central role in the 'war on obesity'. Supposedly driven by science, this crusade continues to recycle the racist history of fatphobia. While the perception of corpulence as evidence of an undisciplined mind and uncivilized soul is alive and well in the United States today, this view is now layered with the medicalized designation of fat as the embodiment of *disease*. The collateral damage that the crusade to eradicate this menace leaves in its wake – from bullying and harassment to stress and self-loathing – harms people of colour most of all. Although Mexican Americans like Annemarie comprise just over 11 per cent of the US population today (Funk and Lopex, 2002), 50.4 per cent of this demographic could be categorized as 'obese' using BMI criteria (Alemán et al., 2023). Similarly, while approximately 13 per cent of Americans are Black, about 51 per cent of Americans who are fat are Black (Harrison, 2021, p. 79). Ultimately, a war that targets adipose tissue disproportionately targets Black and Brown people.

The lingering moral and colonial impulses driving the war on obesity are evident in the bellicose language that saturates medical, self-help and commercial diet discourses, which encourage us to 'Conquer our cravings', 'Blast belly fat', 'Burn calories' and 'Triumph over obesity'.[5] It would be one thing if this crusade actually promoted healthier lifestyles, but research indicates that over 95 per cent of diets fail to keep weight off permanently, and that weight fluctuation puts you at higher risk for health problems than being 'overweight' (Bacon, 2010; Harrison, 2021, p. 41). It's been well documented that the American 2004 Center for Disease Control study that amplified panic about the health threats of obesity in and beyond the medical community was based on outdated data and included significant statistical errors that grossly inflated the negative impacts of being fat (Oliver, 2006). Additionally, there's an abundance of peer-reviewed research that calls into question the automatic association between weight and well-being, suggesting that this relationship is far more complicated than the doctrine that health = thinness assumes (Bacon and Aphramor, 2014).

(Unknowingly) claiming White privilege through thinness

During my bulimic years, it wouldn't have mattered if you had told me that, like the nineteenth-century mathematician who created the BMI, the statistician who invented the Metropolitan Life Insurance 'ideal/desirable weight' charts had never studied medicine. Nor would I have cared that he was White. At the time, I wouldn't have understood that these men's membership in the dominant/default racial group probably contributed to their failure to consider differences in body composition between members of diverse racial and ethnic groups when they concocted their formulas for categorizing health by weight. Yet this negligence is significant. For example, one reason Black people tend to score higher in the BMI is that they typically have greater muscle mass and/or bone density than their White counterparts (Strings, 2019).

More broadly, as a teenager, I never saw my obsessive pursuit of thinness as having anything to do with securing the unearned advantages of being White. Nor did I connect my passion for thinness with an attempt to distance myself from the negativity – the shameful out-of-controlness – that's stereotypically associated with Blackness. I had no idea that my desire to be – or at least *look* – 'in control', which is what I believed a perfect/thin body communicated to the world, was deeply implicated in the long-standing, racialized perception of fat as 'uncivilized' and 'barbaric' – that is, as undisciplined, unsightly, unsophisticated and sinful. Lacking both introspection and critical thinking skills, it seemed both natural and self-evident that every girl should want to be thin. I didn't understand the extent to which US culture had indoctrinated me with this desire. Like so many girls of my age, I had eagerly consumed a commercially driven iconography that encouraged me to pursue a kind of toxic femininity that associated slenderness with social privilege: all the female models and film stars whose sculpted bodies everyone adored appeared to be rich, refined, able-bodied, heterosexual and disproportionately White. Ultimately, I didn't know that *my devotion to thinness was infused with a desire to claim those privileges for myself.* Unwittingly, my drive for the perfection of thinness masked and perpetuated a kind of superiority complex – not unlike the kind you find in exclusivist approaches to religions.

In *The Sin of White Supremacy* (2017), Jeannine Hill Fletcher describes how a theology of White Christian supremacy was used to justify the terrors of slavery and various other racist institutions, ideologies and systems in US history. In their writings and sermons, academic theologians and ministers alike conflated White supremacy with Christian supremacy, with American exceptionalism, to the point at which being a 'Christian' was virtually synonymous with being 'White' for much of US history. These men's belief that it was God's intention for everyone to become Christian provided the conceptual scaffolding for the hierarchy of race around which the United States' dominant culture became organized. Implicitly, this racist, one-size-fits-all theology provided a template for US devotion to thinness as the singular body ideal.

Perfectionism's imprisoning impact

The connections I'm making here between the United States' 'original sin' of slavery[6] and the Religion of Thinness are not immediately obvious. But the way I treated my body during my teenage eating disorder mirrors the master/slave relationship that generated centuries of unimaginable suffering for African Americans. I didn't use a whip to subdue my appetite, but I made sure my hunger knew who was boss, punishing my body when it dared to disobey – when my flesh had the audacity to have a 'mind' of its own.

Bulimia is not illegal. As a teenager, I was never worried about being arrested for engaging in behaviour that most people would consider desperate, harmful or just plain gross. Nonetheless, during the three-plus years I spent bingeing and purging, I lived in a fog of secrecy and shame so thick you'd have thought I'd committed the most horrific crime. Not only did I treat my body as if it were a slave – separate from and inferior to 'me' – but I monitored my appetite as if it were a dangerous criminal who needed constant surveillance and punishment to keep her in line. All the while, I was terrified that I'd be caught bingeing and purging, that someone would discover my secret, revolting compulsion. Though as a middle-class White girl I didn't worry about going to prison, I felt as though I was living in one.

Punishing bodies for being 'big'

Several years ago, I began noticing the parallels between how I used to monitor and mortify my body and how the US criminal legal system often targets and treats people who get in trouble with the law. Since early 2018, I've been taking students in my Religion, Race and Social Justice course to the local detention centre, where we spend time talking with incarcerated teenagers.[7] The youth we visit are disproportionately kids of colour. The vast majority of them come from horrific backstories of poverty, trauma and abuse. Invariably, whatever harm they inflicted on others is rooted in the unhealed pain of what they have survived.

Initially, I didn't understand the connections between my history of disordered eating and the experiences of incarcerated youth. With time, however, I've come to see these obviously different experiences as oddly connected by the shame surrounding them. More specifically, the shame that girls and women are encouraged to direct at the 'flaws' or 'defects' of our individual bodies mirrors the shame many people with privilege direct at members of the social body who we often perceive to be 'bad', 'out-of-control', 'deserving of punishment'. Moreover, both the disobedient parts of our personal bodies that we've been trained to fear and disdain and those members of the social body who we've been taught to view as threatening and delinquent are connected by humans' tendency to judge and shun whatever – or whoever – we perceive to be untameable and 'other'.

In their fascinating (though disturbing) book *Belly of the Beast* (2021), Da'Shaun L. Harrison explores various threads connecting fat shame and the racist criminalization of Black bodies in the United States. Harrison demonstrates that the same fatphobic culture that motivated my adolescent crusade for the moral/social rewards of thinness continues to endanger a population of youth who don't fit the stereotypical profile of who is harmed by Western culture's quasi-religious devotion to thinness. Fat (or larger-than-average) young Black males from low-income communities are particularly vulnerable to harassment and violence by police officers who assume they're older than they are *because of their size*. In some of the most widely publicized police killings of unarmed Black boys in the United States, the 'large' body of the victim was listed as a reason for police aggression. The officer who killed Tamir Rice, a 12-year-old who was playing with a toy gun in a park in Cleveland, Ohio, described the boy's 'big' body – saying he was 'the size of a full-grown man' – as part of his explanation for shooting him just seconds after getting out of his police car. The officer who shot and killed Mike Brown characterized the 18-year-old as 'Hulk Hogan', explaining that he looked like a 'demon' (Harrison, 2021, p. 49).

The issue of body size also surfaces in cases of police killings of unarmed Black men. Those defending the officer who suffocated Eric Garner said it was not the illegal chokehold that killed him, but 'obesity' (as well as asthma and a heart condition). In the case of George Floyd's murder, the initial autopsy identified underlying health conditions associated with obesity (e.g. heart disease) as the cause of death. (Floyd's family ordered a second autopsy that confirmed he died of asphyxiation from the pressure that officer Chauvin applied to his back and neck.) Harrison concludes his analysis of the stereotypes many law officers have internalized of Black males as 'beasts' by stating that fat Black boys and men 'experience police brutality at disproportionate rates because their "largeness" coupled with their Blackness is read as dangerous, destructive, and inherently violent' (Harrison, 2021, p. 66). In the United States, the role that size plays in the policing of Black bodies may partially explain why Black youth are more likely than their White peers to be tried as adults (Campaign for Youth Justice, 2019; Lahey, 2016; Sawyer, 2019; Stevenson, 2015). Body size may also play a role in the stereotypical tendency to perceive Black girls to be older than they are – a pattern that contributes to the greater likelihood of their being arrested in school (compared to their White counterparts; Epstein, Blake and Gonzalez, 2020; Morris, 2016).

White supremacy and the pain of perfectionism

Connecting the dots between Euro-America's ongoing legacy of White Christian supremacy, the racist history of fatphobia, police violence against larger-than-average Black bodies, and the constant state of surveillance and punishment I imposed on my own unruly flesh as a teenager, reveals the banality of racism.[8] Most of the time, White supremacy is not perpetuated by evil people, but by those of us who perceive ourselves to be morally upright. Already by the time I was ten, I'd learned that following the rules – that is, obeying the gender/body norms dictated to me by my White, middle-class, Christian family and culture – made me 'good'. Behaviours as seemingly innocuous, normal and praiseworthy as counting calories, skipping lunch and weighing my body were, unbeknown to me, strategies for embracing the elevated virtue and status associated with Whiteness. The fact that my efforts to claim White privilege by perfecting my body were *unintentional* doesn't make them less racist.

In their challenging book *White Women: Everything You Already Know About Your Own Racism and How to Do Better* (2022), Regina Jackson and Saira Rao suggest that White women's pursuit of perfection is a classic habit of White supremacy. The habit has painful consequences all around. A mythical belief in the necessity of perfection prompts us/White women to pursue not just the tantalizing fantasy of an impeccably sculpted body, but the tortuous illusion of a perfect partner, perfect children, perfect job (or academic) performance, perfect home, perfect life. Not only does our pursuit of perfection generate a chronically painful sense of never being (or looking) 'good enough', but our belief that we need to be 'perfect' in order to be loved stokes our desperate desire for others' approval, of which there will never be enough. This same longing for approval makes many of us conflict-avoidant and thus reluctant to speak out against racism. Worried about 'making a mistake' or being called out for our unintentionally racist assumptions or behaviours, we remain silent, leaving it to people of colour to shoulder the burden of dismantling racism. Not only does the pursuit of perfection create a lot of internal suffering, but imagine how much energy White women could dedicate to challenging White supremacy if we relinquished the never-ending quest to feel good enough inside our own skin by being perfect!

To be sure, people of all genders, races, classes, ages, sexualities, nationalities and religious backgrounds develop body-image and eating problems. The origins of these struggles are diverse and complicated because they are *both* structurally/culturally patterned *and* unique to each individual's biology, psyche, heredity and history. I can't speak for other survivors of disordered eating – certainly not for women of colour, and not even for White, middle-class, able-bodied women like myself. But I see my own history of devotion to the Religion of Thinness – specifically my pursuit of perfection through thinness – as an unwitting strategy for embracing the unearned advantages of Whiteness. The harrowing consequences of this quest are a poignant reminder that White supremacy isn't good for anyone.

Transforming the shame that shadows the pursuit of perfection

In her beautiful book *The Body Is Not an Apology* (2018), Sonja Renee Taylor offers a hopeful reminder that it's never 'too late' to transform the shame that shadows the quest for the 'perfect' body. For her, practising 'radical self-love', including loving your body *as it is*, is the foundation for this transformation, which is simultaneously social and spiritual. After all, Taylor writes: 'When we speak of the ills of the world – violence, poverty, injustice – we are not speaking conceptually; we are talking about things that happen to bodies' (Taylor, 2018, pp. 4–5). The work of creating a more equitable, peaceful and loving society begins with the most proximate practice of appreciating, nurturing and honouring the flesh – both our own flesh and that of others. Consciously or not, how we view and treat our own physicality is a blueprint for how we relate to the embodiment of others. As Taylor points out, body shame not only makes you miserable, it creates misery for others: 'The bodies you share space with are afraid you are judging them with the same venom they have watched you use to judge yourself' (Taylor, 2018, p. 24). Conversely, practising radical self-love as an antidote to body shame has the power to liberate you and others from the painful pursuit of physical perfection and from the moral superiority complex that drives that quest, imprisons your spirit and marginalizes others.

Taylor is not a theologian, but I see her summons to practise radical self-love as a clarion call for *every body* – regardless of size, shape, colour or creed – to embrace the indelible goodness of our flesh in its glorious diversity and manifest divinity.

Moved by the Spirit of Radical Self-love, I find myself wanting to apologize to people of colour for the ways I sought to claim the benefits of Whiteness through my devotion to thinness. And I offer another apology to that nine-year-old girl holding the fish. I'm sorry for believing the lie that our bodies are not already good enough, that we are not already perfect.

Notes

1 The 90 per cent figure includes both men and women in Western societies or 'communities touched by globalization' (McBride, 2021, p. 7).

2 The biggest differences in levels of body acceptance between women of different racial groups appears to be between White and Black women, with the latter expressing somewhat higher levels of body satisfaction than their White counterparts.

3 Erdman Farrell's account builds on previous work on the history of dieting, especially Schwartz (1986) and Stearns (1997).

4 On the 'Americanization' of ethnic minority and working-class cultures through monitoring body size and eating habits, see also Levenstein (1988) and Seid (1989). R. Marie Griffith describes the form of Christianity that most influenced Americans' pursuit of physical perfectibility as 'white, middle-class Protestantism', noting that many of the 'somatic disciplines and devotions' that characterize this pursuit 'draw their source and momentum from specific Protestant patterns' (2004, pp. 4, 8–9).

5 For a more in-depth discussion of the colonial rhetoric that permeates diet culture, see chapter 5 of my book *Shameful Bodies* (Lelwica, 2017b).

6 Clint Smith uses this language in his interview with Kerri Miller (2023). See also Smith (2021).

7 I describe the Religion, Race, and Social Justice class in *Liberal Education* (AAC&U's journal): 'The Power of Proximity' (Lelwica, 2022), and I elaborate

what I've learned from my visits with justice-involved youth in *Hurting Kids: What Incarcerated Youth are Teaching Me About Whiteness, Compassion, Accountability, and Healing* (Lelwica, 2024).

8 This is a reference to Hannah Arendt's (1977) insight about the origins and dynamics of evil.

Bibliography

Alemán, J. O. et al., 2023, 'Obesity among Latinx People in the United States: A Review', *Obesity*, vol. 31, no. 2, pp. 329–37.

Arendt, H., 1977, *Eichmann in Jerusalem: A Report on the Banality of Evil*, New York: Viking Penguin.

Bacon, L., 2010, *Health at Every Size: The Surprising Truth About Your Weight*, Dallas, TX: BenBella Books.

Bacon, L. and Aphramor, L., 2014, *Body Respect: What Conventional Health Books Get Wrong, Leave Out, and Just Plain Fail to Understand About Weight*, Dallas, TX: BenBella Books.

Bordo, S., 2009, 'Not Just "a White Girl's Thing": The Changing Face of Food and Body Image Problems', in H. Malson and M. Burns (eds), *Critical Feminist Approaches to Eating Dis/Orders*, New York: Routledge, pp. 46–60.

Brumberg, J. J., 2000, *Fasting Girls: The History of Anorexia Nervosa*, New York: Vintage Books.

Campaign for Youth Justice, 2019, 'If Not the Adult System Then Where? Alternatives to Adult Incarceration for Youth Certified as Adults', Washington, DC, http://www.campaignforyouthjustice.org/images/ALT_INCARCERATION_FINAL.pdf, accessed 31.08.2024.

Clare, E., 2017, *Brilliant Imperfection: Grappling with Cure*, Durham, NC: Duke University Press.

Epstein, R., Blake, J. and Gonzalez, T., 2020, 'Girlhood Interrupted: The Erasure of Black Girls' Childhood', Washington, DC: Center on Poverty and Inequality, Georgetown Law, https://genderjusticeandopportunity.georgetown.edu/wp-content/uploads/2020/06/girlhood-interrupted.pdf, accessed 31.08.2024.

Farrell, A. E., 2011, *Fat Shame: Stigma and the Fat Body in American Culture*, New York: New York University Press.

Funk, C. and Lopex, M. H., 2002, 'A Brief Statistical Portrait of U.S. Hispanics', June, Pew Research Center, https://www.pewresearch.org/science/2022/06/14/a-brief-statistical-portrait-of-u-s-hispanics/, accessed 31.08.2024.

Gagne, D. A. et al., 2012, 'Eating Disorder Symptoms and Weight and Shape Concerns in a Large Web-Based Convenience Sample of Women Ages 50 and Above: Results of the Gender and Body Image (GABI) Study', *International Journal of Eating Disorders*, vol. 45, no. 7, pp. 832–44.

Glaude, E., 2017, *Democracy in Black: How Race Still Enslaves the American Soul*, New York: Broadway Books.

Grabe, S. and Hyde, J. S., 2006, 'Ethnicity and Body Dissatisfaction among Women in the United States: A Meta-Analysis', *Psychological Bulletin*, vol. 132, no. 4, pp. 622–40.

Greenhalgh, S., 2015, *Fat-Talk Nation: The Human Costs of America's War on Fat*, Ithaca, NY: Cornell University Press.

Griffith, R. M., 2004, *Born Again Bodies: Flesh and Spirit in American Christianity*, Berkeley, CA: University of California Press.

Harrison, D. S. L., 2021, *Belly of the Beast: The Politics of Anti-Fatness as Anti-Blackness*, Berkeley, CA: Atlantic Books.

Hill Fletcher, J., 2017, *The Sin of White Supremacy: Christianity, Racism, and Religious Diversity in America*, Maryknoll, NY: Orbis Books.

Jackson, C. and Lemay, M.-P., 2018, 'Most Americans Experience Feeling Dissatisfied with How Their Body Looks', *Ipsos News*, 13 February, https://www.ipsos.com/en-us/news-polls/most-americans-experience-feeling-dissatisfied-with-body-looks-from-time-to-time, accessed 31.08.2024.

Jackson, R. and Rao, S., 2022, *White Women: Everything You Already Know About Your Own Racism and How to Do Better*, New York: Penguin.

Lahey, J., 2016, 'The Steep Costs of Keeping Juveniles in Adult Prisons', *The Atlantic*, 8 January, https://www.theatlantic.com/education/archive/2016/01/the-cost-of-keeping-juveniles-in-adult-prisons/423201/, accessed 31.08.2024.

Lelwica, M., 1999, *Starving for Salvation: The Spiritual Dimensions of Eating Problems among American Girls and Women*, New York: Oxford University Press.

Lelwica, M., 2010, *The Religion of Thinness: Satisfying the Spiritual Hungers Behind Women's Obsession with Food and Weight*, Carlsbad, CA: Gürze Books.

Lelwica, M., 2011, 'The Religion of Thinness', in T. Ahlbäck and B. Dahla (eds), *Scripta Instituti Donneriani Aboensis*, Abo, Finland: Donner Institute for Research in Religious and Cultural History, vol. 23, pp. 257–85.

Lelwica, M., 2017a, 'Losing Their Way to Salvation: Women, Weight Loss, and the Religion of Thinness', in B. Forbes and J. Mahan (eds), *Religion and Popular Culture in America*, 3rd edn, Oakland, CA: University of California Press, pp. 262–87.

Lelwica, M., 2017b, *Shameful Bodies: Religion and the Culture of Physical Improvement*, London: Bloomsbury Publishing.

Lelwica, M., 2019, 'Depriving the Body to Save the Soul: Women, Weight Loss, and the Religion of Thinness', in R. Gounelle, A.-L. Zwilling and Y. Lehmann (eds), *Religions Et Alimentation*, Turnhout, Belgium: Brepols, pp. 49–68.

Lelwica, M., 2022, 'The Power of Proximity: Embodying Anti-Racist Learning', *Liberal Education*, Spring, https://www.aacu.org/liberaleducation/articles/the-power-of-proximity, accessed 31.08.2024.

Lelwica, M., 2024, *Hurting Kids: What Incarcerated Youth Are Teaching Me About Whiteness, Compassion, Accountability, and Healing*, Eugene, OR: Cascade Books.

Lelwica, M., Hoglund, E. and McNallie, J., 2009, 'Spreading the Religion of Thinness from California to Calcutta: A Critical Feminist Postcolonial Analysis', *Journal of Feminist Studies in Religion*, vol. 25, no. 1, pp. 19–41.

Levenstein, H., 1988, *Revolution at the Table: The Transformation of the American Diet*, New York: Oxford University Press.

McBride, H. L., 2021, *The Wisdom of Your Body: Finding Healing, Wholeness, and Connection through Embodied Living*, Grand Rapids, MI: Brazos Press.

McDow, K. B. et al., 2019, 'Attempts to Lose Weight among Adolescents Aged 16–19 in the United States, 2013–2016', in *NCHS Data Brief*, Hyattsville, MD: National Center for Health Statistics, vol. 340, pp. 1–8, https://pubmed.ncbi. nlm.nih.gov/31442192/, accessed 31.08.2024.

Miller, K., 2023, 'Clint Smith on How to Reckon with Slavery as America's Original Sin', 27 January, Minnesota Public Radio, https://www.mprnews.org/ episode/2023/01/27/clint-smith-on-how-to-reckon-with-slavery-as-americas-original-sin, accessed 31.08.2024.

Morris, M., 2016, *Pushout: The Criminalization of Black Girls in Schools*, New York: The New Press.

National Organization for Women, 2024, 'Get the Facts', https://now.org/now-foundation/love-your-body/love-your-body-whats-it-all-about/get-the-facts/, accessed 31.08.2024.

Oliver, E., 2006, *Fat Politics: The Real Story Behind America's Obesity Epidemic*, New York: Oxford University Press.

Sawyer, W., 2019, 'Youth Confinement: The Whole Pie 2019', *Prison Policy Initiative*, 19 December, https://www.prisonpolicy.org/reports/youth2019.html, accessed 31.08.2024.

Schwartz, H., 1986, *Never Satisfied: A Cultural History of Diets, Fantasies, and Fat*, New York: Free Press.

Seid, R. P., 1989, *Never Too Thin: Why Women Are at War with Their Bodies*, New York: Prentice-Hall.

Smith, C., 2021, *How the Word is Passed: A Reckoning with the History of Slavery across America*, Boston, MA: Little, Brown & Co.

Stearns, P. N., 1997, *Fat History: Bodies and Beauty in the Modern West*, New York: New York University Press.

Stevenson, B., 2015, *Just Mercy: A Story of Justice and Redemption*, New York: One World.

Strings, S., 2019, *Fearing the Black Body: The Racial Origins of Fat Phobia*, New York: New York University Press.

Taylor, S. R., 2018, *The Body Is Not an Apology: The Power of Radical Self-Love*, Oakland, CA: Berrett-Koehler Publishers.

Questions for reflection and discussion

1 At the start of the chapter, the author describes the 'Religion of Thinness' and unpacks five key observations. How do you observe these in your own life and that of your community?

2 The threads of shame are traced through the author's personal experience of eating disorders and through the development of the culturally ideal female form. Where do you see shame active in your own relationship with your body and in the way you think about and relate to others' bodies?

3 How are shame and perfectionism related? Have you experienced them as connected? If you struggle with perfectionism and shame, how have religious narratives contributed to your struggles – or, perhaps, helped you resolve them?

4 The author unpacks how 'White girls' and women's quasi-religious devotion to thinness is deeply entangled with racism.' Consider the dynamics at play in your thinking and being and that of your community. This may involve you sitting with significant discomfort, either individually or as a group, so endeavour to do so with patience and humility; listen well to the stories of others.

11

Conclusion

MAJA WHITAKER

The Christian Scriptures open with a rich depiction of the creation narrative, in which glorious diversity flows forth from the abundant imagination and inventiveness of our creator God. Reflecting on this creative work, each day God proclaims that it is 'good', until after the culmination of creation in the human being, when God exclaims that it is 'very good' (Gen. 1.31).

Can we imagine a world in which those are the words that we speak to ourselves and to others about our bodies? As a mother to four daughters, my heart aches every time I hear them express something that contradicts that, whatever part is under scrutiny, whatever metrics might be used and whatever conclusion is reached. I have worked hard to promote body positivity in the culture of our family, despite the onslaught of friends, media and the insufficiency of my accounting of my own body. I am coming to understand that my approach, however, well intended as it is, is fundamentally skewed, as the question 'What kind of body is a good body?' is still grounded in an assessment of goodness that is ethically conceived.

As Walter Brueggemann (1997) points out, the proclamation 'it was very good' is not primarily, or at least not only, an ethical or moral descriptor. An overemphasis on this ethical dimension can lead to conceptions of holiness becoming overbearing or even 'oppressive modes of social control' (p. 339), characterized by 'coercive harshness' (p. 340). To balance this, Brueggemann directs us towards the aesthetic dimension, writing:

> In Gen 1:31, at the conclusion of the sixth day of creation, Yahweh exclaimed, 'It was very good.' Most probably this is an aesthetic judgment and response to a brilliant act of creation. The sense of beauty or loveliness evokes on Yahweh's part a doxological response to the created order, a sense of satisfaction on the part of the artist, a

glad acknowledgment of success. Here and in some other places, a glad affirmation of creation is moved more by awe and delight than by ethical insistence or command. Thus Prov 8:30–31, in speaking of creation, culminates in a statement of 'delight' and 'rejoicing'. (Brueggemann, 1997, p. 339)

As we have seen throughout this book, the moral and aesthetic are inextricably linked in our habits of thinking and in our cultural discourses. Each element needs to be explicitly addressed and the connection between the two fundamentally critiqued: What is moral goodness when it comes to bodies? How can we describe aesthetic goodness? How might the two be related, or not? As this book has consistently argued, our conclusions become something along the lines of: Are fat bodies good bodies? Yes. Are disabled bodies good bodies? Yes. Are 'underperforming' bodies good bodies? Yes. Are 'unsexy' bodies good bodies? Yes. Are undisciplined bodies good bodies? Yes. Yes.

Yet as we expand our comprehension of the goodness of human bodies to include diversity on all manner of biological criteria, we can find that we are still complicit in promulgating the oppression of our selves and of others. In all this we must be gentle as well as resolute. The Lord knows that we are but dust (Ps. 103.14). He is not surprised by the brokenness of our humanity – it is we whose attempt to live in denial of our dustiness and limitation reveals our brokenness. We are creatures, and that is good.

Throughout this book, the authors have stirred the pot on a range of issues, complexifying and confronting the ways we think about bodies and their behaviour: sex, eating, spirituality, weight loss and beyond. Much of the focus has been centred on diet culture and fatphobia. These issues take centre stage not because they are the only kind of harm or even the most prevalent one, but because they remain the most acceptable. Where other forms of implicit bias (such as that against sexual orientation, race, age and disability) appear to be on the decrease, fatphobia is on the rise (Charlesworth and Banaji, 2019). This means that a conscious and generous embrace of fat bodies can flow over into discourse around other forms of systemic bias and model for us new ways forward.

This must be paired with the necessary acceptance of the fluidity of the body and the ambiguity of the lived experience of fatness. As Hannah Bacon points out in her chapter, there is an insidious current within the fat-acceptance movement to reject the fluidity of fatness and only accept those who are committed to maintaining a fat status quo, even in the face of health issues. She calls us to 'hear to speech the complex and sometimes conflicting messy lived experiences of fat women committed to fat acceptance, giving space to the shifting and fluid ways in which fat women might perform their size' (p. 92 above). The danger here is that control and conformity can remain at play. The desired norm may have shifted to a more generous body weight, but the norm has retained its normative power.

We must be careful not to move from broad claims about the need for cultural reform to claims about what actions individuals should or should not take in relation to their own bodies. In her book *Perfect Me*, Heather Widdows is careful to reject this and to avoid promoting 'natural' beauty, which could arise as a new ethical ideal. This is a move that might seem promising but would only continue harm and the segregation of economic, social and cultural power to a few. She writes:

> I have rejected the approach of telling women what to do and not do. Such an approach is women-blaming and divisive, and it does not address the beauty ideal. Only collectively can change happen, and if we seek to mitigate the harms and costs of the emerging inhuman and punishing beauty ideal, we should focus collectively. (Widdows, 2018, pp. 257–8)

The dangerous temptation to make judgements about the actions and bodies of others persists. Back in the Garden we grasped for the power to determine good from evil according to our own value systems, and we have been making poor judgements ever since. Instead, we must be content to wrestle with the 'complexity and the "mixed blessing" of life and bodies, without living in despair' (Eiesland, 1994, p. 102).

The moral philosopher Kate Manne proposes that instead of body positivity or body neutrality, we adopt 'body reflexivity'. In doing so, she names how both body positivity and body neutrality are out of reach for many people, particularly women. Body positivity can become yet another form of 'toxic positivity' when people are pressured to express body acceptance and an absence of this is problematized. It is no simple matter to change the way we think about or relate to our bodies, entrenched as we are in cultural discourses and practices, deeply formed by the stories we have told about our bodies and others'. Instead, Manne promotes a reflexivity that pins everything on one's relating to one's own body:

This notion – 'body reflexivity,' as I'll call it – differs from both body positivity and body neutrality. It does not prescribe any particular evaluative stance toward one's form. It is compatible with finding oneself beautiful, or sexy – or not, as the case may be. We may decline to think about our appearance much whatsoever. Body reflexivity prescribes a radical reevaluation of whom we exist in the world *for*, as bodies: ourselves, and no one else. We are not responsible for pleasing others. (Manne, 2024, p. 196; her emphasis)

'[M]y *body is for me*. Your body is for you', she writes (p. 195; her emphasis). I appreciate the spaciousness of this proposal, providing as it does room for diverse expressions and preferences, and for change in these over time. However, followers of Christ will note something missing from the individualistic and self-referential nature of Manne's proposal. My body is not just mine and your body is not just yours. We belong to one another, and we belong to God.

Paul writes in 1 Corinthians 6:

Don't you realize that your body is the temple of the Holy Spirit, who lives in you and was given to you by God? You do not belong to yourself, for God bought you with a high price. So you must honour God with your body. (1 Cor. 6.19–20, NLT)

These verses are clearly located in a passage discussing 'sexual sin'. Despite this, the passing reference to food and eating in verse 13 (intended to illustrate the Corinthians' belief in the meaninglessness of bodily action) has been used to build an argument for diet restriction as the desirable behaviour that Paul had in mind here. Countless women have denied their appetites by telling themselves that the Spirit's temple requires careful keeping. Here again we see the entrenched connection between aesthetics and moral judgement. What I believe Paul is getting at here is the broad claim that our actions have impacts; as people constituted by and embedded in community, we must consider the effects of our bodily actions and being in the world on those we are in relationship with – God, others and creation. The orientation of our bodily being should be towards loving God and loving neighbour, but in a way that is not incompatible with loving self.

In the twelfth century, Bernard of Clairvaux articulated four degrees of love, the fourth of which is 'love of self for God's sake', which, somewhat surprisingly, surpasses the third degree of 'love of God for God's sake'.[1] That is, we love this self that God loves, in the same manner and degree, and this need not detract from our loving of God. While Bernard promotes a forgetting of the body and an inattention to its immediate needs in order to pursue this perfection of love, I suggest that it is in and with our bodies that we love God, and so it is in and with our bodies that we must love ourselves.

And so let us offer our bodies to God (Rom. 12.1). We can do this in full confidence that they are 'holy and acceptable' (Rom. 12.1, ESV) in their current state. No change is needed to receive this approval. 'Very good' are the words that were spoken over our first parent in creation, and are still the words that are spoken over our embodied life. Let us speak them over ourselves and over others, but let this not lead to complacency. For as Paul goes on in Romans, this offering of our embodiment is paired with the transforming work of the Spirit who renews our minds. This requires deeply counter-cultural work, in which we resist not only the lies of that 'old deluder'[2] and those powers of this age with which we wrestle (Eph. 6.12), but also the thought and behaviour patterns of this world (Rom. 12.2) and the brokenness of our embedded and enculturated ways of thinking.[3] This is no easy task, however. Learning to embrace the body involves more than attending to its simple needs. It requires asking difficult questions that complexify that which we had taken for granted. Too often I am preoccupied and wearied by wrestling with my own body, both its form and its being in the world, to take on the world, the devil and my own sinful nature. Women, particularly poor, Black, fat and disabled women, are already carrying disproportionate burdens by merely being themselves. And so in all this we must be gentle with ourselves and with others. We must participate in the work of the Spirit rather than drive it, in order that we might echo God's response to our bodies in also calling them 'very good', and live in them, care for them and relate to them as such.

Notes

1 See chapters IX–XI of *On Loving God*, available at https://www.ccel.org/ccel/bernard/loving_god.toc.html, accessed 31.08.2024.

2 This name for the devil is enshrined in the Massachusetts School Laws of 1647, and to my mind neatly captures his nature as one whose character is defined by lying (John 8.44).

3 I have in mind here the framework of 'the flesh, the world, and the devil' as articulated historically by Evagrius of Pontus.

Bibliography

Brueggemann, W., 1997, *Theology of the Old Testament: Testimony, Dispute, Advocacy*, Minneapolis, MN: Fortress Press.

Charlesworth, T. E. and Banaji, M. R., 2019, 'Patterns of Implicit and Explicit Attitudes: I. Long-Term Change and Stability from 2007 to 2016', *Psychological Science*, vol. 30, no. 2, pp. 174–92.

Eiesland, N., 1994, *The Disabled God: Toward a Liberatory Theology of Disability*, Nashville, TN: Abingdon Press.

Manne, K., 2024, *Unshrinking: How to Face Fatphobia*, New York: Crown Publishing Group.

Widdows, H., 2018, *Perfect Me: Beauty as an Ethical Ideal*, Princeton, NJ: Princeton University Press.

A Liturgy and Benediction

O Lord.
We are often weary of trying to shape ourselves into something that
we are not,
of wrestling with our world and with our selves,
wrestling with our very flesh.

We grieve for the ways that we have dismissed, denied, despised and
denigrated the bodies we have and the bodies of others.
We justify and excuse shame in the name of seeking health, seeking
performance, seeking beauty and seeking perfection.
Forgive us, Lord.

Refine our definitions and teach us to order our values aright.
May we pursue you and your kingdom,
rather than the shadow of perfection offered to us.
Turn our eyes away from worthless things and redeem our perceptions,
that we might perceive beauty where beauty is rightly found,
that we might perceive the beauty and goodness of our bodies.

Lord, you know how deeply entrenched we are in the inhospitableness
of our cultures.
Bodies are forever labelled as either too much or not enough.
We look at others' bodies and name them too much or not enough.
We look at our own and name them too much or not enough.
Heaping shame and bearing shame,
when we should echo you,
naming all bodies 'very good'.

In the midst of our broken and beautiful realities,
we call to mind that which you say is true.

Bodies are good.

Disabled bodies are good,
fat bodies are good,
thin bodies are good,
bony bodies are good,
hairy bodies are good,
aged bodies are good,
youthful bodies are good,
chronically ill bodies are good,
toned bodies are good,
underperforming bodies are good.

We look forward to their ultimate redemption, whatever that might
involve.
Yet for now, we endeavour to welcome what is.

Our bodies are good.
May we receive them as such,
enjoy them as such
and share them as such with the world.

Index of Bible References

Old Testament

Genesis

1.20–25	106
1.26–17	55, 67
1.31	3, 8, 173
6.1–4	84
12.12–14	150n3
32	17

Exodus

24.10	148

Deuteronomy

21.11	150n3

1 Samuel

16.6–13	33
16.7	26
25.3	150n3

2 Samuel

13.1	150n3
14.27	150n3

1 Kings

1.3–4	150n3
17.17–24	112n2

Esther

2.7	150n3

Job

42.15	150n3

Psalms

103.14	174

Proverbs

8.30–31	173
11.22	150n3
31	34
31.30	30

Song of Songs

1.8	150n3
2.1–2	146
4.10–11	145, 146, 149
5.9–16	133–50
6.1–3	146, 150n3
6.4–10	141, 149
7.1–6	135, 146, 147, 150n3

Isaiah

18.4	139
53.2	42

Jeremiah

4.11	139
29.11	14

Ezekiel

1.26	148

Amos

8.13	150n3

New Testament

Matthew

5.43–48	28–9, 36
5.48	25, 28, 105
5—7	69
15.10–11	45
19	28
19.21	63
22.37–40	54
23	26, 33
23.27	31
26.26–28	74

Mark

5.35–42	112n2

Luke

6.20–26	51
7.11–17	112n2
10.7–8	46
10.38–21	45
11.28	45
21.18	85
24.13–43	49, 101, 104
24.50–51	49

John

1.14	48, 67
4.4–30	45
7.24	26
8.44	177
11.38–45	112n2
20.11–18	18
20.27	19, 101

Acts

1.11	18

Romans

1.18–32	27
2.25–29	26
5	36, 39
5.6–11	29
6.4–5	21
8.1–4	49
8.5–8	27
8.19–25	69, 108
8.31–39	73
12.1–2	9, 28, 46, 50, 106, 110, 177
15.13	15

1 Corinthians

2.6–16	27, 112n3
6.19–20	45, 176
7.25–31	90
11.1	36
11.20–26	74
14.20	112n3
15.42–44	104

2 Corinthians

4.16–18	41
5.11–21	26, 37, 67, 73
12.9	38

Galatians

3.28	65
5.14	45

Ephesians

4.13	112n3
5.1	36
6.12	177

Philippians

2.5–8	41, 67
3.15	112n3
4.13	9

Colossians

1.28	112n3
2.20–23	11
3.3	102

1 Timothy

2.9	31

2 Timothy

2.15	46

James

1.4	28
3.2	112

1 Peter

3.3–4	31, 34

Revelation

2.14	20
5.6	19
21	69

Index of Names and Subjects

ableism 9–11, 82, 106, 109
abstinence 118–19
abuse 115, 133–6, 137, 140–2, 147–50
adolescence 24, 43, 69, 163, 164
advertising 24, 66, 72, 108–9, 123
ageing 24, 108, 109
anorexia 60, 62, 64, 74, 153
anthropology 10, 47, 62, 64, 68, 110, 154, *see also* ontology
anxiety 45, 64, 65–6, 155
asceticism 9–11, 62–3
Augustine of Hippo 63, 72, 79, 83–90, 93–5, 105
autopsy 80–1, 87, 94n4, 165–6

baldness 47, 153
baptism 21–2, 73
bariatric surgery 77, 91
beauty 2, 24–38, 41, 45, 70–1, 73, 82, 86, 88–90, 93, 105, 107–9, 110, 111, 124, 136, 139–40, 143, 159, 175
bingeing 50, 52, 164
BMI (Body Mass Index) 47, 50, 161–2, 163
bulimia 43, 153, 157, 163, 164

chastity 63, 84, 118, 119, 132, 140
church 3, 10, 45–6, 54–5, 62–3, 67, 68–9, 73–4, 110–11, 116, 129, 130, 135, 137–8, 140, 144
colonialism 82–3, 120, 124, 125, 158–9, 162–4
cosmetic surgery 12, 34, 48, 55, 107
creation 8, 17, 27, 117, 173–4, 177
crime 164–6

diet culture 3, 43–59, 67, 111, 168n5, 174, *see also* slimming
dieting 9, 12, 13, 43–59, 60, 63–5, 66–7, 71, 87, 92, 107, 124, 155, 159–60, 162, 168n3, 168n5, 176
depression 45, 50, 66
disability 19, 21, 88, 92, 99–103, 108–9, 111–12, 174
discipleship 51, 61–2, 69, 72, 74
discipline 3, 10–11, 14, 44, 52–3, 55, 62, 66, 67, 69, 109, 118, 163, 168n4
discrimination 44–5, 50, 55, 65, 99, 101, 105, 115, 137
disgust 45, 61, 80–1, 86, 105, 109

eating disorders 51, 60, 66, 69, 72, 73, 160, *see also* anorexia, bulimia

education 44, 119, 121, 124–5,
129–31, 135
Eiesland, Nancy 21, 92, 100–1,
102, 108, 175
emotion 44, 48, 50, 66, 70–1,
85, 109
erotic 84, 115, 123, 126–8,
136–7
eschatology 16, 83–7, 99–103,
108, 110–12 see also new
creation, resurrection body
Eucharist 21–2, 71, 73–4
exercise 14, 43, 44, 47, 54, 60,
65, 71

fasting 9–10, 62–4
fatness 14, 44–8, 50, 64, 78–81,
86–7, 90–3, 100, 106, 109–12,
153–6, 158–62, 164–6, 174–5
fatphobia 98, 99, 174, see also
discrimination
feasting 62, 63
fertility 47
food 12, 21, 30, 46, 49, 53 60,
73

gender 44–5, 80, 81–2, 89, 92,
121, 122, 127, 128, 133–8,
140–1, 143–9, 154, 166
genitalia 84, 119, 121, 124, 126,
147
gluttony 12, 64–5, 159

hair 47, 86, 105, 111, 137,
142–3
healing 85, 88
health 3, 11, 44–9, 54–5, 63, 67,
77, 82, 91, 103, 106, 109–11,
141, 160–2, 165–6
Health At Every Size (HAES) 51,
55

heaven see new creation
height 2, 26, 33, 89, 148, 160–1
hope 7, 9, 13–16, 19, 20–2, 70,
73, 100, 108
hunger 48, 51, 52–3, 60, 74, 89,
95n11, 157, 158, 159, 164

identity 49, 64, 68–9, 92, 93,
100–1, 102, 107, 121, 159
imago Dei 55, 106, 107
incarnation 8, 9, 10–11, 21, 67,
73, 116–17, 124, 129, 130, 131
individualism 68–9, 91, 176
intuitive eating 51, 56n1

Jesus, resurrection of 15–16,
17–19, 29, 49, 100–1, see also
incarnation
justice 7, 21, 32, 65, 126, 131,
164, 167

kenosis 40–1

limitation 1–2, 78, 89–90, 101,
103, 106, 174
liturgy 21, 71, 107, 130–1,
179–80

marriage 8, 30, 35, 115, 118–19,
126–7, 129
masculinity 105, 121, 125–6,
130, 131, 134–5, 140–1, 142,
143, 145, 146–7, 148, 149
masturbation 118
media 10, 24, 30, 43, 44, 49, 53,
72, 78, 80, 109
misogyny 82, 90, 125–6, 154
money 49, 66, 107, 127, 159

neighbour 8, 11–12, 28–9, 45,
55, 176

new creation 16, 19, 20, 69, 90,
    99–103, 106, 108, 111
normality 49–50, 65–6, 71,
    84–5, 99, 100, 101, 104, 106,
    108, 115, 117
normativity 82, 92, 103, 126,
    175

obesity 30, 45, 47–8, 64, 80–1,
    161–2, 165–6
'obesity epidemic' 52, 67
ontology, human 8, 47–8,
    55, 62–3, 68, 104, see also
    anthropology
orgasm 122, 124, 152

patriarchy 67, 94n1, 117,
    118–19, 121, 124, 125–6, 127,
    129–30, 140–1, 143, 154
pleasure 50, 63, 121–3, 124,
    129, 130–1
police 165–6 see also crime
porn 115, 124
post-mortem see autopsy
prayer 9–10, 12, 18, 38–41, 63,
    70–1, 73
preaching 3, 45, 69, 111, 159
prison see crime
promiscuity 116, 131, 140, see
    also chastity

racism 65, 81–2, 94n4, 125, 129,
    130, 158–60, 162–3, 164–7,
    177
reproduction 85, 110, 121, 131,
    160
resurrection body 3, 9, 15–16,
    19, 20–1, 49, 79, 85–7, 89,
    94n9, 95n10, 95n11, 99–106,
    110–11

sex 88, 115–32, 147, 148
sexuality 77, 92, 110, 116,
    120–3, 125, 126, 128, 130,
    136, 138, 147
shame 14, 45, 61, 65–7, 69, 70,
    85, 88, 93, 109–10, 115, 155,
    156–7, 158, 161, 164, 165,
    167–8
sin 27, 37–8, 64, 65, 67, 69, 88,
    108, 157–8, 163, 164, 176
slimming 14, 44–53, 60, 64–7,
    72, 77, 87, 88, 93, 174 see also
    dieting
social media 7, 11, 49, 56n1, 78
stigma see discrimination

teenagers see adolescence
telos 7, 9–10, 16, 17, 20–2, 25,
    61, 70, 72–3, 103, 106–7, 108,
    110
thinness see fatness, slimming

violence 65, 115–16, 121, 122,
    131, 133–7, 142, 143, 165–6,
    167
virginity 118, 119, 129, 140 see
    also chastity

weight loss see slimming
Whiteness 43, 65, 82, 100, 105,
    119, 154, 158–60, 163–4,
    166–7, 168n2, 172, see also
    racism
willpower see discipline
woundedness 18–19, 20, 101

youthfulness 2, 107–8, 111, 124,
    141, 143, see also ageing